An Introductory Mathematics To Business and Economics

An Introductory Mathematics To Business and Economics

Dr. G. Surya Prakasa Rao

AKANSHA PUBLISHING HOUSE
NEW DELHI • GUWAHATI • VISAKHAPATNAM

AKANSHA PUBLISHING HOUSE
4649-B/21, Ansari Road
Darya Ganj, New Delhi - 110 002
Ph.: 23263193 / 9811582579 / 09435116718
Fax: 011-23263193
Email: ektabooks@yahoo.com
www.akanshapublishinghouse.com

An Introductory Mathematics to Business and Economics

First Published 2011
ISBN 978-81-8370-299-7

PRINTED IN INDIA

Published by Akansha Publishing House, New Delhi and Printed at Harmain Offset Press, Delhi.

Dedicated

To

Bhagavan

Sri Satya Sai Baba

"Help Ever - Hurt Never"

Contents

Preface

This book is specially designed to practitioners and students of Economics both Graduate and Under-Graduate courses. Nowadays Mathematics plays an important role in Economics and Business. For this reason many this has been included in the syllabi in various universities. Dr. C. Rangarajan, Economist and Chairman, 12th Finance Commission of India has aptly noted *"Without Mathematics there is no Economics"*.

The present book consists of seven chapters, well organized in a coherent manner. Chapter-One deals with Functions, Limits and Continuity. Matrices, types, rules, determinants and various methods for solving system of equations and its applications are presented in Chapter-Two.

Chapter-Three presents differentiation, rules of differentiation, methods and its applications like market equilibrium, elasticities, cost and revenue concepts, cost minimization and profit maximization of a single variable function, and Chapter-Four deals with partial differentiation and rules of partial differentiation, homogeneous functions, Euler's theorem and its applications like production function, marginal productivity, Cobb-Douglas and CES production functions and profit maximization with a multivariable function in different markets. Chapter-Five presents Integration, simple concepts, definite integrals and its applications like consumer's surplus and producer's surplus. Input-Output analysis has been carried out with suitable applications in Chapter-Six. The last Seventh chapter deals with Linear Programming and Game theory. In a Linear Programming- Formulation and Graphical methods only, and in Game theory- concept, types of games, maxmin and minmax principle, optimum and mixed strategies, 2 x n and m x 2 games with a graphical representation.

With great pleasure, I turn to the acknowledgements. I wish to express my deep sense of gratitude to my teacher and well-wisher Prof. P. V. Sarma, School of Management Studies, Gayatri Vidya Parishad College for P.G. Courses, Visakhapatnam, for encouraging me constantly to complete my Text Book. I express my profound sense of gratitude to my Research Director Prof. P.Narasimha Rao, Department of Economics & Applied Economics, Acharya Nagarjuna University.

I would like to thak Head, Department of Economics and my teachers in the Department of Economics, Andhra University for their encoragement for completing the Text Book.

I would also like to place on record my sincere gratitude to "Gayatri Vidya Parishad" (G.V.P) with whom I have been employed as a faculty in Economics for the last 9 years. I thank the Governing body of our college.

I express my gratitude to my colleagues especially P. Raju and P. Srinivasa Rao and a few of my friends for their support at all stages of this work.

Last but not least, I specially thank my Parents, Wife, Son, Brother and Marital Parents for their cooperation and moral support, which helped me a lot in completing this endeavour.

G.S. Prakasa Rao

1

Functions, Limits & Continuity

We shall introduce some different types of functions, which are particularly useful in Business and Economics.

Definition: The relationship between two real variables say x and y which are so related that corresponding to every value of 'a' of x defined as the domain, we get a finite value 'b' of y defined as the range, then y is said to be the function of x.

'y' is a function of a variable x is expressed symbolically by equations;

$$y=f(x),\quad y=f(x),\quad y=\phi(x), etc.......$$

1. Explicit function

A function expressed directly in terms of the dependent variable is said to be an explicit function, for example is $y=x^2+2x-5$

2. Polynomial function

A function of the form:

$$y=f(x)=a_n\,x^n+a_{n-1}\,x^{n-1}+......a_0 x^0$$

Where a_i's are real numbers (i = 0,1,2, ... n), a_i ““‘ 0 and n_i, *a* positive integer, is called a polynomial of degree 'n'.

(*a*) If n = 1, then the polynomial function of degree 1 and is called a linear function i.e. for n = 1 function is written as:

$$y = a_1 x^1 + a_0 x^0$$

$y = a + bx$, where a & b are constants

3. Quadratic function

If n = 2, then the polynomial function is of degree 2 and is called a quadratic function. The function can be written as

This is usually written as $y = ax^2 + bx + c$

Where a, b, c are constants

The graph of quadratic function $y = f(x) = ax^2 + bx + c$ is parabola that opens upwards according as $a > 0$ or $a < 0$. Each parabola has a vertical axis of symmetric and turning point called a vertex. Typical graphs of parabola are shown in the following figures

Figure-1: upward open parabola

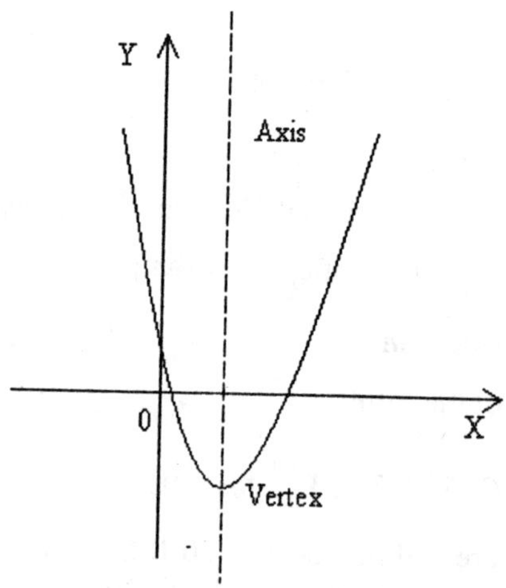

Figure-2: downward open parabola

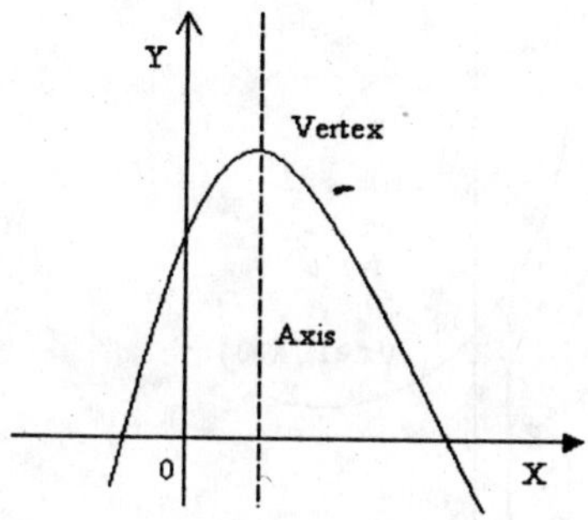

4. Exponential function

A function having a variable base and a constant exponent viz. $y = x, x^3, x^9$ etc., is called a power function while a function having a constant base and variable exponent is called an exponential function.

For example $y = a^x$, $(a > 0)$ is an exponential function.

Where 'a' is the base and x is a real number exponent.

Graphs of exponential function:

Case (i) when $a > 1$ Case (ii) when $0 < a < 1$

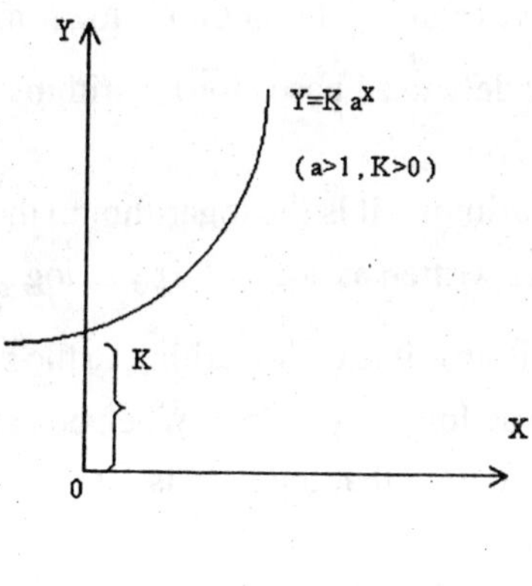

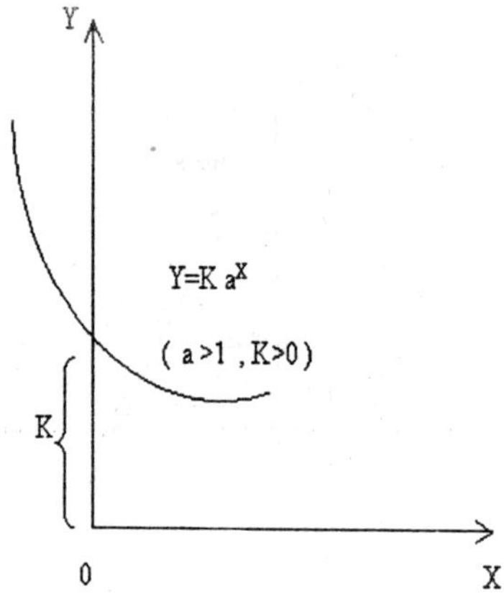

5. Logarithmic function: A logarithmic function is expressed as

$$y = \log_e x$$

Where $a \neq 1$ and $x > 0$ is the base. It is read as y is the log to the base a of x. This can be written as

$$x = a^y$$

Thus from exponential function $y = a^x$ we may construct the logarithmic function x $=a^4$ by interchanging the variables. This shows that the inverse of an exponential function is logarithmic function.

The two most widely used bases for logarithms are 10 and e (= 2.7182).

(i) Common logarithm – it is the logarithm to the base of 10 of a number x, it is written as $\log_{10} x$. If y = $\log_{10} x$ then $x = 10^y$.

(ii) Natural logarithm – it is the logarithm to the base of a number x. It is written as $\log_e x$. (or) ln x. When no base is mentioned, it will be understood that the base is 10.

Graph of the logarithmic function

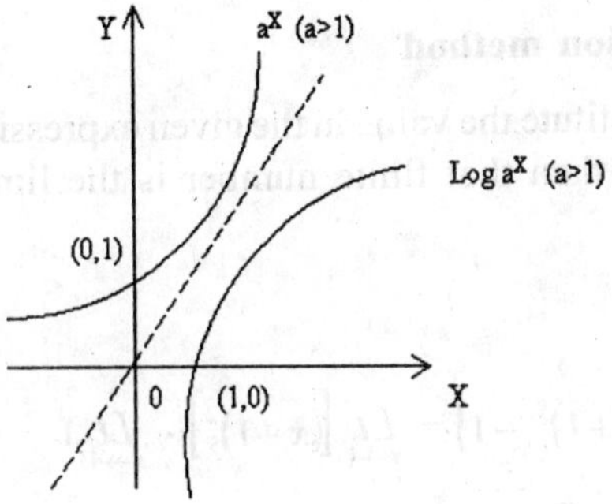

Limits

The concept of limit is the foundation of calculus and this concept plays an important role throughout the whole structure of the calculus.

If x be a real variable and '*a*' be a fixed number, then by '*x*' tends to '*a*' it is written as $x \to a$, here we mean that *x* assumes successively values i.e. either greater than '*a*' or less than '*a*' whose numerical differences from '*a*' i.e. $|x-a|$ becomes smaller and smaller and can ultimately be taken to be less than any small positive quantity. In this case, *x* is very close to '*a*' but $x \neq a$ and we say that '*x*' approaches to '*a*'.

If '*x*' approaches '*a*' only through values greater than '*a*' such that $x-a$ becomes smaller and smaller, then we say that '*x*' trends to '*a*' from the right side and we express it by $x \to a^+$. In this case, is very close to '*a*' and greater than '*a*'.

Similarly, if '*x*' approaches '*a*' through values less than '*a*' such that '$a-x$' becomes smaller and smaller, then we say that '*a*' from the left side and we express if by '$x \to a^-$. In this case, *x* is very close to '*a*' and less than '*a*'.

Methods

There are mainly three methods for finding the limit to a function f (x) as tends to a finite quantity say 'a'.

Direct substitution method

Directly substitute the value in the given expression and if we get a finite number, then that finite number is the limit of the given expression.

For example

$$\underset{x\to 4}{Lt}\left[(x+1)^2-1\right]=\underset{x\to 4}{Lt}\left[(x+1)^2\right]-\underset{x\to 4}{Lt}\,1$$

$$=(4+1)^2-1$$

$$=(5)^2-1=25-1=24$$

Factorization method

We have to factorize both the numerator and the denominator and cancel out the common factor.

For example:

$$\underset{x\to 2}{Lt}\frac{x^2-4x+12}{x^2-4}=\underset{x\to 3}{Lt}\frac{(x-6)(x-2)}{(x+2)(x-2)}$$

$$\underset{x\to 2}{Lt}=\frac{(x-6)}{(x-2)}=\frac{-4}{0}=\infty$$

Rationalization method

This method is useful for where the radical sings are involved either in the numerator or the denominator. The numerator or the denominator is rationalized and limit taken.

For example,

$$\underset{x\to 0}{Lt}\frac{x}{1-\sqrt{1-x}} = \underset{x\to 0}{Lt}\frac{x}{1-\sqrt{1-x}}\times\frac{1+\sqrt{1-x}}{1+\sqrt{1-x}}$$

$$= \underset{x\to 0}{Lt}\frac{x\left(1+\sqrt{1-x}\right)}{(1)^2-\left(\sqrt{1-x}\right)^2}$$

$$= \underset{x\to 0}{Lt}\frac{x\left(1+\sqrt{1-x}\right)}{1-(1-x)}$$

$$= \underset{x\to 0}{Lt}\frac{x\left(1+\sqrt{1-x}\right)}{1-1+x}$$

$$= \underset{x\to 0}{Lt}\, 1+\sqrt{1-x}$$

$$= 1+1 = 2$$

Infinite limits

For finding the limit of f(x)= $\frac{g(x)}{h(x)}$ as →, divide the numerator and the denominator of the fraction by the highest power of present in the fraction and then use $\frac{1}{x},\frac{1}{x^2}$ .... → 0 as x → ∞.

For example,

$$\underset{x\to\infty}{Lt}\frac{2x^2+5x+3}{3x^2+10x+8}$$

$$\underset{x\to\infty}{Lt}\frac{x^2\left(2+\frac{5}{x}+\frac{3}{x^2}\right)}{x^2\left(3+\frac{10}{x}+\frac{8}{x^2}\right)}$$

$$\underset{\frac{1}{x}\to\infty}{Lt}\frac{2+5(0)+3(0)}{3+10(0)+8(0)}$$

$$= \frac{2}{3}$$

Problems

Example-1: Evaluate $\underset{x \to 1}{Lt} \dfrac{x-1}{2x^2-7x+5}$

Solution: we have $\underset{x \to 1}{Lt} \dfrac{x-1}{2x^2-7x+5}$

$$= \frac{1-1}{2(1)^2-7(1)+5}$$

$$= \frac{0}{2-7+5} = 0$$

Example-2: Evaluate $\underset{x \to 3}{Lt} \dfrac{x^2-4+3}{x^2-2x+3}$

Solution: we have $\underset{x \to 3}{Lt} \dfrac{x^2-4+3}{x^2-2x+3}$

$$= \frac{(3)^2-4(3)+3}{(3)^2-2(3)-3}$$

$$= \frac{9-12+3}{9-6-3} = \frac{0}{0} \text{ it is undefined.}$$

Then we go for factorization method

The factors of is and for $x^2 + 4x + 3$ is $(x-3)$ $(x-1)$ and $x^2 - 2x-3$ for $(x-3)$ $(x+1)$.

Then $\underset{x \to 3}{Lt} \dfrac{(x-3)(x-1)}{(x-3)(x+1)}$

$$\underset{x \to 3}{Lt} \frac{x-1}{x+1}$$

$$= \frac{3-1}{3+1} = \frac{2}{4} = \frac{1}{2}$$

Example-3: Evaluate $\underset{x\to 1}{Lt}\dfrac{x^4-3x^3+2}{x^3-5x^2+3x+1}$

Solution: we have $\underset{x\to 1}{Lt}\dfrac{x^4-3x^3+2}{x^3-5x^2+3x+1}$

$$=\frac{(1)^4-3(1)^3+2}{(1)^3-5(1)^2+3(1)+1}$$

$$=\frac{1-3+2}{1-5+3+1}=\frac{0}{0}$$

It is undefined, so that we go for factorization method.

Here by using Horner method we can find out the factors for both numerator and denominator.

First we take numerator i.e. x^4-3x^3+2

	1	–3	0	0	2
$x=1$	0	1	–2	–2	–2
	1	–2	–2	–2	0

The factors are $(x-1)(x^3-2x^2-2x-2)$

Similarly for denominator i.e. x^3-5x^2+3x+1

	1	–5	3	1
$x=1$	0	1	–4	–1
	1	–4	–1	0

The factors are $(x-1)(x^2-4x-1)$

Now we applying the limit

$$=\underset{x\to 1}{Lt}\frac{(x-1)(x^3-2x^2-2x-2)}{(x-1)(x^2-4x-1)}$$

$$= \underset{x \to 1}{Lt} \frac{x^3 - 2x^2 - 2x - 2}{x^2 - 4x - 1}$$

$$= \frac{(1)^3 - 2(1)^2 - 2(1) - 2}{(1)^2 - 4(1) - 1}$$

$$= \frac{1 - 2 - 2 - 2}{1 - 4 - 1} = \frac{-5}{-4} = \frac{5}{4}$$

Example-4: Evaluate $\underset{x \to 3}{Lt} \left[\frac{1}{x-3} - \frac{3}{x(x^2 - 5x - 6)} \right]$

Solution: we have $\underset{x \to 3}{Lt} \left[\frac{1}{x-3} - \frac{3}{x(x^2 - 5x - 6)} \right]$

Now we have to find out the factors for $x^2 - 5x + 6$

$x^2 - 5x + 6$

$x^2 - 3x - 2x + 6$

$x(x-3) - 2(x-3)$

$(x-3)(x-2)$

Then we can write the above limit as

$$= \underset{x \to 3}{Lt} \left[\frac{1}{x-3} - \frac{3}{x(x-3)(x-2)} \right]$$

$$= \underset{x \to 3}{Lt} \left[\frac{x(x-2) - 3}{x(x-3)(x-2)} \right]$$

$$= \underset{x \to 3}{Lt} \left[\frac{x^2 - 2x - 3}{x(x-3)(x-2)} \right]$$

Then again the factors for is $x^2 - 2x - 3$ is $(x - 3)(x + 1)$

Then $\underset{x\to 3}{Lt} \dfrac{(x-3)(x+1)}{x(x-3)(x-2)}$

$$\underset{x\to 3}{Lt} \frac{(x+1)}{x(x-2)}$$

$$= \frac{3+1}{3(x-2)}$$

$$= \frac{4}{3}$$

Example-5: Evaluate $\underset{x\to\infty}{Lt} \dfrac{6-5x^2}{4x-15x^2}$

Solution: In this case we dividing both numerator and denominator by the highest power of x in the denominator then use $\frac{1}{x}, \frac{1}{x^2}, \ldots\ldots\ldots \to 0$ as $x \to \infty$

$$\underset{x\to\infty}{Lt} \frac{\frac{6}{x^2} - \frac{5x^2}{x^2}}{\frac{4}{x} + \frac{15x^2}{x^2}}$$

$$\underset{x\to\infty}{Lt} \frac{\frac{6}{x^2} - 5}{\frac{4}{x} + 15}$$

$$\underset{x\to\infty}{Lt} \frac{6(0)-5}{4(0)+15} = \frac{-5}{15} = \frac{-1}{3}$$

Example-6: Evaluate $\underset{x\to\infty}{Lt} \dfrac{2x^3+3x^2+5}{-5x^3+8x-17}$

Solution: In this case we dividing both numerator and denominator by the highest power of 'x' in the denominator then use $\frac{1}{x}, \frac{1}{x^2}, \ldots\ldots \rightarrow 0$ as $x \rightarrow \infty$

$$\underset{x\to\infty}{Lt} \frac{\frac{2x^3}{x^3}+\frac{3x^2}{x^3}+\frac{5}{x^3}}{\frac{-5x^3}{x^3}+\frac{8x}{x^3}-\frac{17}{x^3}}$$

$$\underset{x\to\infty}{Lt} \frac{2+\frac{3}{x}+\frac{5}{x^3}}{-5+\frac{8}{x^2}-\frac{17}{x^3}}$$

$$\underset{x\to\infty}{Lt} \frac{2+3(0)+5(0)}{-5+8(0)-17(0)}$$

$$= \frac{2}{-5} \quad = \frac{-2}{5}$$

Some Standard Formula results

1. $\underset{x\to a}{Lt} \frac{x^n - a^n}{x-a} = n\cdot a^{n-1}$

2. $\underset{x\to a}{Lt} \frac{x^m - a^m}{x^n - a^n} = \frac{m}{n}\cdot a^{m-n}$

Example-1: Evaluate $\underset{x\to a}{Lt} \frac{x^3-27}{x-3}$

Solution: we have $\underset{x\to a}{Lt} \frac{x^3-27}{x-3}$

$$= \frac{(3)^3-27}{3-3}$$

$$= \frac{27-27}{3-3}$$

$= \frac{0}{0}$ It is undefined

By applying the formula is $\underset{x \to a}{Lt} \frac{x^n - a^n}{x-a}$

Here a = 3, n = 3

$= 3 \cdot 3^{3-1}$

$= 3 \cdot 3^2 = 3.9 = 27$

Example-2: Evaluate $\underset{x \to 2}{Lt} \frac{x^2-4}{x-2}$

Solution: Given $\underset{x \to 2}{Lt} \frac{x^2-4}{x-2}$

$$= \frac{(2)^2-4}{2-2}$$

$$= \frac{4-4}{2-2}$$

$= \frac{0}{0}$ It is undefined

By applying the formula $\underset{x \to a}{Lt} \frac{x^n - a^n}{x-a} = n \cdot a^{n-1}$

$$\underset{x \to 2}{Lt} \frac{(x)^2-(2)^2}{x-2}$$

Here n = 2, a = 2

$= 2 \cdot 2^{2-1} = 2 \cdot 2^1$

$= 2 \cdot 2$

$= 4$

Example-3: Evaluate $\underset{x\to 3}{Lt} \dfrac{x^5 - 243}{x^2 - 9}$

Solugion: We have, $\underset{x\to 3}{Lt} \dfrac{x^5 - 243}{x^2 - 9}$

$$= \frac{(3)^5 - 243}{3^2 - 9}$$

$$= \frac{243 - 243}{9 - 9}$$

$$= \frac{0}{0} \text{ It is undefined.}$$

By applying the formula $\underset{x\to a}{Lt} \dfrac{x^m - a^m}{x^n - a^n} = \dfrac{m}{n} \cdot a^{m-n}$

The given problem can be written as

$$\underset{x\to 3}{Lt} \frac{(x)^5 - (3)^5}{(x)^2 - (3)^2}$$

Here m = 5, a = 3, n = 2

$$= \frac{5}{2} \cdot 3^{5-2}$$

$$= \frac{5}{2} 3^3$$

$$= \frac{5}{2} \cdot 27 = \frac{135}{2}$$

Example-4: Evaluate $\underset{x\to a}{Lt} \dfrac{(x)^{3/5}-(a)^{3/5}}{x^{1/3}-a^{1/3}}$

Solution: Given $\underset{x\to a}{Lt} \dfrac{(x)^{3/5}-(a)^{3/5}}{x^{1/3}-a^{1/3}}$

$$= \frac{a^{3/5}-a^{3/5}}{a^{1/3}-a^{1/3}}$$

$= \dfrac{0}{0}$ It is undefined.

By applying the formula is $\underset{x\to a}{Lt} \dfrac{x^m-a^m}{x^n-a^n} = \dfrac{m}{n}\cdot a^{m-n}$

Hence, the given problem can be written as

$$\underset{x\to a}{Lt} \frac{(x)^{3/5}-(a)^{3/5}}{(a)^{1/3}-(a)^{1/3}}$$

Here, m $=\dfrac{3}{5}$, $a = a$, $n = \dfrac{1}{3}$

$$= \frac{\frac{3}{5}}{1/3} a^{\frac{3}{5}-\frac{1}{3}}$$

$$= \frac{3}{5}\times\frac{3}{1} a^{\frac{9-5}{15}}$$

$$= \frac{9}{5} a^{\frac{4}{15}}$$

Exercise – 1

Evaluate the following limits

1. $\underset{x\to 0}{Lt}\ 4x+5$

2. $\underset{x\to 3}{Lt}\ \dfrac{2x-4}{x-2}$

3. $\underset{x\to 1}{Lt}\ \dfrac{x^2-2}{x}$

4. $\underset{x\to 3}{Lt}\ \dfrac{x^2-4x+3}{x^2-2x+3}$

5. $\underset{x\to 1}{Lt}\ \dfrac{x^2-x\log x+\log x-1}{x-1}$

6. $\underset{x\to 0}{Lt}\ \dfrac{\sqrt{2-x}-\sqrt{2+x}}{x}$

7. $\underset{x\to 3}{Lt}\ \dfrac{x^2-4}{\sqrt{3x-2}-\sqrt{x+2}}$

8. $\underset{x\to 3}{Lt}\ \dfrac{x^2+x-12}{x-3}$

9. $\underset{x\to 1}{Lt}\ \dfrac{x^2-3x+2}{x^2-4x+3}$

10. $\underset{x\to \infty}{Lt}\ \dfrac{2x+3}{4x-5}$

11. $\underset{x\to 0}{Lt}\ \dfrac{\sqrt{1+x}-1}{x}$

12. $\underset{x\to \infty}{Lt}\ \dfrac{3-2x^2}{5x+4x^2}$

13. $\underset{x\to 3}{Lt}\ \left(\dfrac{x}{x-3}-\dfrac{9}{x^2-3x}\right)$

14. $\underset{x\to\infty}{Lt} \dfrac{5x^2+3x-6}{2x^2-5x-1}$

15. $\underset{x\to\infty}{Lt} \left(\sqrt{x^2+5x+4}-\sqrt{x^2-3x+4}\right)$

16. $\underset{x\to\infty}{Lt} \dfrac{2x^3+3x^2+5}{-5x^3+8x-17}$

17. $\underset{x\to2}{Lt} \dfrac{x^3-3x^2+4}{x^4-8x^2+16}$

18. $\underset{x\to5}{Lt} \dfrac{x^3-625}{x^3-125}$

19. $\underset{x\to\infty}{Lt} \dfrac{4x^2-5x+7}{2x-3}$

20. $\underset{x\to2}{Lt} \dfrac{x^4-16}{x^2-4}$

Continuity

A function *f(x)* is said to be continuous at $x=a$ if $\underset{x\to a}{Lt} f(x)$ exists and equals *f(a)*. Thus, *f(x)* is continuous at *x=a*, if $\underset{x\to a^+}{Lt} f(x)= \underset{x\to a^-}{Lt} f(x)=f(a)$

If *f(x)* is not continuous at a point, it is said to be discontinuous at that point.

In general, the word continuity is used to indicate the absence of any break or group in the graph of a function. If there is any break at a point corresponding to $x = a$, then we say that the function is not continuous at $x = a$.

Cauchy's definition of continuity

A function *f(x)* is said to be continuous at $x = a$ if *f(a)* exists and corresponding to an arbitrary positive number '$\in$', however small, we can find a positive number 'δ' such that

$$|f(x)-f(a)| < \in, \text{ whenever } |x-a| < \delta$$

Properties of continuous function

1) The sum, difference and product of two functions which are continuous at a point are continuous at that point.
2) A polynomial function is continuous everywhere.
3) The exponential and the logarithmic functions are continuous in their respective domains.
4) If *f(x)* is continuous at $x = a$, then $|f(x)|$ is also continuous at $x = a$.
5) A rational function is continuous at every point in its domain.

Example -1: Given y = $f(x) = \dfrac{x^2 - x - 12}{x - 4}$

a) Evaluate the limit of y as x → 4
b) Is this function continuous at x = 4? Why?

Solution: a) $\underset{x\to 4}{Lt}\ y = \underset{x\to 4}{Lt} \dfrac{x^2 - x - 12}{x - 4}$

$$= \underset{x\to 4}{Lt} \frac{(x+3)(x-4)}{x-4}$$

$$= \underset{x\to 4}{Lt} (x-4)(x+3) = 4 + 3 = 7$$

The function is discontinuous at $x = 4$, as it is not defined at $x = 4$

Example-2: A function *f(x)* is defined as follows:

$f(x) = 3 + 2x$, for $\dfrac{-3}{2} \leq x < 0$

$= 3 - 2x$, for $0 \le x < \frac{3}{2}$

$= -3 - 2x$, for $x \ge \frac{3}{2}$

Discuss the continuity of $f(x)$ at $x = 0, \frac{3}{2}$

Solution: continuity at $x = 0$

$$\underset{x \to 0}{Lt} f(x) = \underset{x \to 0^+}{Lt} (3 - 2x) = 3 - 2.0 = 3 \quad [\because f(x) = 3 - 2x \ \ when \ \ x > 0]$$

$$\underset{x \to 0}{Lt} f(x) = \underset{x \to 0^-}{Lt} (3 - 2x) = 3 + 2.0 = 3 \quad [\because f(x) = 3 - 2x \ \ when \ \ x < 0]$$

At $x = 0, f(x) = 3 - 2x$ $\quad \therefore f(0) = 3 - 2.0 = 3$

Thus $\underset{x \to 0}{Lt} f(x) = \underset{x \to 0^-}{Lt} f(x) = f(0)$

Hence, $f(x)$ is continuous at $x = 0$

Continuity at $x = \frac{3}{2}$

$$\underset{x \to \frac{3^+}{2}}{Lt} f(x) = \underset{x \to \frac{3^+}{2}}{Lt} (-3 - 2x) = -6 \left[\because f(x) = -3 - 2x \ when \ x > \frac{3}{2}\right]$$

$$\underset{x \to \frac{3^-}{2}}{Lt} f(x) = \underset{x \to \frac{3^-}{2}}{Lt} (-3 - 2x) = -6 \left[\because f(x) = -3 - 2x \ when \ x < \frac{3}{2}\right]$$

Also at $x = \frac{3}{2}, f(x) = -3 - 2x$ $\quad \therefore f\left(\frac{3}{1}\right) = -6$

Thus, $\underset{x \to \frac{3^+}{2}}{Lt} f(x) \ne \underset{x \to \frac{3^-}{2}}{Lt} f(x) \ne f\left(\frac{3}{2}\right)$

2
Matrices

Matrix

A matrix is a rectangular array of numbers enclosed by a pair of brackets [ ] or ( ) subject to certain rules of operation. A set of *mn* numbers $a_{11}, a_{12}, \ldots\ldots\ldots, a_{mn}$ arranged in a rectangular array of m rows and n columns like $\begin{bmatrix} a_{11} & a_{12} & a_{13} & \ldots & a_{1n} \\ a_{21} & a_{22} & a_{23} & \ldots & a_{2n} \\ \ldots & \ldots & \ldots & \ldots & \ldots \\ a_{m1} & a_{m2} & a_{m3} & \ldots & a_{mn} \end{bmatrix}$ and subject to certain rules of operation is called as '$m \times n$' Matrix.

The numbers $a_{11}, a_{12}, \ldots\ldots\ldots, a_{mn}$ are called an '$m \times n$' matrix.

Equality of matrices

Two matrices A =[*aij*] and B = [*bij*] are said to be equal if

a) They have the same order i.e. the number of rows and columns in both the matrices are same.

b) Their corresponding elements are equal i.e. for each *i* and *j*.

Types of matrices

Row and column Matrix: A matrix having one row is called a row matrix.

For example [2 3 4] is a 1 x 3 row matrix and $[a_{11}, a_{12}, \ldots\ldots\ldots a_{1n}]$ is a $1 \times n$ row matrix.

A matrix having only one column is called a column matrix.

For example $\begin{bmatrix} 1 \\ 2 \\ 3 \end{bmatrix}$ is a 3×1 column matrix and $\begin{bmatrix} a_{11} \\ a_{21} \\ \vdots \\ a_{n1} \end{bmatrix}$ is an $n \times 1$ column matrix.

Null Matrix

A Matrix of any order whose all elements are zero is called a null matrix.

For example $\begin{bmatrix} 0 & 0 \\ 0 & 0 \end{bmatrix}$ and $\begin{bmatrix} 0 & 0 & 0 \\ 0 & 0 & 0 \\ 0 & 0 & 0 \end{bmatrix}$ are null matrices for order 2×2 and 3 x 3 respectively.

Diagonal Matrix

A square matrix whose all elements except those in the main diagonal are Zero is called a diagonal matrix.

For example $\begin{bmatrix} 3 & 0 \\ 0 & 5 \end{bmatrix}$ and $\begin{bmatrix} 2 & 0 & 0 \\ 0 & 3 & 0 \\ 0 & 0 & 6 \end{bmatrix}$ are diagonal matrices of order 2 x 2 and 3 x 3 respectively.

Scalar Matrix

A square matrix is said to be a scalar matrix if its non – diagonal elements are Zero and diagonal elements are equal

For example $\begin{bmatrix} 2 & 0 \\ 0 & 2 \end{bmatrix}$ and $\begin{bmatrix} 3 & 0 & 0 \\ 0 & 3 & 0 \\ 0 & 0 & 3 \end{bmatrix}$ are scalar matrices of order 2×2 & 3 x 3 respectively.

Unit Matrix

A square matrix is said to be a unit matrix if its non – diagonal elements are zero and diagonal elements are all equal to one.

For example $\begin{bmatrix} 1 & 0 \\ 0 & 1 \end{bmatrix}$ is a unit matrix of order 2 x 2 and is denoted by I_2.

Triangular Matrix

A matrix A= $[aij]$ is said to be a triangular matrix if aij = 0 whenever i>j (or i < j)

For example $\begin{bmatrix} 3 & 4 & 5 \\ 0 & 1 & 2 \\ 0 & 0 & 1 \end{bmatrix}$ and $\begin{bmatrix} 3 & 0 & 0 \\ 2 & 4 & 0 \\ 3 & 4 & 6 \end{bmatrix}$ are triangular matrices.

Transpose of a Matrix

The transpose of a matrix A is the Matrix obtained from A by interchanging its rows and columns and it is denoted by A^T The order of the transpose of an m x n matrix is n x m.

For example If $A = \begin{bmatrix} 3 & -1 & 2 \\ 0 & 4 & -7 \end{bmatrix}$ then

$$A^T = \begin{bmatrix} 3 & 0 \\ -1 & 4 \\ 2 & 7 \end{bmatrix}$$

Rules of Operations

1. Additional of Matrices

Two matrices A and B can be added only when they are of the same order, i.e., each of the two matrices must have the same number of rows and columns. When this condition is satisfied the process of addition consists of adding the corresponding elements of the two matrices.

For example if $A = \begin{bmatrix} 1 & 2 & 3 \\ 0 & 4 & 5 \end{bmatrix}_{2X3}$ and $B = \begin{bmatrix} 3 & 1 & 5 \\ 2 & 0 & 1 \end{bmatrix}_{2X3}$

Then $A+B = \begin{bmatrix} 1+3 & 2+1 & 3+5 \\ 0+2 & 4+0 & 5+1 \end{bmatrix} = \begin{bmatrix} 4 & 3 & 8 \\ 2 & 4 & 6 \end{bmatrix}$

2. Scalar Multiplication

Let A be a matrix and k be a scalar, multiplication of A by k is effected by multiplying each element of A by K.

For example $A = \begin{bmatrix} 1 & 2 & 3 \\ 4 & 5 & 6 \end{bmatrix}$ and k= 3 then

kA is $\begin{bmatrix} 3 & 6 & 9 \\ 12 & 15 & 18 \end{bmatrix}$

Subtraction of two Matrices

Let A and B be two Matrices of same order.

For Example of $A = \begin{bmatrix} 2 & 5 & -3 \\ 4 & -6 & 7 \end{bmatrix}$ and $B = \begin{bmatrix} -1 & 3 & 2 \\ 6 & -4 & 8 \end{bmatrix}$

Then $A\text{-}B = \begin{bmatrix} 2 & 5 & -3 \\ 4 & -6 & 7 \end{bmatrix} - \begin{bmatrix} -1 & 3 & 2 \\ 6 & -4 & 8 \end{bmatrix}$

$= \begin{bmatrix} 3 & 2 & -5 \\ -2 & -2 & -1 \end{bmatrix}$

Matrix Multiplication

The product AB of two matrices A and B is defined only when the number of columns in A is equal to the number of rows in B.

Let A be an m x n Matrix and B be an n x p matrix. Then their product AB in an m x p matrix whose (i, j)[th] element is obtained by multiplying the elements of ith row of A with the Corresponding elements of jth column of B and then adding the products.

Symbolically,

$$\begin{bmatrix} a_{11} & a_{12} & \cdots & \cdots & a_{1n} \\ a_{21} & a_{22} & \cdots & \cdots & a_{2n} \\ \cdots & \cdots & \cdots & \cdots & \cdots \\ a_{m1} & a_{m2} & \cdots & \cdots & a_{mn} \end{bmatrix} \begin{bmatrix} b_{11} & b_{12} & \cdots & \cdots & b_{1p} \\ b_{21} & b_{22} & \cdots & \cdots & b_{2p} \\ \cdots & \cdots & \cdots & \cdots & \cdots \\ b_{n1} & b_{n2} & \cdots & \cdots & b_{np} \end{bmatrix}$$

$$= \begin{bmatrix} c_{11} & c_{12} & \cdots & \cdots & c_{1p} \\ c_{21} & c_{22} & \cdots & \cdots & c_{2p} \\ \cdots & \cdots & \cdots & \cdots & \cdots \\ c_{m1} & c_{m2} & \cdots & \cdots & c_{pn} \end{bmatrix}$$

When $c_{ij} = a_{i1} b_{1j} + a_{i2} b_{2j} + \ldots\ldots\ldots + a_{in} b_{nj}$

Properties of Matrix multiplication

1. Matrix multiplication is associative. If A,B,C are m x n, n x p and p x q matrices respectively, then

   A (BC) = (AB) C

2. Matrix multiplication is distributive with respect to addition. If A,B,C are m x n, n x p and n x p matrices respectively, then

   A (B+C) = AB + AC

3. If A be a square matrix of order n and I be the unit matrix of the same order, then AI = IA = A

4. If AB = 0 where A, B are two matrices, then, in general, A ≠ 0 or B ≠ 0 or A ≠ 0 and B ≠ 0.

Example-1: If $A=\begin{bmatrix} 2 & -1 \\ 3 & 4 \\ 1 & 5 \end{bmatrix}$ and $B=\begin{bmatrix} -1 & 3 \\ 2 & 1 \end{bmatrix}$ find AB. Does BA exist?

Solution: Here A is a 3 × 2 order matrix and B is 2 × 2 order matrix. Clearly the number of columns in A equals the number of rows in B

$$AB=\begin{bmatrix} 2 & -1 \\ 3 & 4 \\ 1 & 5 \end{bmatrix}\begin{bmatrix} -1 & 3 \\ 2 & 1 \end{bmatrix}$$

$$=\begin{bmatrix} 2\times(-1)+(-1)\times 2 & : & 2\times 3+(-1)\times 1 \\ 3\times(-1)+4\times 2 & : & 3\times 3+4\times 1 \\ 1\times(-1)+5\times 2 & : & 1\times 3+5\times 1 \end{bmatrix}$$

$$=\begin{bmatrix} -4 & 5 \\ 5 & 13 \\ 9 & 8 \end{bmatrix}$$

Further, B is a 2 × 2 matrix and A is a 3 × 2 matrix. So the number of columns in B is not equal to the number of rows in A. Therefore, BA does not exist.

Example-2: If $A=\begin{bmatrix} 1 & -1 \\ -1 & 1 \end{bmatrix}$ and $B=\begin{bmatrix} 1 & 1 \\ 1 & 1 \end{bmatrix}$ find AB and BA.

Solution: $AB=\begin{bmatrix} 1 & -1 \\ -1 & 1 \end{bmatrix}\begin{bmatrix} 1 & 1 \\ 1 & 1 \end{bmatrix}$

$$= \begin{bmatrix} 1\times1+(-1)\times1 & : 1\times1+(-1)\times1 \\ (-1)\times1+1\times1 & : -1\times1+1\times1 \end{bmatrix}$$

$$= \begin{bmatrix} 1-1 & : & 1-1 \\ -1+1 & : & -1+1 \end{bmatrix}$$

$$= \begin{bmatrix} 0 & 0 \\ 0 & 0 \end{bmatrix}$$

$$BA = \begin{bmatrix} 1 & 1 \\ 1 & 1 \end{bmatrix} \begin{bmatrix} 1 & -1 \\ -1 & 1 \end{bmatrix}$$

$$= \begin{bmatrix} 1\times1+1\times(-1) & : & 1\times(-1)+1\times1 \\ 1\times1+1\times(-1) & : & 1\times(-1)+1\times1 \end{bmatrix}$$

$$= \begin{bmatrix} 1-1 & : & -1+1 \\ 1-1 & : & -1+1 \end{bmatrix}$$

$$= \begin{bmatrix} 0 & 0 \\ 0 & 0 \end{bmatrix}$$

Example-3: If $A = \begin{bmatrix} 2 & 3 \\ 3 & 5 \end{bmatrix}$, show that $A^2 = 7A - I$ when

$$I = \begin{bmatrix} 1 & 0 \\ 0 & 1 \end{bmatrix}$$

Solution: $A^2 = A \times A = \begin{bmatrix} 2 & 3 \\ 3 & 5 \end{bmatrix} \begin{bmatrix} 2 & 3 \\ 3 & 5 \end{bmatrix}$

$$= \begin{bmatrix} 2\times2+3\times3 & : 2\times3+3\times5 \\ 3\times2+5\times3 & : 3\times3+5\times5 \end{bmatrix}$$

$$= \begin{bmatrix} 4+9 & : 6+15 \\ 6+15 & : 9+25 \end{bmatrix}$$

$$= \begin{bmatrix} 13 & 21 \\ 21 & 34 \end{bmatrix}$$

$$7\,A = 7\begin{bmatrix} 2 & 3 \\ 3 & 5 \end{bmatrix} = \begin{bmatrix} 14 & 21 \\ 21 & 35 \end{bmatrix}$$

$$\therefore\ 7A - I = \begin{bmatrix} 14 & 21 \\ 21 & 35 \end{bmatrix} - \begin{bmatrix} 1 & 0 \\ 0 & 1 \end{bmatrix}$$

$$= \begin{bmatrix} 13 & 21 \\ 21 & 34 \end{bmatrix}$$

Hence, we get $A^2 = 7A - I$

Example-4: Find matrix A such that

$$A = \begin{bmatrix} 0 & 1 \\ 2 & -1 \end{bmatrix} = \begin{bmatrix} 2 & 1 \\ -1 & 0 \end{bmatrix}$$

Solution: Let $A = \begin{bmatrix} a_1 & a_2 \\ a_3 & a_4 \end{bmatrix}$

We have $\begin{bmatrix} a_1 & a_2 \\ a_3 & a_4 \end{bmatrix} \begin{bmatrix} 0 & 1 \\ 2 & -1 \end{bmatrix} = \begin{bmatrix} 2 & 1 \\ -1 & 0 \end{bmatrix}$

$$= \begin{bmatrix} a_1 \times 0 + a_2 \times 2 & : & a_1 \times 1 + a_2 \times (-1) \\ a_3 \times 0 + a_4 \times (2) & : & a_3 \times 1 + a_4 (-1) \end{bmatrix} = \begin{bmatrix} 2 & 1 \\ -1 & 0 \end{bmatrix}$$

$$= \begin{bmatrix} 0 + 2a_2 & : & a_1 - a_2 \\ 0 + 2a_4 & : & a_3 - a_4 \end{bmatrix} = \begin{bmatrix} 2 & 1 \\ -1 & 0 \end{bmatrix}$$

$$2a_2 = 2$$

$$a_2 = \frac{2}{2} = 1 \qquad a_1 - a_2 = 1$$

$$a_1 = 1 + a_2$$

$$a_1 = 1 + 1 = 2$$

$$2a_4 = -1$$

$$a_4 = \frac{-1}{2} \qquad a_3 - a_4 = 0$$

$$a_3 = a_4$$

$$a_3 = \frac{-1}{2}$$

Hence, $A = \begin{bmatrix} 2 & 1 \\ -1/2 & -1/2 \end{bmatrix}$

Example-5: Find the Matrix A such that

$$A \begin{bmatrix} 3 & 4 \\ 6 & 2 \end{bmatrix} = \begin{bmatrix} 2 & 8 \\ 9 & 4 \end{bmatrix}$$

Solution: Let $A = \begin{bmatrix} a_1 & a_2 \\ a_3 & a_4 \end{bmatrix}$

We have $\begin{bmatrix} a_1 & a_2 \\ a_3 & a_4 \end{bmatrix} \begin{bmatrix} 3 & 4 \\ 6 & 2 \end{bmatrix} = \begin{bmatrix} 2 & 8 \\ 9 & 4 \end{bmatrix}$

$$= \begin{bmatrix} a_1 \times 3 + a_2 \times 6 & : & a_1 \times 4 + a_2 \times 2 \\ a_3 \times 3 + a_4 \times 6 & : & a_3 \times 4 + a_4 \times 2 \end{bmatrix} = \begin{bmatrix} 2 & 8 \\ 9 & 4 \end{bmatrix}$$

$$\begin{bmatrix} 3a_1 + 6a_2 & : & 4a_1 + 2a_2 \\ 3a_3 + 6a_4 & : & 4a_3 + 2a_4 \end{bmatrix} = \begin{bmatrix} 2 & 8 \\ 9 & 4 \end{bmatrix}$$

$3a_1 + 6a_2 = 2 \rightarrow (1)$ $\quad$ $3a_3 + 6a_4 = 9 \rightarrow (3)$

$4a_1 + 2a_2 = 8 \rightarrow (2)$ $\quad$ $4a_3 + 2a_4 = 4 \rightarrow (4)$

By solving equations (1) and (2), we get $a_1 = \frac{22}{9}$, $a_2 = \frac{-8}{9}$

and similarly (3) and (4), we get $a_3 = \frac{-1}{3}$, $a_4 = \frac{5}{3}$

Hence, $A = \begin{bmatrix} \frac{22}{9} & \frac{-8}{9} \\ \frac{-1}{3} & \frac{5}{3} \end{bmatrix}$

Example-6: Given that $A = \begin{bmatrix} 2 & 3 & 1 \\ 1 & 2 & 3 \end{bmatrix}$ and $B = \begin{bmatrix} 3 & 1 \\ 2 & 2 \\ 2 & 3 \end{bmatrix}$, show that $(AB)^T = B^T A^T$.

Solution: $AB = \begin{bmatrix} 2 & 3 & 1 \\ 1 & 2 & 3 \end{bmatrix} \begin{bmatrix} 3 & 1 \\ 2 & 2 \\ 2 & 3 \end{bmatrix}$

$$= \begin{bmatrix} 2\times3+3\times2+1\times2 & : & 2\times1+3\times2+1\times3 \\ 1\times3+2\times2+3\times2 & : & 1\times1+2\times2+2\times3 \end{bmatrix}$$

$$= \begin{bmatrix} 6+6+2 & 2+6+3 \\ 3+4+6 & 1+4+9 \end{bmatrix}$$

$$AB = \begin{bmatrix} 14 & 11 \\ 13 & 14 \end{bmatrix}$$

$$(AB)^T = \begin{bmatrix} 14 & 13 \\ 11 & 14 \end{bmatrix}$$

$$B^T = \begin{bmatrix} 3 & 2 & 2 \\ 1 & 2 & 3 \end{bmatrix}$$

$$A^T = \begin{bmatrix} 2 & 1 \\ 3 & 2 \\ 1 & 3 \end{bmatrix}$$

$$\therefore B^T A^T = \begin{bmatrix} 3 & 2 & 2 \\ 1 & 2 & 3 \end{bmatrix} \begin{bmatrix} 2 & 1 \\ 3 & 2 \\ 1 & 3 \end{bmatrix}$$

$$= \begin{bmatrix} 3\times2+2\times3+2\times1 & : & 3\times1+2\times2+2\times3 \\ 1\times2+2\times3+3\times1 & : & 1\times1+2\times2+2\times3 \end{bmatrix}$$

$$= \begin{bmatrix} 6+6+2 & 3+4+6 \\ 2+6+3 & 1+4+9 \end{bmatrix}$$

$$AB = \begin{bmatrix} 14 & 13 \\ 11 & 14 \end{bmatrix}$$

$$\therefore\ (AB)^T = B^T A^T$$

Example-7: If $A = \begin{bmatrix} 1 & 1 & 2 \\ 2 & 1 & 3 \end{bmatrix}$, $B = \begin{bmatrix} 4 & -1 & 6 \\ 6 & 2 & 3 \end{bmatrix}$ verify $(A+B)^T = A^T + B^T$

Solution: $A + B = \begin{bmatrix} 1 & 1 & 2 \\ 2 & 1 & 3 \end{bmatrix} + \begin{bmatrix} 4 & -1 & 6 \\ 6 & 2 & 3 \end{bmatrix}$

$$= \begin{bmatrix} 1+4 & 1+(-1) & 2+6 \\ 2+6 & 1+2 & 3+3 \end{bmatrix}$$

$$= \begin{bmatrix} 5 & 0 & 8 \\ 8 & 3 & 6 \end{bmatrix}$$

$$(A+B)^T = \begin{bmatrix} 5 & 8 \\ 0 & 3 \\ 8 & 6 \end{bmatrix}$$

$$A^T = \begin{bmatrix} 1 & 2 \\ 1 & 1 \\ 2 & 3 \end{bmatrix}$$

$$B^T = \begin{bmatrix} 4 & 6 \\ -1 & 2 \\ 6 & 3 \end{bmatrix}$$

$$A^T+B^T=\begin{bmatrix}1 & 2\\1 & 1\\2 & 3\end{bmatrix}+\begin{bmatrix}4 & 6\\-1 & 2\\6 & 3\end{bmatrix}$$

$$=\begin{bmatrix}1+4 & 2+6\\1+(-1) & 1+2\\2+6 & 3+3\end{bmatrix}$$

$$=\begin{bmatrix}5 & 8\\0 & 3\\8 & 6\end{bmatrix}$$

$\therefore\ (A+B)^T\ = A^T+B^T$

Exercise – 1

1. If $A=\begin{bmatrix}0 & 2 & 3\\2 & 1 & 4\end{bmatrix}$ and $B=\begin{bmatrix}7 & 6 & 3\\1 & 4 & 5\end{bmatrix}$ find the value of

$2A + 3B$.

2. If $A=\begin{bmatrix}3 & 5 & 7\\9 & 3 & 2\\1 & 2 & 5\end{bmatrix}$, $B=\begin{bmatrix}3 & 5 & 4\\4 & 7 & 8\\3 & 2 & 1\end{bmatrix}$ find the matrix '*X*' such that

$3A + 2B - 2X = 0$

3. If $A=\begin{bmatrix}0 & 1\\1 & 0\end{bmatrix}$, $B=\begin{bmatrix}0 & -i\\i & 0\end{bmatrix}$, where $i^2 = -1$ verify

$(A+B)^2 = A^2 + B^2$.

4. If $A=\begin{bmatrix}1 & -1\\ -1 & 1\end{bmatrix}$ show that $A^2 = 2A$ and $A^3 = 4A$

5. If $A=\begin{bmatrix}1 & 2 & 3\\ 1 & 2 & 3\\ -1 & -2 & -3\end{bmatrix}$, show that $A^2 = 0$

6. If $A=\begin{bmatrix}1 & 2 & 1\\ 0 & 1 & -1\\ 3 & -1 & 1\end{bmatrix}$ show that $A^3 - 3A^2 - A + 9I = 0$

7. Find x if $y=\begin{bmatrix}2 & 3\\ -1 & 5\end{bmatrix}$ and $2x + y = \begin{bmatrix}4 & -1\\ 5 & 3\end{bmatrix}$

8. Find the values of x and y when

$$\begin{bmatrix}3 & x+2\\ y & 5\end{bmatrix} = \begin{bmatrix}x-1 & 6\\ x-3y & 5\end{bmatrix}$$

9. If $A=\begin{bmatrix}1 & 1 & 2\\ 2 & 1 & 0\end{bmatrix}$ and $B=\begin{bmatrix}1 & 2\\ 2 & 0\\ -1 & 1\end{bmatrix}$, verify that

(i) $B^T A^T = (AB)^T$

(ii) $(A^T B^T)^T = BA$

10. If $A=\begin{bmatrix}2 & 2 & 0\\ 2 & 1 & 1\\ -7 & 2 & -3\end{bmatrix}$, verity that $A^3 - 13A + 12I = 0$

Determinants

With every square matrix A of certain order, we associate a

number called the determinant of 'A' and it is denoted by |A| or det.A. If a matrix is not a square, we cannot associate a determinant with it.

Definition: For the square matrix $A = \begin{bmatrix} a_1 & b_1 \\ a_2 & b_2 \end{bmatrix}$ of second order

the symbol $|A| = \begin{vmatrix} a_1 & b_1 \\ a_2 & b_2 \end{vmatrix}$ is called a determinant of second order.

And its value is defined by $\begin{bmatrix} a_1 & b_1 \\ a_2 & b_2 \end{bmatrix} = a_1 b_2 - a_2 b_1$

The four numbers a_1, b_1, a_2, b_2 are called elements of the determinant.

In case of a square matrix of order 3

$$\text{i.e} \quad A = \begin{bmatrix} a_1 & b_1 & c_1 \\ a_2 & b_2 & c_2 \\ a_3 & b_3 & c_3 \end{bmatrix}$$

$$\text{Then} \quad |A| = \begin{bmatrix} + & - & + \\ a_1 & b_1 & c_1 \\ a_2 & b_2 & c_2 \\ a_3 & b_3 & c_3 \end{bmatrix}$$

$$|A| = +a_1 \begin{vmatrix} b_2 & c_2 \\ b_3 & c_3 \end{vmatrix} - b_1 \begin{vmatrix} a_2 & c_2 \\ a_3 & c_3 \end{vmatrix} + c_1 \begin{vmatrix} a_2 & b_2 \\ a_3 & b_3 \end{vmatrix}$$

$$= a_1(b_2c_3 - b_3 c_2) - b_1 (a_2 c_3 - a_3c_2) + c_1 (a_2 b_3 - a_3b_2)$$

$$= a_1b_2c_3 - a_1b_3c_2 - a_2b_1c_3 + a_3b_1c_2 + a_2b_3c_1 - a_3 b_2c_1$$

Example-1: If $A = \begin{bmatrix} 3 & -1 \\ 2 & 3 \end{bmatrix}$ then find out |A|

Solution: $|A| = \begin{vmatrix} 3 & -1 \\ 2 & 3 \end{vmatrix} = (3\times 3)-(-1\times 2)$

$= 9 - (1 - 2)$

$= 9 + 2 = 11$

Example-2: If $A = \begin{bmatrix} 1 & -2 & 3 \\ 4 & -1 & -2 \end{bmatrix}$ find |A|

$$\begin{matrix} + & - & + \end{matrix}$$

Solution: $|A| = \begin{vmatrix} 1 & -2 & 3 \\ 4 & -1 & -2 \\ -2 & 1 & 5 \end{vmatrix}$

$$= +_1\begin{vmatrix} -1 & -2 \\ 1 & 5 \end{vmatrix} + 2\begin{vmatrix} 4 & -2 \\ -2 & -5 \end{vmatrix} + 3\begin{vmatrix} 4 & -1 \\ -2 & 1 \end{vmatrix}$$

$= +1(-5+2)+2(20-4)+3(4-2)$

$= -3 + 32 + 6$

$= 35$

Properties of Determinants

1. The value of a determinant remains unaltered if the rows and columns are interchanged i.e.

$$\begin{vmatrix} a_1 & b_1 & c_1 \\ a_2 & b_2 & c_2 \\ a_3 & b_3 & c_3 \end{vmatrix} = \begin{vmatrix} a_1 & a_2 & a_3 \\ b_1 & b_2 & b_3 \\ c_1 & c_2 & c_3 \end{vmatrix}$$

2. If any two rows or columns of a determinant are interchanged, then the value of the determinant so obtained is the negative of the value of the original determinant.

i.e. $$\begin{vmatrix} a_1 & a_2 & a_3 \\ b_1 & b_2 & b_3 \\ c_1 & c_2 & c_3 \end{vmatrix} = -\begin{vmatrix} b_1 & b_{2_3} & b_3 \\ a_1 & a_2 & a_3 \\ c_1 & c_2 & c_3 \end{vmatrix}$$

3. If two rows or columns of a determinant are identical, the value of the determinant is zero

i.e. $$\begin{vmatrix} a_1 & a_2 & a_3 \\ a_1 & a_2 & a_3 \\ c_1 & c_2 & c_3 \end{vmatrix} = 0 \quad \text{or} \quad \begin{vmatrix} a_1 & b_1 & c_1 \\ a_2 & b_2 & c_2 \\ a_3 & b_3 & c_3 \end{vmatrix} = 0$$

4. If all the elements of any one row or column are multiplied by the same constant, then the original determinant is multiplied by that constant i.e.

$$\begin{vmatrix} Ka_1 & Kb_1 & Kc_1 \\ a_2 & b_2 & c_2 \\ a_3 & b_3 & c_3 \end{vmatrix} = K\begin{vmatrix} a_1 & b_1 & c_1 \\ a_2 & b_2 & c_2 \\ a_3 & b_3 & c_3 \end{vmatrix}$$

5. If all the elements of any one row or column are proportional, then its value is zero

i.e. $$\begin{vmatrix} a_1 & a_2 & a_3 \\ b_1 & b_2 & b_3 \\ Ka_1 & Ka_2 & Ka_3 \end{vmatrix} = 0$$

6. If each elements of a row or column of a determinant is expressed as a sum of two or more terms, then the determinant can be expressed as the sum of two or more determinants.

i.e. $\begin{vmatrix} a_1+\alpha_1 & b_1+\beta_1 & c_1+\Gamma_1 \\ a_2 & b_2 & c_2 \\ a_3 & b_3 & c_3 \end{vmatrix} = \begin{vmatrix} a_1 & b_1 & c_1 \\ a_2 & b_2 & c_2 \\ a_3 & b_3 & c_3 \end{vmatrix} + \begin{vmatrix} \alpha_1 & \beta_1 & \Gamma_1 \\ a_2 & b_2 & c_2 \\ a_3 & b_3 & c_3 \end{vmatrix}$

7. If to any row or column is added K times the corresponding elements of another row, the determinant remains unchanged.

i.e. $\begin{vmatrix} a_1+Kb_1 & a_2+Kb_2 & a_3+Kb_3 \\ b_1 & b_2 & b_3 \\ c_1 & c_2 & c_3 \end{vmatrix} = \begin{vmatrix} a_1 & b_2 & a_3 \\ b_1 & b_2 & b_3 \\ c_1 & c_2 & c_3 \end{vmatrix}$

8. If all the elements of any row or column are zero, the determinant vanishes

Example-1: Find the value of determinant $\begin{vmatrix} 2 & 5 & 4 \\ 1 & 4 & 3 \\ 6 & 8 & 10 \end{vmatrix}$

Solution: $\begin{vmatrix} 2 & 5 & 4 \\ 1 & 4 & 3 \\ 6 & 8 & 10 \end{vmatrix} = \begin{vmatrix} 1 & 1 & 1 \\ 1 & 4 & 3 \\ 6 & 8 & 10 \end{vmatrix} \quad (R_1 - R_2)$

$= \begin{vmatrix} 1 & 0 & 0 \\ 1 & 3 & 2 \\ 6 & 2 & 4 \end{vmatrix} \quad (C_2 - C_1 \text{ and } C_3 - C_1)$

$= +1 \begin{vmatrix} 3 & 2 \\ 2 & 4 \end{vmatrix} = 12 - 4 = 8$

Example-2: Find the value of $\begin{vmatrix} 43 & 1 & 6 \\ 35 & 7 & 4 \\ 17 & 3 & 2 \end{vmatrix}$

Solution: $\begin{vmatrix} 43 & 1 & 6 \\ 35 & 7 & 4 \\ 17 & 3 & 2 \end{vmatrix} = \begin{vmatrix} 42 & 1 & 6 \\ 35 & 7 & 4 \\ 14 & 3 & 2 \end{vmatrix}$ [applying $C_1 \rightarrow C_1 - C_2$]

$= 7\begin{vmatrix} 6 & 1 & 6 \\ 4 & 7 & 4 \\ 2 & 3 & 2 \end{vmatrix}$ [Taking 7 common from C_1]

$= 7 \times 0$ [as C_1 and C_2 are identical]

Example-3: $\begin{vmatrix} 1^2 & 2^2 & 3^2 & 4^2 \\ 2^2 & 3^2 & 4^2 & 5^2 \\ 3^2 & 4^2 & 5^2 & 6^2 \\ 4^2 & 5^2 & 6^2 & 7^2 \end{vmatrix}$ Find the value of

Solution: $\begin{vmatrix} 1^2 & 2^2 & 3^2 & 4^2 \\ 2^2 & 3^2 & 4^2 & 5^2 \\ 3^2 & 4^2 & 5^2 & 6^2 \\ 4^2 & 5^2 & 6^2 & 7^2 \end{vmatrix} = \begin{vmatrix} 1 & 3 & 5 & 7 \\ 4 & 5 & 7 & 9 \\ 9 & 7 & 9 & 11 \\ 16 & 9 & 11 & 13 \end{vmatrix}$ $\begin{bmatrix} \text{Applying } C_2 \rightarrow C_2 - C_1 \\ C_3 \rightarrow C_3 - C_2 \\ C_4 \rightarrow C_4 - C_3 \end{bmatrix}$

$= \begin{vmatrix} 1 & 3 & 5 & 2 \\ 4 & 5 & 7 & 2 \\ 9 & 7 & 9 & 2 \\ 16 & 9 & 11 & 2 \end{vmatrix}$ $\begin{bmatrix} \textit{Applying} \\ C_4 \rightarrow C_4 - C_3 \end{bmatrix}$

$= \begin{vmatrix} 1 & 3 & 2 & 2 \\ 4 & 5 & 2 & 2 \\ 9 & 7 & 2 & 2 \\ 16 & 9 & 2 & 2 \end{vmatrix}$ $\begin{bmatrix} \textit{Applying} \\ C_3 \rightarrow C_3 - C_2 \end{bmatrix}$

$= 0$ [as C_3 & C_4 are identical]

Example-4: Prove that $\begin{vmatrix} 1 & 1 & 1 \\ a & b & c \\ a^2 & b^2 & c^2 \end{vmatrix} = (a-b)\ (b-c)\ (c-a)$

Solution:

$$\begin{vmatrix} 1 & 1 & 1 \\ a & b & c \\ a^2 & b^2 & c^2 \end{vmatrix} = \begin{vmatrix} 1 & 0 & 0 \\ a & b-a & c-b \\ a^2 & b^2-a^2 & c^2-b^2 \end{vmatrix} \begin{bmatrix} applying \\ C_2 \to C_2 - C_1 \\ C_3 \to C_3 - C_2 \end{bmatrix}$$

$$\begin{vmatrix} 1 & 0 & 0 \\ a & b-a & c-b \\ a^2 & (b-a)(b+a) & (c-b)(c+b) \end{vmatrix} \begin{bmatrix} Taking (b-a)\ as\ common factor from C_2 \\ and\ (c-b)\ from C_3 \end{bmatrix}$$

$$= \text{(b-a)(c-b)} \begin{vmatrix} 1 & 0 & 0 \\ a & 1 & 1 \\ a^2 & b+a & c+b \end{vmatrix}$$

$$= (b-a)\ (c-b)\ [1(c+b) - 1\ (b+a)]$$

$$= (b-a)\ (c-b)\ [c+b-b-a]$$

$= (b-a)\ (c-b)\ (c-a)$ proved

Exercise-2

1. Show that $\begin{vmatrix} 13 & 16 & 19 \\ 14 & 17 & 20 \\ 15 & 18 & 21 \end{vmatrix} = 0$

2. Show that $\begin{vmatrix} (b+c)^2 & a^2 & a^2 \\ b^2 & (c+a)^2 & b^2 \\ c^2 & c^2 & (a+b)^2 \end{vmatrix} = 2abc\,(a+b+c)^3$

3. Find the value of $\begin{vmatrix} 2 & 5 & 7 \\ 3 & 6 & 10 \\ 8 & 4 & 15 \end{vmatrix}$

4. Find the value of $\begin{vmatrix} 46 & 32 & 15 \\ 27 & 21 & 9 \\ 17 & 16 & 7 \end{vmatrix}$

5. Find the value of $\begin{vmatrix} 1 & 2 & 0 \\ 0 & 1 & 2 \\ 1 & 0 & 2 \end{vmatrix}$

6. Find the value of $\begin{vmatrix} 91 & 94 & 96 \\ 92 & 95 & 97 \\ 93 & 96 & 98 \end{vmatrix}$

7. Prove that $\begin{vmatrix} 1+a & 1 & 1 \\ 1 & 1+a & 1 \\ 1 & 1 & 1+a \end{vmatrix} = a^2(a+3)$

8. Prove that $\begin{vmatrix} 1+a_1 & a_2 & a_3 \\ a_1 & 1+a_2 & a_3 \\ a_1 & a_2 & 1+a_3 \end{vmatrix} = 1+a_1+a_2+a_3$

9. Show that $\begin{vmatrix} b+c & a & a \\ b & c+a & b \\ c & c & a+b \end{vmatrix} = 4abc$

10. Show that $\begin{vmatrix} 1 & x & x^2 - yz \\ 1 & y & y^2 - zx \\ 1 & z & z^2 - xy \end{vmatrix} = 0$

Cramer's rule for solving a system of linear equations:

The solution of the system of equations

$$a_1x + b_1y + c_1z = d_1$$

$$a_2x + b_2y + c_2z = d_2$$

$$a_3x + b_3y + c_3z = d_3$$

is given by $x = \dfrac{D_1}{D}$, $y = \dfrac{D_2}{D}$, $z = \dfrac{D_3}{D}$

Where $D = \begin{vmatrix} a_1 & b_1 & c_1 \\ a_2 & b_2 & c_2 \\ a_3 & b_3 & c_3 \end{vmatrix}$

$D_1 = \begin{vmatrix} d_1 & b_1 & c_1 \\ d_2 & b_2 & c_2 \\ d_3 & b_3 & c_3 \end{vmatrix}$

$$D_2 = \begin{vmatrix} a_1 & d_1 & c_1 \\ a_2 & d_2 & c_2 \\ a_3 & d_3 & c_3 \end{vmatrix}$$

$$D_3 = \begin{vmatrix} a_1 & b_1 & d_1 \\ a_2 & b_2 & d_2 \\ a_3 & b_3 & d_3 \end{vmatrix}$$

Example-1: Solve the following system of equations by using Cramer's rule.

$$x + y + z = 9$$

$$2x + 5y + 7z = 52$$

$$2x + y - z = 0$$

Solution: We have

$$\begin{matrix} + & - & + \end{matrix}$$

$$D = \begin{vmatrix} 1 & 1 & 1 \\ 2 & 5 & 7 \\ 2 & 1 & -1 \end{vmatrix}$$

$$= +1\begin{vmatrix} 5 & 7 \\ 1 & -1 \end{vmatrix} - 1\begin{vmatrix} 2 & 7 \\ 2 & -1 \end{vmatrix} +1\begin{vmatrix} 2 & 5 \\ 2 & 1 \end{vmatrix}$$

$$= +1(-5-7) -1(-2-14) +1(2-10)$$

$$= -12 + 16 - 8$$

$$= -4 \neq 0$$

$$D_1 = \begin{vmatrix} \overset{+}{9} & \overset{-}{1} & \overset{+}{1} \\ 52 & 5 & 7 \\ 0 & 1 & -1 \end{vmatrix}$$

$$= +9\begin{vmatrix} 5 & 7 \\ 1 & -1 \end{vmatrix} -1\begin{vmatrix} 52 & 7 \\ 0 & -1 \end{vmatrix} +1\begin{vmatrix} 52 & 5 \\ 0 & 1 \end{vmatrix}$$

$$= +9(-5-7) -1(-52-0) +1(52-0)$$

$$= -108 + 52 + 52$$

$$= -108 + 104$$

$$= -4$$

$$D_2 = \begin{vmatrix} \overset{+}{1} & \overset{-}{9} & \overset{+}{1} \\ 2 & 52 & 7 \\ 2 & 0 & -1 \end{vmatrix}$$

$$= +1\begin{vmatrix} 52 & 7 \\ 0 & -1 \end{vmatrix} -9\begin{vmatrix} 2 & 7 \\ 2 & -1 \end{vmatrix} +1\begin{vmatrix} 2 & 52 \\ 2 & 0 \end{vmatrix}$$

$$= +1(-52-0) -9(-2-14) +1(0-104)$$

$$= -52 + 144 - 104$$

$$= -156 + 144 = -12$$

$$D_3 = \begin{vmatrix} \overset{+}{1} & \overset{-}{1} & \overset{+}{9} \\ 2 & 5 & 52 \\ 2 & 1 & 0 \end{vmatrix}$$

$$= +1\begin{vmatrix} 5 & 52 \\ 1 & 0 \end{vmatrix} - 1\begin{vmatrix} 2 & 52 \\ 2 & 0 \end{vmatrix} +9\begin{vmatrix} 2 & 5 \\ 2 & 1 \end{vmatrix}$$

$$= +1(0-52) -1(0-104) +9(2-10)$$

$$= -52 + 104 - 72$$

$$= -124 + 104 = -20$$

Therefore by using Cramer's rule

$$x = \frac{D_1}{D} = \frac{-4}{-4} = 1$$

$$y = \frac{D_2}{D} = \frac{-12}{-4} = 3$$

$$z = \frac{D_3}{D} = \frac{-20}{-4} = 5$$

Verification: Take the first equation i.e.

$$x + y + z = 9$$

$$1 + 3 + 5 = 9$$

$$\therefore 9 = 9$$

Example-2: Solve the following system of equations by using Cramer's rule

$$2y - 3z = 0$$

$$x + 3y = -4$$

$$3x + 4y = 3$$

Solution: we have $D = \begin{matrix} + & - & + \\ \end{matrix}$

$$D = \begin{vmatrix} 0 & 2 & -3 \\ 1 & 3 & 0 \\ 3 & 4 & 0 \end{vmatrix}$$

$$= +0\begin{vmatrix}3 & 0\\4 & 0\end{vmatrix} - 2\begin{vmatrix}1 & 0\\3 & 0\end{vmatrix} - 3\begin{vmatrix}1 & 3\\3 & 4\end{vmatrix}$$

= 0- 2 (0 – 0) -3 (4-9)

= 0 – 3 (-5)

D = 15, $\quad \therefore D \neq 0$

$$D_1 = \begin{vmatrix} \overset{+}{0} & \overset{-}{2} & \overset{+}{-3}\\ -4 & 3 & 0\\ 3 & 4 & 0\end{vmatrix}$$

$$= +0\begin{vmatrix}3 & 0\\4 & 0\end{vmatrix} - 2\begin{vmatrix}-4 & 0\\3 & 0\end{vmatrix} - 3\begin{vmatrix}-4 & 3\\3 & 4\end{vmatrix}$$

= 0 – 2 (0-0) -3 (-16 – 9)

= 0 – 3 (-25)

= 75

$$D_2 = \begin{vmatrix} \overset{+}{0} & \overset{-}{0} & \overset{+}{-3}\\ 1 & -4 & 0\\ 3 & 3 & 0\end{vmatrix}$$

$$= +0\begin{vmatrix}-4 & 0\\3 & 0\end{vmatrix} - 0\begin{vmatrix}1 & 0\\3 & 0\end{vmatrix} - 3\begin{vmatrix}1 & -4\\3 & 3\end{vmatrix}$$

= 0 +0 -3 (3+12)

= -3 (15)

D_2 = -45

$$D_3 = \begin{vmatrix} \overset{+}{0} & \overset{-}{2} & \overset{+}{0} \\ 1 & 3 & -4 \\ 3 & 4 & 3 \end{vmatrix}$$

$$= +0\begin{vmatrix} 3 & -4 \\ 4 & 3 \end{vmatrix} - 2\begin{vmatrix} 1 & -4 \\ 3 & 3 \end{vmatrix} + 0\begin{vmatrix} 1 & 3 \\ 3 & 3 \end{vmatrix}$$

$= 0 - 2(3 + 12) + 0$

$= -2(15)$

$D_3 = -30$

Therefore by using Cramer's rule

$$x = \frac{D_1}{D} = \frac{75}{15} = 5$$

$$y = \frac{D_2}{D} = \frac{-45}{15} = -3$$

$$z = \frac{D_3}{D} = \frac{-30}{15} = -2$$

Verification: take the first equation

$2y - 3z = 0$

$2(-3) - 3(-2) = 0$

$-6 + 6 = 0$

$0 = 0$

Example-3: Solve the following equation by Cramer rule

$5x - 6y + 4z = 15$

$7x + 4y - 3z = 19$

$2x + y + 6z = 46$

Solution: Here $D = \begin{vmatrix} \overset{+}{5} & \overset{-}{-6} & \overset{+}{4} \\ 7 & 4 & -3 \\ 2 & 1 & 6 \end{vmatrix}$

$$= +5\begin{vmatrix} 4 & -3 \\ 1 & 6 \end{vmatrix} +6\begin{vmatrix} 7 & -3 \\ 2 & 6 \end{vmatrix} +4\begin{vmatrix} 7 & 4 \\ 2 & 1 \end{vmatrix}$$

$= 5(24+3) + 6(42 + 6) +4 (7\text{-}8)$

$= 135 + 288 - 4$

$= 423 - 4$

$D = 419 \quad \therefore D \neq 0$

$$D_1 = \begin{vmatrix} \overset{+}{15} & \overset{-}{-6} & \overset{+}{4} \\ 19 & 4 & -3 \\ 46 & 1 & 6 \end{vmatrix}$$

$$= +15\begin{vmatrix} 4 & -3 \\ 1 & 6 \end{vmatrix} +6\begin{vmatrix} 19 & -3 \\ 46 & 6 \end{vmatrix} +4\begin{vmatrix} 19 & 4 \\ 46 & 1 \end{vmatrix}$$

$= 15(24 + 3) +6(114 + 138) +4(19\text{-}184)$

$= 405 + 1512 - 660$

$= 1257$

$$D_2 = \begin{vmatrix} \overset{+}{5} & \overset{-}{15} & \overset{+}{4} \\ 7 & 19 & -3 \\ 2 & 46 & 6 \end{vmatrix}$$

$$= +5\begin{vmatrix} 19 & -3 \\ 46 & 6 \end{vmatrix} -15\begin{vmatrix} 7 & -3 \\ 2 & 6 \end{vmatrix} +4\begin{vmatrix} 7 & 19 \\ 2 & 46 \end{vmatrix}$$

$= 5(114 + 138) -15(42 +6) +4(322 - 38)$

$= 5(252) -15(48) +4(284)$

$= 1260 - 720 + 1136$

$= 1676$

$$\begin{matrix} + & - & + \end{matrix}$$

$$D_3 = \begin{vmatrix} 5 & -6 & 15 \\ 7 & 4 & 19 \\ 2 & 1 & 46 \end{vmatrix}$$

$$= +5\begin{vmatrix} 4 & 19 \\ 1 & 46 \end{vmatrix} +6\begin{vmatrix} 7 & 19 \\ 2 & 46 \end{vmatrix} +15\begin{vmatrix} 7 & 4 \\ 2 & 1 \end{vmatrix}$$

$= 5(184 - 19) + 6(322 - 38) + 15 (7- 8)$

$= 5(165) + 6(284) + 15 (-1)$

$= 825 + 1704 - 15$

$= 2529 - 15$

$= 2514$

Now, by using Crammers rule

$$x = \frac{D_1}{D} = \frac{1257}{419} = 3$$

$$y = \frac{D_2}{D} = \frac{1676}{419} = 4$$

$$z = \frac{D_3}{D} = \frac{2514}{419} = 6$$

Verification: Take the first equation,

$$5x-6y+4z=15$$

$$5(3)-6(4)+4(6)=15$$

$$15-24+24=15$$

$$15=15$$

Exercise-3

1. Solve the following system of equations by Crammers rule.

$$2x+y+2z=10$$
$$x-y+2z=5$$
$$x+y+z=16$$

2. Solve the following equation by Crammers rule

$$3x+2y=8$$
$$5x-3y=7$$

3. Solve the following equation by Crammers rule

$$x+y+z=3$$
$$2x+3y+4z=9$$
$$x+2y-4z=-1$$

4. Solve the following equation by Crammers rule

$$x+y+z=3$$
$$2x-3y+5z=4$$
$$x+2y-4z=-1$$

5. Solve the following equation by Crammers rule

$$3x+y+z=10$$
$$x+y-z=0$$
$$5x-9y=1$$

6. Solve the following equation by Crammers rule

$x+3y=4$

$y+3z=7$

$z+4x=6$

7. Solve the following equation by Crammers rule

$x-2y+z=-1$

$3x+y-2z=4$

$y-z=1$

8. Solve the following equation by Crammers rule

$2x+y+z=7$

$3x-y-z=-2$

$x+2y-3z=-4$

9. Solve the following equation by Crammers rule

$x+2y-z=-3$

$3x+y+z=4$

$x-y+2z=6$

10. Solve the following equation by Crammers rule

$2x-7y=13$

$5x+6y=9$

Adjoint of a matrix

Let A = [*aij*]be a square matrix of order 'n' and let Cij denote the co–factor of aij in $|A|$. Then, the matrix of cofactors of 'A' is given by

$$A=\begin{bmatrix} A_1 & A_2 & \cdots\cdots & \cdots A_n \\ B_1 & B_2 & \cdots\cdots & .B_n \\ \cdots\cdots & \cdots\cdots & \cdots\cdots \\ \cdots\cdots & \cdots\cdots & \cdots\cdots \\ C_{n1} & C_{n2} & \cdots\cdots & C_{m} \end{bmatrix}$$

Thus, the adjoint of A, denoted by "adj. A" is defined as the transpose of the matrix of cofactors of A.

$$\text{Adj. A} = \begin{bmatrix} A_1 & A_2 \ldots\ldots\ldots & \ldots C_{n1} \\ B_1 & B_2 & \ldots\ldots\ldots .C_{n2} \\ \ldots\ldots\ldots & \ldots\ldots\ldots & \ldots\ldots\ldots \\ \ldots\ldots\ldots & \ldots\ldots\ldots & \ldots\ldots\ldots \\ A_{1n} & B_{2n} & \ldots\ldots\ldots C_{m} \end{bmatrix}$$

Example-1: Find the adjoint of the Matrix

$$A = \begin{bmatrix} 1 & -2 & 4 \\ 0 & 2 & 1 \\ -4 & 5 & 3 \end{bmatrix}$$

Solution: Let $A = \begin{bmatrix} A_1 & A_2 & A_3 \\ B_1 & B_2 & B_3 \\ C_1 & C_2 & C_3 \end{bmatrix} = \begin{bmatrix} + & - & + \\ 1 & -2 & 4 \\ - & + & - \\ 0 & 2 & 1 \\ + & - & + \\ -4 & 5 & 3 \end{bmatrix}$

$$\text{Co-factor of } A_1 = +\begin{vmatrix} 2 & 1 \\ 5 & 3 \end{vmatrix} = +(6-5) = 1$$

$$\text{Co-factor of } A_2 = -\begin{vmatrix} 0 & 1 \\ -4 & 3 \end{vmatrix} = -(0+4) = -4$$

$$\text{Co-factor of } A_3 = +\begin{vmatrix} 0 & 2 \\ -4 & 5 \end{vmatrix} = +(0+8) = 8$$

$$\text{Co-factor of } B_1 = -\begin{vmatrix} -2 & 4 \\ 5 & 3 \end{vmatrix} = -(-6-20) = -26$$

$$\text{Co-factor of } B_2 = +\begin{vmatrix} 1 & 4 \\ -4 & 3 \end{vmatrix} = +(3+16) = 19$$

$$\text{Co-factor of } B_3 = -\begin{vmatrix} 1 & -2 \\ -4 & 5 \end{vmatrix} = +(5-8) = 3$$

$$\text{Co-factor of } C_1 = +\begin{vmatrix} -2 & 4 \\ 2 & 1 \end{vmatrix} = +(-2-8) = -10$$

$$\text{Co-factor of } C_2 = -\begin{vmatrix} 1 & 4 \\ 0 & 1 \end{vmatrix} = -(1-0) = -1$$

$$\text{Co-factor of } C_3 = +\begin{vmatrix} 1 & -2 \\ 0 & 2 \end{vmatrix} = +(2-0) = 2$$

$$\text{Therefore } A = \begin{bmatrix} 1 & -4 & 8 \\ 26 & 19 & 3 \\ -10 & -1 & 2 \end{bmatrix}$$

Then Adj A. is the transport of A.

$$\text{Therefore, Adj } A = \begin{bmatrix} 1 & 26 & -10 \\ -4 & 19 & -1 \\ 8 & 3 & 2 \end{bmatrix}$$

Example-2: Find the adjoint Matrix of the following

$$A = \begin{bmatrix} 1 & -1 & 1 \\ 2 & 3 & 0 \\ 18 & 3 & 2 \end{bmatrix}$$

Solution: Let $A = \begin{bmatrix} A_1 & A_2 & A_3 \\ B_1 & B_2 & B_3 \\ C_1 & C_2 & C_3 \end{bmatrix} = \begin{bmatrix} + & - & + \\ 1 & -1 & 1 \\ - & + & - \\ 2 & 3 & 0 \\ + & - & + \\ 18 & 2 & 10 \end{bmatrix}$

$$\text{Co-factor of } A_1 = +\begin{vmatrix} 3 & 0 \\ 2 & 10 \end{vmatrix} = +(30-0) = 30$$

$$\text{Co-factor of } A_2 = -\begin{vmatrix} 2 & 0 \\ 18 & 10 \end{vmatrix} = -1(20-0) = -20$$

$$\text{Co-factor of } A_3 = -\begin{vmatrix} 2 & 0 \\ 18 & 10 \end{vmatrix} = -1(20-0) = -20$$

$$\text{Co-factor of } B_1 = -\begin{vmatrix} -1 & 1 \\ 2 & 10 \end{vmatrix} = -(-10-2) = 12$$

$$\text{Co-factor of } B_2 = +\begin{vmatrix} 1 & 1 \\ 18 & 10 \end{vmatrix} = +(10-18) = -8$$

$$\text{Co-factor of } B_3 = -\begin{vmatrix} 1 & -1 \\ 18 & 2 \end{vmatrix} = -(2+18) = -20$$

$$\text{Co-factor of } C_1 = +\begin{vmatrix} -1 & 1 \\ 3 & 0 \end{vmatrix} = (0-3) = -3$$

$$\text{Co-factor of } C_2 = -\begin{vmatrix} 1 & 1 \\ 2 & 0 \end{vmatrix} = -(0-2) = 2$$

$$\text{Co -factor of } C_3 = +\begin{vmatrix} 1 & -1 \\ 2 & 3 \end{vmatrix} = +(3+2) = 5$$

$$\text{Thus, Co-factor of A} = \begin{bmatrix} A_1 & A_2 & A_3 \\ B_1 & B_2 & B_3 \\ C_1 & C_2 & C_3 \end{bmatrix}$$

$$= \begin{bmatrix} 30 & -20 & -50 \\ 12 & -8 & -20 \\ -3 & 2 & 5 \end{bmatrix}$$

Then, the transpose of co-factor of A is

$$\text{Adj. A} = \begin{bmatrix} 30 & 12 & -3 \\ -20 & -8 & 2 \\ -50 & -20 & 5 \end{bmatrix}$$

Example-3: Find the adjoint of the matrix

$$A = \begin{bmatrix} 1 & 2 & -3 \\ 2 & 3 & 2 \\ 3 & -3 & -4 \end{bmatrix}$$

Solution: Let $A = \begin{bmatrix} A_1 & A_2 & A_3 \\ B_1 & B_2 & B_3 \\ C_1 & C_2 & C_3 \end{bmatrix} = \begin{bmatrix} + & - & + \\ 1 & 2 & -3 \\ - & + & - \\ 2 & 3 & 2 \\ + & - & + \\ 3 & -3 & -4 \end{bmatrix}$

Co-factor of $A_1 = +\begin{vmatrix} 3 & 2 \\ -3 & -4 \end{vmatrix} = +(-12+6) = -6$

Co-factor of $A_2 = -\begin{vmatrix} 2 & 2 \\ 3 & -4 \end{vmatrix} = -(-8-6) = +14$

Co-factor of $A_3 = +\begin{vmatrix} 2 & 3 \\ 3 & -3 \end{vmatrix} = +(-6-9) = -15$

Co-factor of $B_1 = -\begin{vmatrix} 2 & -3 \\ -3 & -4 \end{vmatrix} = -(8-9) = -17$

Co-factor of $B_2 = +\begin{vmatrix} 1 & -3 \\ 3 & -4 \end{vmatrix} = -(-4+9) = 5$

Co-factor of $B_3 = -\begin{vmatrix} 1 & 2 \\ 3 & -3 \end{vmatrix} = -(-3-6) = -9$

Co-factor of $C_1 = +\begin{vmatrix} 2 & -3 \\ 3 & 2 \end{vmatrix} = +(4+9) = 13$

Co-factor of $C_2 = -\begin{vmatrix} 1 & -3 \\ 2 & 2 \end{vmatrix} = -(2+6) = -8$

Co-factor of $C_3 = +\begin{vmatrix} 1 & 2 \\ 2 & 3 \end{vmatrix} = +(3-4) = -1$

$$\therefore A = \begin{bmatrix} -6 & 14 & -15 \\ 17 & 5 & 9 \\ 13 & -8 & -1 \end{bmatrix}$$

Then Adj. a is Transpose of A

$$\therefore \text{ There Adj. A} = \begin{bmatrix} -6 & 17 & 13 \\ 14 & 5 & -8 \\ -15 & 9 & -1 \end{bmatrix}$$

Example-4: Find the Adjoint of the following Matrix

$$A = \begin{bmatrix} 4 & -2 & 1 \\ 7 & 3 & 3 \\ 2 & 0 & 1 \end{bmatrix}$$

Solution: Let $A = \begin{bmatrix} A_1 & A_2 & A_3 \\ B_1 & B_2 & B_3 \\ C_1 & C_2 & C_3 \end{bmatrix} = \begin{bmatrix} + & - & + \\ 4 & -2 & 1 \\ - & + & - \\ 7 & 3 & 3 \\ + & - & + \\ 2 & 0 & 1 \end{bmatrix}$

$$\text{Co-factor of } A_1 = +\begin{vmatrix} 3 & 3 \\ 0 & 1 \end{vmatrix} = +(3-0) = 3$$

$$\text{Co-factor of } A_2 = -\begin{vmatrix} 7 & 3 \\ 2 & 1 \end{vmatrix} = -(7-6) = -1$$

$$\text{Co-factor of } A_3 = +\begin{vmatrix} 7 & 3 \\ 2 & 0 \end{vmatrix} = -(0-6) = -6$$

$$\text{Co-factor of } B_1 = -\begin{vmatrix} -2 & 1 \\ 0 & 1 \end{vmatrix} = -(-2-0) = 2$$

Co-factor of $B_2 = +\begin{vmatrix} 4 & 1 \\ 2 & 1 \end{vmatrix} = +(4-2) = 2$

Co-factor of $B_3 = -\begin{vmatrix} 4 & -2 \\ 2 & 0 \end{vmatrix} = -(0+4) = -4$

Co-factor of $C_1 = +\begin{vmatrix} -2 & 1 \\ 3 & 3 \end{vmatrix} = +(-6-3) = -9$

Co-factor of $C_2 = -\begin{vmatrix} 4 & 1 \\ 7 & 3 \end{vmatrix} = -(12-7) = -5$

Co-factor of $C_3 = +\begin{vmatrix} 4 & -2 \\ 7 & 3 \end{vmatrix} = +(12+14) = 26$

$$\therefore A = \begin{bmatrix} 3 & -1 & -6 \\ 2 & 2 & -4 \\ -9 & -5 & 26 \end{bmatrix}$$

Then Adj. a is Transpose of A

$$\text{Then Adj.A} = \begin{bmatrix} 3 & 2 & -9 \\ -1 & 2 & -5 \\ -6 & -4 & 26 \end{bmatrix}$$

Exercise-4

1. Find the adjoint of the following matrix

$$\begin{bmatrix} 3 & -1 & 1 \\ -15 & 6 & -5 \\ 5 & -2 & 2 \end{bmatrix}$$

2. Find the adjoint of the following matrix

$$\begin{bmatrix} 1 & 2 & 1 \\ 0 & -3 & 1 \\ -1 & 4 & 2 \end{bmatrix}$$

3. If $A = \begin{bmatrix} 1 & -1 & 1 \\ 2 & 3 & 0 \\ 18 & 2 & 10 \end{bmatrix}$ and prove that A. (Adj.A) = 0

4. Find the adjoint of the following matrix.

$$\begin{bmatrix} 1 & 2 & 3 \\ 2 & 3 & 2 \\ 3 & 3 & 4 \end{bmatrix}$$

5. Find the adjoint of the following matrix.

$$\begin{bmatrix} 1 & 0 & -1 \\ 3 & 4 & 5 \\ 0 & -6 & -7 \end{bmatrix}$$

Solving a system of linear equation:

Consider the following systems of linear equation are:

$$a_1x + b_1y + c_1z = d_1$$
$$a_2x + b_2y + c_2z = d_2$$
$$a_3x + b_3y + c_3z = d_3$$

The above system of linear equation can be written in matrix form as AX = B

Where $A = \begin{bmatrix} a_1 & b_1 & c_1 \\ a_2 & b_2 & c_2 \\ a_3 & b_3 & c_3 \end{bmatrix}$ $X = \begin{bmatrix} x \\ y \\ z \end{bmatrix}$ *and* $B = \begin{bmatrix} d_1 \\ d_2 \\ d_3 \end{bmatrix}$

Then, if A^{-1} exists, we get $x = A^{-1} . B$

Example-1: Find the inverse of the following matrix

$$\begin{bmatrix} 2 & -1 & 1 \\ -1 & 2 & -1 \\ 1 & -1 & 2 \end{bmatrix}$$

$$\text{Let } A = \begin{bmatrix} 2 & -1 & -1 \\ -1 & 2 & -1 \\ 1 & -1 & 2 \end{bmatrix}$$

$$A^{-1} = \frac{1}{|A|} adj.\ A$$

$$\begin{matrix} + & - & + \end{matrix}$$

$$|A| = \begin{bmatrix} 2 & -1 & 1 \\ -1 & 2 & -1 \\ 1 & -1 & 2 \end{bmatrix}$$

$$= +2\begin{vmatrix} 2 & -1 \\ -1 & 2 \end{vmatrix} +1\begin{vmatrix} -1 & -1 \\ 1 & 2 \end{vmatrix} +1\begin{vmatrix} -1 & 2 \\ 1 & -1 \end{vmatrix}$$

$$= 2(4-1) + 1(-2+1) + 1(1-2)$$

$$= 2(4-1) + 1(-2+1) + 1(1-2)$$

$$= 6 - 1 - 1$$

$$|A| = 4$$

$$\text{Now Let A}=\begin{bmatrix} A_1 & A_2 & A_3 \\ B_1 & B_2 & B_3 \\ C_1 & C_2 & C_3 \end{bmatrix} = \begin{bmatrix} + & - & + \\ 2 & -1 & 1 \\ - & + & - \\ -1 & 2 & -1 \\ + & - & + \\ 1 & -1 & 2 \end{bmatrix}$$

$$\text{The co-factor of } A_1 = +\begin{vmatrix} 2 & -1 \\ -1 & 2 \end{vmatrix} = (4-1) = 3$$

$$\text{The co-factor of } A_2 = -\begin{vmatrix} -1 & -1 \\ 1 & 2 \end{vmatrix} = -(-2+1) = 1$$

$$\text{The co-factor of } A_3 = +\begin{vmatrix} -1 & 2 \\ 1 & -1 \end{vmatrix} = (1-2) = -1$$

$$\text{The co-factor of } B_1 = -\begin{vmatrix} -1 & 1 \\ -1 & 2 \end{vmatrix} = -(-2+1) = 1$$

$$\text{The co-factor of } B_2 = +\begin{vmatrix} 2 & 1 \\ 1 & 2 \end{vmatrix} = (4-1) = 3$$

$$\text{The co-factor of } B_3 = -\begin{vmatrix} 2 & -1 \\ 1 & -1 \end{vmatrix} = -(-2+1) = 1$$

$$\text{The co-factor of } C_1 = +\begin{vmatrix} -1 & 1 \\ 2 & -1 \end{vmatrix} = (1-2) = -1$$

$$\text{The co-factor of } C_2 = -\begin{vmatrix} 2 & 1 \\ -1 & -1 \end{vmatrix} = -(-2+1) = 1$$

$$\text{The co-factor of } C_3 = -\begin{vmatrix} 2 & -1 \\ -1 & 2 \end{vmatrix} = (4-1) = 3$$

$$\therefore \text{ The co-factor of A} = \begin{bmatrix} 3 & 1 & -1 \\ 1 & 3 & 1 \\ -1 & 1 & 3 \end{bmatrix}$$

Then the Transpose of Co-factors of A is

$$\text{Adj. A} = \begin{bmatrix} 3 & 1 & -1 \\ 1 & 3 & 1 \\ -1 & 1 & 3 \end{bmatrix}$$

$$A^{-1} = \frac{1}{4}\begin{bmatrix} 3 & 1 & -1 \\ 1 & 3 & 1 \\ -1 & 1 & 3 \end{bmatrix}$$

$$\therefore A^{-1} = \begin{bmatrix} 3/4 & 1/4 & -1/4 \\ 1/4 & 3/4 & 1/4 \\ -1/4 & 1/4 & 3/4 \end{bmatrix}$$

Example-2: If $A = \begin{bmatrix} 2 & -3 & 3 \\ 2 & 2 & 3 \\ 3 & -2 & 2 \end{bmatrix}$ find A^{-1}

Solution: Given $A = \begin{bmatrix} 2 & -3 & 3 \\ 2 & 2 & 3 \\ 3 & -2 & 2 \end{bmatrix}$

$$\text{Thus, } |A| = \begin{bmatrix} \overset{+}{2} & \overset{-}{-3} & \overset{+}{3} \\ 2 & 2 & 3 \\ 3 & -2 & 2 \end{bmatrix}$$

$$= +2\begin{vmatrix} 2 & 3 \\ -2 & 2 \end{vmatrix} +3\begin{vmatrix} 2 & 3 \\ 3 & 2 \end{vmatrix} +3\begin{vmatrix} 2 & 2 \\ 3 & -2 \end{vmatrix}$$

$= 2(4 + 6) \quad +3(4 - 9) +3(-4 - 6)$

$= 2(10) +3 (-5) +3(-10)$

$= 20 - 15 -30$

$|A| = -25$

Then we can find out adjoint A.

$$\text{Let } A = \begin{bmatrix} A_1 & A_2 & A_3 \\ B_1 & B_2 & B_3 \\ C_1 & C_2 & C_3 \end{bmatrix} = \begin{bmatrix} + & - & + \\ 2 & -3 & 3 \\ - & + & - \\ 2 & 2 & 3 \\ + & - & + \\ 3 & -2 & 2 \end{bmatrix}$$

$$\text{The co-factor of } A_1 = +\begin{vmatrix} 2 & 3 \\ -2 & 2 \end{vmatrix} = (4+6) = 10$$

$$\text{The co-factor of } A_2 = -\begin{vmatrix} 2 & 3 \\ 3 & 2 \end{vmatrix} = -(4-9) = 5$$

$$\text{The co-factor of } A_3 = +\begin{vmatrix} 2 & 2 \\ 3 & -2 \end{vmatrix} = +(-4-6) = -10$$

The co-factor of $B_1 = -\begin{vmatrix} -3 & 3 \\ -2 & 2 \end{vmatrix} = -(-6+6) = 0$

The co-factor of $B_2 = +\begin{vmatrix} 2 & 3 \\ 3 & 2 \end{vmatrix} = +(4-9) = -5$

The co-factor of $B_3 = -\begin{vmatrix} 2 & -3 \\ 1 & -2 \end{vmatrix} = -(-4+9) = -5$

The co-factor of $C_1 = +\begin{vmatrix} -3 & 3 \\ 2 & 3 \end{vmatrix} = +(-9-6) = -15$

The co-factor of $C_2 = -\begin{vmatrix} 2 & 3 \\ 2 & 3 \end{vmatrix} = -(6-6) = 0$

The co-factor of $C_2 = -\begin{vmatrix} 2 & -3 \\ 2 & 2 \end{vmatrix} = (4+6) = 10$

$\therefore$ The co-factors of $A = \begin{bmatrix} 10 & 5 & -10 \\ 0 & -5 & -5 \\ -15 & 0 & 10 \end{bmatrix}$

Then the Transpose of Co-factors of A is

$$\text{Adj. A} = \begin{bmatrix} 10 & 0 & -15 \\ 5 & -5 & 0 \\ -10 & -5 & 10 \end{bmatrix}$$

$$A^{-1} = \frac{1}{-25}\begin{bmatrix} 10 & 0 & -15 \\ 5 & -5 & 0 \\ -10 & -5 & 10 \end{bmatrix}$$

$$= \begin{bmatrix} \frac{-10}{25} & \frac{0}{-25} & \frac{-15}{-25} \\ \frac{-5}{25} & \frac{-5}{-25} & \frac{0}{-25} \\ \frac{-10}{-25} & \frac{-5}{-25} & \frac{10}{-25} \end{bmatrix}$$

$$\therefore \quad A^{-1} = \begin{bmatrix} -2/5 & 0 & -3/5 \\ -1/5 & 1/5 & 0 \\ 2/5 & 1/5 & -2/5 \end{bmatrix}$$

Example-3: If $A = \begin{bmatrix} 1 & 2 & 2 \\ 2 & 1 & 2 \\ 2 & 2 & 1 \end{bmatrix}$ find out A^{-1}

Solution: we have $A = \begin{bmatrix} 1 & 2 & 2 \\ 2 & 1 & 2 \\ 2 & 2 & 1 \end{bmatrix}$

$$A^{-1} = \frac{1}{|A|} \, adj. \, A$$

$$\begin{matrix} + & - & + \end{matrix}$$

$$|A| = \begin{bmatrix} 1 & 2 & 2 \\ 2 & 1 & 2 \\ 2 & 2 & 1 \end{bmatrix}$$

$$= +\begin{vmatrix} 1 & 2 \\ 2 & 2 \end{vmatrix} -2\begin{vmatrix} 2 & 2 \\ 2 & 1 \end{vmatrix} +2\begin{vmatrix} 2 & 1 \\ 2 & 2 \end{vmatrix}$$

$= +(1 - 4) \quad -2(2 - 4) +2(4 -2)$

$= -3 + 4 + 4$

$|A| = 5$

Thus we have to find out adjoint A.

$$\text{Let } A = \begin{bmatrix} A_1 & A_2 & A_3 \\ B_1 & B_2 & B_3 \\ C_1 & C_2 & C_3 \end{bmatrix} = \begin{bmatrix} + & - & + \\ 1 & 2 & 2 \\ - & + & - \\ 2 & 1 & 2 \\ + & - & + \\ 2 & 2 & 1 \end{bmatrix}$$

$$\text{The co-factor of } A_1 = +\begin{vmatrix} 1 & 2 \\ 2 & 1 \end{vmatrix} = +(1-4) = -3$$

$$\text{The co-factor of } A_2 = -\begin{vmatrix} 2 & 2 \\ 2 & 1 \end{vmatrix} = -(2-4) = 2$$

$$\text{The co-factor of } A_3 = +\begin{vmatrix} 2 & 1 \\ 2 & 2 \end{vmatrix} = +(4-2) = 2$$

$$\text{The co-factor of } B_1 = -\begin{vmatrix} 2 & 2 \\ 2 & 1 \end{vmatrix} = -(2-4) = 2$$

$$\text{The co-factor of } B_2 = +\begin{vmatrix} 1 & 2 \\ 2 & 1 \end{vmatrix} = +(1-4) = -3$$

The co-factor of $B_3 = -\begin{vmatrix} 1 & 2 \\ 2 & 2 \end{vmatrix} = -(2-4) = 2$

The co-factor of $C_1 = +\begin{vmatrix} 2 & 2 \\ 1 & 2 \end{vmatrix} = +(4-2) = 2$

The co-factor of $C_2 = -\begin{vmatrix} 1 & 2 \\ 2 & 2 \end{vmatrix} = -(2-4) = 2$

The co-factor of $C_3 = +\begin{vmatrix} 1 & 2 \\ 2 & 1 \end{vmatrix} = +(1-4) = -3$

$\therefore$ The co-factors of $A = \begin{bmatrix} -3 & 2 & 2 \\ 2 & -3 & 2 \\ 2 & 2 & -3 \end{bmatrix}$

Then the transpose of co-factors of A is

$$\text{Adj. A} = \begin{bmatrix} -3 & 2 & 2 \\ 2 & -3 & 2 \\ 2 & 2 & -3 \end{bmatrix}$$

$$\therefore A^{-1} = \frac{1}{5}\begin{bmatrix} -3 & 2 & 2 \\ 2 & -3 & 2 \\ 2 & 2 & -3 \end{bmatrix}$$

$$\therefore A^{-1} = \begin{bmatrix} -3/5 & 2/5 & 2/5 \\ 2/5 & -3/5 & 2/5 \\ 2/5 & 2/5 & -3/5 \end{bmatrix}$$

Example-4: Solve the following system of equations by using matrix inversion method.

$$x + 2y - 3z = 4$$
$$2x + 3y + 2z = 2$$
$$3x - 3y - 4z = 11$$

Solution: The given system of equations of can be written in the matrix form as AX = B

$$\text{Where } A = \begin{bmatrix} 1 & 2 & -3 \\ 2 & 3 & 2 \\ 3 & -3 & -4 \end{bmatrix} \quad X = \begin{bmatrix} x \\ y \\ x \end{bmatrix} \quad \textit{and} \quad B = \begin{bmatrix} 4 \\ 2 \\ 11 \end{bmatrix}$$

$X = A^{-1} . B$

$$\therefore \ A^{-1} = \frac{1}{|A|} \ adj. A$$

$$\begin{matrix} & + & - & + \end{matrix}$$

$$|A| = \begin{vmatrix} 1 & 2 & -3 \\ 2 & 3 & 2 \\ 3 & -3 & -4 \end{vmatrix}$$

$$= +1 \begin{vmatrix} 3 & 2 \\ -3 & -4 \end{vmatrix} - 2 \begin{vmatrix} 2 & 2 \\ 3 & -4 \end{vmatrix} - 3 \begin{vmatrix} 2 & 3 \\ 3 & -3 \end{vmatrix}$$

$= +1\ (-12 + 6) \ \ -2\ (-8-6) \ \ -3\ (-6-9)$

$= -6 + 28 + 45$

$|A| = 67$

$\therefore \ |A| \neq 0$

Thus, A^{-1} exists

Then we have to find out adj. A

$$\text{Let } A = \begin{bmatrix} A_1 & A_2 & A_3 \\ B_1 & B_2 & B_3 \\ C_1 & C_2 & C_3 \end{bmatrix} = \begin{bmatrix} + & - & + \\ 1 & 2 & -3 \\ - & + & - \\ 2 & 3 & 2 \\ + & - & + \\ 3 & -3 & -4 \end{bmatrix}$$

$$\text{The co-factor of } A_1 = +\begin{vmatrix} 3 & 2 \\ -3 & -4 \end{vmatrix} = +(-12+6) = -6$$

$$\text{The co-factor of } A_2 = -\begin{vmatrix} 2 & 2 \\ 3 & -4 \end{vmatrix} = -(-8-6) = +14$$

$$\text{The co-factor of } A_3 = +\begin{vmatrix} 2 & 3 \\ 3 & -3 \end{vmatrix} = +(-6-9) = -15$$

$$\text{The co-factor of } B_1 = -\begin{vmatrix} 2 & -3 \\ -3 & -4 \end{vmatrix} = -(-8-9) = +17$$

$$\text{The co-factor of } B_2 = +\begin{vmatrix} 1 & -3 \\ 3 & -4 \end{vmatrix} = +(-4+9) = 5$$

$$\text{The co-factor of } B_3 = -\begin{vmatrix} 1 & 2 \\ 3 & -3 \end{vmatrix} = -(-3-6) = 9$$

$$\text{The co-factor of } C_1 = +\begin{vmatrix} 2 & -3 \\ 3 & 2 \end{vmatrix} = +(4+9) = 13$$

The co-factor of $C_2 = -\begin{vmatrix} 1 & -3 \\ 2 & 2 \end{vmatrix} = -(2+6) = -8$

The co-factor of $C_3 = +\begin{vmatrix} 1 & 2 \\ 2 & 3 \end{vmatrix} = -(3-4) = -1$

$\therefore$ The co-factors of $A = \begin{bmatrix} -6 & 14 & -15 \\ 17 & 5 & 9 \\ 13 & -8 & -1 \end{bmatrix}$

Then the transpose of co-factors of A is

$$\text{Adj. } A = \begin{bmatrix} -6 & 17 & 13 \\ 14 & 5 & -8 \\ -15 & 9 & -1 \end{bmatrix}$$

$\therefore X = A^{-1} . B$

$$X = \frac{1}{67}\begin{bmatrix} -6 & 17 & 13 \\ 14 & 5 & -8 \\ -15 & 9 & -1 \end{bmatrix}\begin{bmatrix} -4 \\ 2 \\ 11 \end{bmatrix}$$

$$X = \frac{1}{67}\begin{bmatrix} -6\times-4 + 17\times 2 + 13\times 11 \\ 14\times -4 + 5\times 2 + (-8)\times 11 \\ -15\times-4 + 9\times 2 + (-1)\times 11 \end{bmatrix}$$

$$= \frac{1}{67}\begin{bmatrix} 24 + 34 + 143 \\ -56 + 10 - 88 \\ 60 + 18 - 11 \end{bmatrix}$$

$$= \frac{1}{67}\begin{bmatrix} 201 \\ -134 \\ 67 \end{bmatrix}$$

$$X = \begin{bmatrix} 3 \\ -2 \\ 1 \end{bmatrix}$$

$\therefore$ x = 3, y = –2, z = 1

Verification: Take the first equation

$$x + 2y - 3z = -4$$
$$3 + 2(-2) - 3(1) = -4$$
$$3 - 4 - 3 = -4$$
$$-4 = -4$$

Example-5: Use matrix inversion to issue for the following system of linear equation

$$2x + 4y - 3z = 12$$
$$3x - 5y + 2z = 13$$
$$-x + 3y + 2z = 17$$

Solution: The given system of equations of can be written in the matrix form as AX = B

$$\text{When } A = \begin{bmatrix} 2 & 4 & -3 \\ 3 & -5 & 2 \\ -1 & 3 & 2 \end{bmatrix} \quad X = \begin{bmatrix} x \\ y \\ z \end{bmatrix} \quad \text{and } B = \begin{bmatrix} 12 \\ 13 \\ 17 \end{bmatrix}$$

$$\therefore X = A^{-1} . B$$

$$A^{-1} = \frac{1}{|A|} adj. A$$

$$|A| = \begin{vmatrix} \overset{+}{2} & \overset{-}{4} & \overset{+}{-3} \\ 3 & -5 & 2 \\ -1 & 3 & 2 \end{vmatrix}$$

$$= +2\begin{vmatrix} -5 & 2 \\ 3 & 2 \end{vmatrix} - 4\begin{vmatrix} 3 & 2 \\ -1 & 2 \end{vmatrix} - 3\begin{vmatrix} 3 & 5 \\ -1 & 3 \end{vmatrix}$$

$= +2\ (-10 - 6)\ \ - 4\ (6+2) - 3\ (9-5)$

$= +2(-16)\ \ -4(8)\ \ -3(4)$

$|A| = -76$

$\therefore |A| \neq 0$

Thus A^{-1} exist

Then we have to find out adj. A

$$\text{Let } A = \begin{bmatrix} A_1 & A_2 & A_3 \\ B_1 & B_2 & B_3 \\ C_1 & C_2 & C_3 \end{bmatrix} = \begin{bmatrix} + & - & + \\ 2 & 4 & -3 \\ - & + & - \\ 3 & -5 & 2 \\ + & - & + \\ -1 & 3 & 2 \end{bmatrix}$$

$$\text{The co-factor of } A_1 = +\begin{vmatrix} -5 & 2 \\ 3 & 2 \end{vmatrix} = +(-10-6) = -16$$

$$\text{The co-factor of } A_2 = -\begin{vmatrix} 3 & 2 \\ -1 & 2 \end{vmatrix} = -(6+2) = 8$$

$$\text{The co-factor of } A_3 = +\begin{vmatrix} 3 & -5 \\ -1 & 3 \end{vmatrix} = +(9-5) = 4$$

$$\text{The co-factor of } B_1 = -\begin{vmatrix} 4 & -3 \\ 3 & 2 \end{vmatrix} = -(8+9) = -17$$

$$\text{The co-factor of } B_2 = +\begin{vmatrix} 2 & -3 \\ -1 & 2 \end{vmatrix} = +(4-3) = 1$$

$$\text{The co-factor of } B_3 = -\begin{vmatrix} 2 & 4 \\ -1 & 3 \end{vmatrix} = -(+6+4) = -10$$

$$\text{The co-factor of } C_1 = +\begin{vmatrix} 4 & -3 \\ 3 & 2 \end{vmatrix} = +(8+9) = 17$$

$$\text{The co-factor of } C_2 = -\begin{vmatrix} 2 & -3 \\ 3 & 2 \end{vmatrix} = -(4+9) = -13$$

$$\text{The co-factor of } C_3 = +\begin{vmatrix} 2 & 4 \\ 3 & -5 \end{vmatrix} = +(-10-12) = -22$$

$$\therefore \text{ The co-factors is } = \begin{bmatrix} -16 & 8 & 4 \\ -17 & 1 & -10 \\ 17 & -13 & -22 \end{bmatrix}$$

Then the transpose of co-factors of A is

$$\text{Adj. A} = \begin{bmatrix} -16 & -17 & 17 \\ 8 & 1 & -13 \\ 4 & -10 & -22 \end{bmatrix}$$

$\therefore X = A^{-1} . B$

$$X = \frac{1}{-76}\begin{bmatrix}-16 & -17 & 17\\ 8 & 1 & -13\\ 4 & -10 & -22\end{bmatrix}\begin{bmatrix}12\\13\\17\end{bmatrix}$$

$$X = \frac{1}{-76}\begin{bmatrix}-16\times 12 + (-17)\times 13 + 17\times 17\\ 8\times 12 + 1\times 13 + (-13)\times 17\\ 4\times 12 + (-10)\times 13 + (-22)\times 17\end{bmatrix}$$

$$= \frac{1}{-76}\begin{bmatrix}-124\\-112\\-456\end{bmatrix}$$

$$\therefore X = \begin{bmatrix}1.631\\1.473\\6\end{bmatrix}$$

$\therefore$ x = 1.631, y = 1.473, z = 6

Example-6: Solve the following system of equations by using Cramer rule.

$$x + y + z = 7$$

$$x + 2y + 3z = 16$$

$$x + 3y + 4z = 22$$

Solution: We have

$$\begin{matrix} + & - & + \end{matrix}$$

$$D = \begin{bmatrix}1 & 1 & 1\\ 1 & 2 & 3\\ 1 & 3 & 4\end{bmatrix}$$

$$= +1\begin{vmatrix} 2 & 3 \\ 3 & 4 \end{vmatrix} -1\begin{vmatrix} 1 & 3 \\ 1 & 4 \end{vmatrix} \; 1\begin{vmatrix} 1 & 2 \\ 1 & 3 \end{vmatrix}$$

$= +1\ (8 - 9) -1(4 - 3) +1(3 - 2)$

$= -1\ \ -1\ \ +1 = -1$

$= -1 \neq 0$

$$D_1 = \begin{bmatrix} \overset{+}{7} & \overset{-}{1} & \overset{+}{1} \\ 16 & 2 & 3 \\ 22 & 3 & 4 \end{bmatrix} = +7\begin{vmatrix} 2 & 3 \\ 3 & 4 \end{vmatrix} -1\begin{vmatrix} 16 & 3 \\ 22 & 4 \end{vmatrix} +1\begin{vmatrix} 16 & 2 \\ 22 & 3 \end{vmatrix}$$

$= +7\ (8 - 9) -1\ (64 - 66) +1\ (48 - 44)$

$= -7 + 2 + 4 = -1$

$$D_2 = \begin{bmatrix} \overset{+}{1} & \overset{-}{7} & \overset{+}{1} \\ 1 & 16 & 3 \\ 1 & 22 & 4 \end{bmatrix}$$

$$= +1\begin{vmatrix} 16 & 3 \\ 22 & 4 \end{vmatrix} -7\begin{vmatrix} 1 & 3 \\ 1 & 4 \end{vmatrix} +1\begin{vmatrix} 1 & 16 \\ 1 & 22 \end{vmatrix}$$

$= +1\ (64\text{-}66) - 7\ (4\text{-}3) + 1\ (22\text{-}16)$

$= -2-7+6$

$= -3$

$$D_3 = \begin{bmatrix} \overset{+}{1} & \overset{-}{1} & \overset{+}{7} \\ 1 & 2 & 16 \\ 1 & 2 & 22 \end{bmatrix}$$

$$= +1\begin{vmatrix} 2 & 16 \\ 3 & 22 \end{vmatrix} - 1\begin{vmatrix} 1 & 16 \\ 1 & 22 \end{vmatrix} + 7\begin{vmatrix} 1 & 2 \\ 1 & 3 \end{vmatrix}$$

$= +1\ (44 - 48) - 1(22 - 16) + 7\ (3 - 2)$

$= -4 - 6 + 7$

$= -3$

Therefore by using Cramer rule

$$x = \frac{D_1}{D} = \frac{-1}{-1} = 1$$

$$y = \frac{D_2}{D} = \frac{-3}{-1} = 3$$

$$z = \frac{D_3}{D} = \frac{-3}{-1} = 3$$

Verification: Take the first equation

$x + y + z = 7$

$1 + 3 + 3 = 7$

$\therefore\ 7 = 7$

Example-7: Find A^{-1} where $A = \begin{bmatrix} 1 & 2 & -3 \\ 2 & 3 & 2 \\ 3 & -3 & -4 \end{bmatrix}$

Solution: $A^{-1} = \dfrac{1}{|A|}\ Adj.\ A$

$$\begin{matrix} + & - & + \end{matrix}$$

$$|A| = \begin{bmatrix} 1 & 2 & -3 \\ 2 & 3 & 2 \\ 3 & -3 & -4 \end{bmatrix}$$

$$= +1\begin{vmatrix} 3 & 2 \\ -3 & -4 \end{vmatrix} - 2\begin{vmatrix} 2 & 2 \\ 3 & -4 \end{vmatrix} + (-3)\begin{vmatrix} 2 & 3 \\ 3 & -3 \end{vmatrix}$$

$= + 1\ (-12 + 6) -2(-8 - 6) -3\ (-6 - 9)$

$= - 6 + 28 + 45 = 67$

$|A| = 67$

Then we have to find out Adjoint A

$$\text{Let } A = \begin{bmatrix} A_1 & A_2 & A_3 \\ B_1 & B_2 & B_3 \\ C_1 & C_2 & C_3 \end{bmatrix} = \begin{bmatrix} + & - & + \\ 1 & 2 & -3 \\ - & + & - \\ 2 & 3 & 2 \\ + & - & + \\ 3 & -3 & -4 \end{bmatrix}$$

The co-factor of $A_1 = +\begin{vmatrix} 3 & 2 \\ -3 & -4 \end{vmatrix} = +(-12+6) = -6$

The co-factor of $A_2 = -\begin{vmatrix} 2 & 2 \\ 3 & -4 \end{vmatrix} = -(-8-6) = 14$

The co-factor of $A_3 = +\begin{vmatrix} 2 & 3 \\ 3 & -3 \end{vmatrix} = +(-6-9) = -15$

The co-factor of $B_1 = -\begin{vmatrix} 2 & -3 \\ -3 & -4 \end{vmatrix} = -(-8-9) = 17$

The co-factor of $B_2 = -\begin{vmatrix} 1 & -3 \\ 3 & -4 \end{vmatrix} = +(-4+9) = 17$

The co-factor of $B_3 = -\begin{vmatrix} 1 & 2 \\ 3 & -3 \end{vmatrix} = -(-3-6) = 9$

The co-factor of $C_1 = +\begin{vmatrix} 2 & -3 \\ 3 & 2 \end{vmatrix} = +(4+9) = 13$

The co-factor of $C_2 = -\begin{vmatrix} 1 & -3 \\ 2 & 2 \end{vmatrix} = -(2+6) = -8$

The co-factor of $C_3 = +\begin{vmatrix} 1 & 2 \\ 2 & 3 \end{vmatrix} = +(3-4) = -1$

Then Co-factors of $A = \begin{bmatrix} -6 & 14 & -15 \\ 17 & 5 & 9 \\ 13 & -8 & -1 \end{bmatrix}$

Then the transpose of co-factors of A is

$$\text{Adjoint } A = \begin{bmatrix} -6 & 17 & 13 \\ 14 & 5 & -8 \\ -15 & 9 & -1 \end{bmatrix}$$

$$\therefore A^{-1} = \frac{1}{67}\begin{bmatrix} -6 & 17 & 13 \\ 14 & 5 & -8 \\ -15 & 9 & -1 \end{bmatrix}$$

$$\therefore A^{-1} = \begin{bmatrix} -6/67 & 17/67 & 13/67 \\ 14/67 & 5/67 & -8/67 \\ -15/67 & 9/67 & -1/67 \end{bmatrix}$$

Example-8: Solve the following system of equations by using matrix method.

$$x + 2y + z = 7$$

$$x + 3z = 11$$

$$2x - 3y = 1$$

Solution: The above system of equations are written in the matrix form

: i.e. AX = B

$$\text{Where } A = \begin{bmatrix} 1 & 2 & 1 \\ 1 & 0 & 3 \\ 2 & -3 & 0 \end{bmatrix} \quad X = \begin{bmatrix} x \\ y \\ z \end{bmatrix} \quad and \quad B = \begin{bmatrix} 7 \\ 11 \\ 1 \end{bmatrix}$$

$$\therefore X = A^{-1} . B$$

$$A^{-1} = \frac{1}{|A|} \cdot Adj.\, A$$

$$\begin{matrix} + & - & + \end{matrix}$$

$$|A| = \begin{bmatrix} 1 & 2 & 1 \\ 1 & 0 & 3 \\ 2 & -3 & 0 \end{bmatrix}$$

$$= +1 \begin{vmatrix} 0 & +3 \\ -3 & 0 \end{vmatrix} - 2 \begin{vmatrix} 1 & 3 \\ 2 & 0 \end{vmatrix} + 1 \begin{vmatrix} 1 & 0 \\ 2 & -3 \end{vmatrix}$$

$$= +1\,(0 + 9) \quad -2\,(0 - 6) \quad +1\,(-3 - 0)$$

$$= 9 + 12 - 3$$

$$|A| = 18$$

$$\therefore |A| \neq 0$$

Thus A^{-1} exists

Then we have to find out Adjoint A

$$\text{Let } A = \begin{bmatrix} A_1 & A_2 & A_3 \\ B_1 & B_2 & B_3 \\ C_1 & C_2 & C_3 \end{bmatrix} = \begin{bmatrix} + & - & + \\ 1 & 2 & 1 \\ - & + & - \\ 1 & 0 & 3 \\ + & - & + \\ 2 & -3 & 0 \end{bmatrix}$$

$$\text{The co-factor of } A_1 = +\begin{vmatrix} 0 & 3 \\ -3 & 0 \end{vmatrix} = +(0+9) = 9$$

$$\text{The co-factor of } A_2 = -\begin{vmatrix} 1 & 3 \\ 2 & 0 \end{vmatrix} = -(0-6) = 6$$

$$\text{The co-factor of } A_3 = +\begin{vmatrix} 1 & 0 \\ 2 & -3 \end{vmatrix} = +(-3-0) = -3$$

$$\text{The co-factor of } B_1 = -\begin{vmatrix} 2 & 1 \\ -3 & 0 \end{vmatrix} = -(0+3) = -3$$

$$\text{The co-factor of } B_2 = -\begin{vmatrix} 1 & 1 \\ 2 & 0 \end{vmatrix} = +(0-2) = -2$$

$$\text{The co-factor of } B_3 = -\begin{vmatrix} 1 & 2 \\ 2 & -3 \end{vmatrix} = -(-3-4) = +7$$

$$\text{The co-factor of } C_1 = +\begin{vmatrix} 2 & 1 \\ 0 & 3 \end{vmatrix} = +(6-0) = 6$$

$$\text{The co-factor of } C_2 = -\begin{vmatrix} 1 & 1 \\ 1 & 3 \end{vmatrix} = -(3-1) = -2$$

$$\text{The co-factor of } C_3 = +\begin{vmatrix} 1 & 2 \\ 1 & 0 \end{vmatrix} = +(0-2) = -2$$

$$\text{Then Co-factors of A} = \begin{bmatrix} 9 & 6 & -3 \\ -3 & -2 & 7 \\ 6 & -2 & -2 \end{bmatrix}$$

Then the transpose of co-factors of A is

$$\text{Adj. A} = \begin{bmatrix} 9 & -3 & 6 \\ 6 & -2 & -2 \\ -3 & 7 & -2 \end{bmatrix}$$

$$\therefore X = A^{-1} . B$$

$$X = \frac{1}{18} \begin{bmatrix} 9 & -3 & 6 \\ 6 & -2 & -2 \\ -3 & 7 & -2 \end{bmatrix} \begin{bmatrix} 7 \\ 11 \\ 1 \end{bmatrix}$$

$$X = \begin{bmatrix} 9\times7 + (-3)\times11 + 6\times1 \\ 6\times7 + (-2)\times11 + (-2)\times1 \\ -3\times7 + 7\times11 + (-2)\times1 \end{bmatrix}$$

$$= \frac{1}{18}\begin{bmatrix} 63-33+6 \\ 42-22-2 \\ -21+77-2 \end{bmatrix}$$

$$= \frac{1}{18}\begin{bmatrix} 36 \\ 18 \\ 54 \end{bmatrix} \quad \therefore X = \begin{bmatrix} 2 \\ 1 \\ 3 \end{bmatrix}$$

$\therefore x = 2, \quad y = 1, \quad z = 3$

Verification: Take the first equation

$$x + 2y + z = 7$$
$$2 - 2(1) + 3 = 7$$
$$2 + 2 + 3 = 7$$
$$7 = 7$$

Example-9: Solve the system of equations, using matrix method.

$$x + y - 3z = -4$$
$$2x + 3y + 2z = 2$$
$$3x - 3y - 4z = 11$$

Solution: The above system of equations are written in the matrix form i.e. AX = B

Where $A = \begin{bmatrix} 1 & 1 & -3 \\ 2 & 3 & 2 \\ 3 & -3 & -4 \end{bmatrix}$ $X = \begin{bmatrix} x \\ y \\ z \end{bmatrix}$ *and* $B = \begin{bmatrix} -4 \\ 2 \\ 11 \end{bmatrix}$

$\therefore AX = B$

$X = A^{-1}.B$

$$A^{-1} = \frac{1}{|A|} adj.A.$$

$$|A| = \begin{bmatrix} \overset{+}{1} & \overset{-}{1} & \overset{+}{-3} \\ 2 & 3 & 2 \\ 3 & -3 & -4 \end{bmatrix}$$

$$= +1\begin{vmatrix} 3 & 2 \\ -3 & -4 \end{vmatrix} -1\begin{vmatrix} 2 & 2 \\ 3 & -4 \end{vmatrix} +(-3)\begin{vmatrix} 2 & 3 \\ 3 & -3 \end{vmatrix}$$

$= +1\ (-12 + 6) -1\ (-8 - 6) -3\ (-6 - 9)$

$= +1\ (-6) -1\ (-14) -3(-15)$

$= -6 + 14 + 45$

$|A| = 53$

$\therefore\ |A| \neq 0$

Thus A^{-1} exists

Then we have to find out Adj. A

$$\text{Let } A = \begin{bmatrix} A_1 & A_2 & A_3 \\ B_1 & B_2 & B_3 \\ C_1 & C_2 & C_3 \end{bmatrix} = \begin{bmatrix} + & - & + \\ 1 & 1 & -3 \\ - & + & - \\ 2 & 3 & 2 \\ + & - & + \\ 3 & -3 & -4 \end{bmatrix}$$

The co-factor of $A_1 = +\begin{vmatrix} 3 & 2 \\ -3 & -4 \end{vmatrix} = +(-12+6) = -6$

$$\text{The co-factor of } A_2 = -\begin{vmatrix} 2 & 2 \\ 3 & -4 \end{vmatrix} = -(-8-6) = +14$$

$$\text{The co-factor of } A_3 = +\begin{vmatrix} 2 & 3 \\ 3 & -3 \end{vmatrix} = +(-6-9) = -15$$

$$\text{The co-factor of } B_1 = -\begin{vmatrix} 1 & -3 \\ -3 & -4 \end{vmatrix} = -(-4-9) = 13$$

$$\text{The co-factor of } B_2 = -\begin{vmatrix} 1 & -3 \\ 3 & -4 \end{vmatrix} = +(-4+9) = 5$$

$$\text{The co-factor of } B_3 = -\begin{vmatrix} 1 & 1 \\ 3 & -3 \end{vmatrix} = -(-3-3) = 6$$

$$\text{The co-factor of } C_1 = +\begin{vmatrix} 1 & -3 \\ 3 & 2 \end{vmatrix} = +(2+9) = 11$$

$$\text{The co-factor of } C_2 = -\begin{vmatrix} 1 & -3 \\ 2 & 2 \end{vmatrix} = -(2+6) = -8$$

$$\text{The co-factor of } C_3 = +\begin{vmatrix} 1 & 1 \\ 2 & 3 \end{vmatrix} = +(3-2) = 1$$

$$\text{The co-factors of } A = \begin{bmatrix} -6 & 14 & -15 \\ 13 & 5 & 6 \\ 11 & -8 & 1 \end{bmatrix}$$

Then the transpose of co-factors of A is

$$\text{Adj. } A = \begin{bmatrix} -6 & 13 & 11 \\ 14 & 5 & -8 \\ -15 & 6 & 1 \end{bmatrix}$$

$$\therefore X = A^{-1} . B$$

$$X = \frac{1}{15}\begin{bmatrix} -6 & 13 & 11 \\ 14 & 5 & -8 \\ -15 & 6 & 1 \end{bmatrix}\begin{bmatrix} -4 \\ 2 \\ 11 \end{bmatrix}$$

$$= \frac{1}{53}\begin{bmatrix} (-6)\times(-4) + 13\times 2 + 11\times 11 \\ 14\times(-4) + 5\times 2 + (-8)\times 11 \\ (-15)(-4) + 6\times 2 + 1\times 11 \end{bmatrix}$$

$$= \frac{1}{53}\begin{bmatrix} 24 + 26 + 121 \\ -56 + 10 - 88 \\ 60 + 12 + 11 \end{bmatrix}$$

$$= \frac{1}{53}\begin{bmatrix} 171 \\ -134 \\ 83 \end{bmatrix}$$

$$X = \begin{bmatrix} 171/53 \\ -134/53 \\ 83/53 \end{bmatrix}$$

$$\therefore X = \frac{171}{53} \quad y = \frac{-134}{53}, \quad z = \frac{83}{53}$$

Verification: Take the first equation

$$x + y - 3z = -4$$

$$= \frac{171}{53} - \frac{137}{53} - 3\left(\frac{83}{53}\right) = -4$$

$$= \frac{171 - 134 - 249}{53} = -4$$

$$= \frac{171 - 383}{53} = -4$$

$$= \frac{-212}{53} = -4$$

$$-4 = -4$$

Exercise-5

1. Find the inverse of the following matrix

$$\begin{bmatrix} 0 & 0 & -1 \\ 3 & 4 & 5 \\ -2 & -4 & -7 \end{bmatrix}$$

2. Find the inverse of the following matrix

$$\begin{bmatrix} 1 & 4 & 2 \\ -1 & 2 & 1 \\ 1 & 3 & 2 \end{bmatrix}$$

3. Compute the inverse of the matrix

$$A = \begin{bmatrix} -1 & 0 & 2 \\ 2 & 3 & 0 \\ 0 & 1 & -2 \end{bmatrix}$$

4. Find the inverse of the following matrix

$$\begin{bmatrix} 1 & 0 & 1 \\ 3 & 2 & 1 \\ 0 & 1 & 3 \end{bmatrix}$$

5. Find the inverse of the following matrix

$$\begin{bmatrix} 0 & 4 & 2 \\ 0 & -5 & 1 \\ 3 & -2 & -5 \end{bmatrix}$$

6. Compute the inverse of the following matrix

$$\begin{bmatrix} 1 & -2 & 3 \\ 3 & -1 & 4 \\ 2 & 1 & -2 \end{bmatrix}$$

Applications of Matrix

Example-1: Mr. X has invested a part of his investment in 10% bond A and apart in 15% bond B. His interest income during first year is Re. 4,000. If he invests 20% more in 10% bond A and 15% bond B, his income during second year increases by Re. 500. Find his initial investments and the new investment in bonds A and B using matrix method.

Solution: Let initial investment be are x_1 in 10% bonds and are x_2 in 15% bonds

Then the given information can be written we have

$$0.10\,x_1 + 0.15x_2 = 4{,}000 \Rightarrow 2x_1 + 3x_2 = 80{,}000$$

$$0.12\,x_1 + 0.165x_2 = 4{,}500 \Rightarrow 8x_1 + 11x_2 = 3,00{,}000$$

The given system of equations can be written in the matrix form as AX = B

$$\text{Where } A = \begin{bmatrix} 2 & 3 \\ 8 & 11 \end{bmatrix} \quad X = \begin{bmatrix} x_1 \\ x_2 \end{bmatrix} \quad \text{and} \quad B = \begin{bmatrix} 80{,}000 \\ 3{,}00{,}000 \end{bmatrix}$$

$$A^{-1} = \frac{1}{|A|}\,Adj.\,A$$

Here |A| = ad – bc

= (2) (11) – (3) (8)

= 22 – 24

|A| = –2

The Adjoint Matrix A is $\begin{bmatrix} d & -b \\ -c & a \end{bmatrix}$

$$= \begin{bmatrix} 11 & -3 \\ -8 & 2 \end{bmatrix}$$

$$A^{-1} = \frac{1}{-2}\begin{bmatrix} 11 & -3 \\ -8 & 2 \end{bmatrix}$$

$$= \begin{bmatrix} -11/2 & 3/2 \\ 4 & -1 \end{bmatrix}$$

Then X = A^{-1} B

$$= \begin{bmatrix} -11/2 & 3/2 \\ 4 & -1 \end{bmatrix}\begin{bmatrix} 80{,}000 \\ 3{,}00{,}000 \end{bmatrix}$$

$$= \begin{bmatrix} \frac{-88000}{2} + \frac{900000}{2} \\ 320000 - 3{,}00{,}000 \end{bmatrix}$$

$$= \begin{bmatrix} \frac{20{,}000}{2} \\ 20000 \end{bmatrix} = \begin{bmatrix} 10{,}000 \\ 20{,}000 \end{bmatrix}$$

$\therefore x_1$ = Rs.10,000 x_2 = Rs.20,000

Therefore the initial investments Re. 10,000 and 20,000 the new investments Re. 12,000 and 22,000.

Example-2: To control a crop disease it is necessary to use 8 units of chemical A, 14 units of chemical B and 13 units of chemical C. One barel of spray P contains one unit of A, 2 units of B and 3 units of C. One barrel of spray Q contains 2 units of A, 3 units of B and 2 units of C. One barrel of spray R contains 1 unit of A, 2 units of B and 2 units of C. Find how many barrels or each spray be used to just meet the requirements.

Solution: Let x barrels of spray P

y barrels of spray Q

z barrels of spray R be used to just meet the requirements.

$$x+2y+z = 8$$
$$2x+3y+2z = 14$$
$$3x+2y+2z = 13$$

The given system of equation can be written in the matrix form as AX = B

$$A = \begin{bmatrix} 1 & 2 & 1 \\ 2 & 3 & 2 \\ 3 & 2 & 2 \end{bmatrix} \quad X = \begin{bmatrix} x \\ y \\ z \end{bmatrix} \quad and \ B = \begin{bmatrix} 8 \\ 14 \\ 13 \end{bmatrix}$$

$$X = A^{-1} B$$

$$\therefore A^{-1} = \frac{1}{|A|} . Adj. A$$

$$\begin{matrix} + & - & + \end{matrix}$$

$$|A| = \begin{bmatrix} 1 & 2 & 1 \\ 2 & 3 & 2 \\ 3 & 2 & 2 \end{bmatrix}$$

$$= +1\begin{vmatrix}3 & 2\\2 & 2\end{vmatrix} - 2\begin{vmatrix}2 & 2\\3 & 2\end{vmatrix} + 1\begin{vmatrix}2 & 3\\3 & 2\end{vmatrix}$$

$= 1\,(6-4) - 2\,(4-6) + 1\,(4-9)$

$= 1\,(2) - 2\,(-2) \;\; +1(-5)$

$= 2 + 4 - 5$

$\therefore |A| = 1$

Then we have to find out Adj. A

$$\text{Let } A = \begin{bmatrix} A_1 & A_2 & A_3\\ B_1 & B_2 & B_3\\ C_1 & C_2 & C_3\end{bmatrix} = \begin{bmatrix} + & - & +\\ 1 & 2 & 1\\ - & + & -\\ 2 & 3 & 2\\ + & - & +\\ 3 & 2 & 2\end{bmatrix}$$

The co-factors of $A_1 = +\begin{vmatrix}3 & 2\\2 & 2\end{vmatrix} = +(6-4) = 2$

The co-factors of $A_2 = -\begin{vmatrix}2 & 2\\3 & 2\end{vmatrix} = -(4-6) = 2$

The co-factors of $A_3 = +\begin{vmatrix}2 & 3\\3 & 2\end{vmatrix} = +(4-9) = -5$

The co-factors of $B_1 = -\begin{vmatrix}2 & 1\\2 & 2\end{vmatrix} = -(4-2) = -2$

The co-factors of $B_2 = -\begin{vmatrix}1 & 1\\3 & 2\end{vmatrix} = +(2-3) = -1$

The co-factors of $B_3 = -\begin{vmatrix} 1 & 2 \\ 3 & 2 \end{vmatrix} = -(2-6) = 4$

The co-factors of $C_1 = +\begin{vmatrix} 2 & 1 \\ 3 & 2 \end{vmatrix} = +(4-3) = 1$

The co-factors of $C_2 = -\begin{vmatrix} 1 & 1 \\ 2 & 2 \end{vmatrix} = -(2-2) = 0$

The co-factors of $C_3 = +\begin{vmatrix} 1 & 2 \\ 2 & 3 \end{vmatrix} = +(3-4) = -1$

$$\therefore \text{ The co-factors of A} = \begin{bmatrix} 2 & 2 & -5 \\ -2 & -1 & 4 \\ 1 & 0 & -1 \end{bmatrix}$$

Then the transpose of co-factors of A is

$$\text{Adj. A} = \begin{bmatrix} 2 & -2 & 1 \\ 2 & -1 & 0 \\ -5 & 4 & -1 \end{bmatrix}$$

$\therefore X = A^{-1}.B$

$$X = \frac{1}{1}\begin{bmatrix} 2 & -2 & 1 \\ 2 & -1 & 0 \\ -5 & 4 & -1 \end{bmatrix}\begin{bmatrix} 8 \\ 14 \\ 13 \end{bmatrix}$$

$$= \begin{bmatrix} 2\times 8 & + & (-2)\times 14 & +1\times 13 \\ 2\times 8 & + & (-1)\times 14 & +0\times 13 \\ -5 & + & 4\times 14 & +(-1)\times 13 \end{bmatrix}$$

$$= \begin{bmatrix} 16 - 28 + 13 \\ 16 - 14 + 0 \\ -40 + 56 - 13 \end{bmatrix}$$

$$\therefore X = \begin{bmatrix} 1 \\ 2 \\ 3 \end{bmatrix}$$

$\therefore x = 1, \quad y = 2, \quad z = 3$

Hence 1barrel of P, 2 barrel of Q 3 barrel of R must be used to just meet the requirements

Verification: we take the first equation

$$x + 2y + z = 8$$
$$2 + 2(2) + 3 = 8$$
$$1 + 4 + 3 = 8$$
$$8 = 8$$

Example-3: A firm produces two products P_1 and P_2 passing through two medicines M_1 and M_2 before completion. M_1 can produce either 10 units of P_1 or 15 units of P_2 per hour. M_2 can produce 15 units of either product per hour. Find daily production of P_1 and P_2 if time available is 12 hours on medicine M_1 and 10 hours on M_2 per day using matrix inversion.

Solution: Let the daily production of products P_1 and P_2 be x units and y units respectively.

$\therefore$ We have following equations

$$\frac{x}{10} + \frac{y}{15} = 12$$

$$\frac{3x + 2y}{30} = 12$$

$3x + 2y = 360 \quad \rightarrow (1)$

$\frac{x}{15} + \frac{y}{15} = 10$

$\frac{x+y}{15} = 10$

$x + y = 150 \quad \rightarrow (2)$

The above equations can be written in the matrix form as AX = B

Where $A = \begin{bmatrix} 3 & 2 \\ 1 & 1 \end{bmatrix}$ $X = \begin{bmatrix} x \\ y \end{bmatrix}$ *and* $B = \begin{bmatrix} 360 \\ 150 \end{bmatrix}$

$A^{-1} = \frac{1}{|A|} \, adj.\, A$

Where $|A| = ad - bc = (3)(1) - (2)(1)$

$= 3 - 2$

$= 1$

The adjoint matrix A is $\begin{bmatrix} d & -b \\ -c & a \end{bmatrix}$

$= \begin{bmatrix} 1 & -2 \\ -1 & 3 \end{bmatrix}$

$A^{-1} = \frac{1}{1} \begin{bmatrix} 1 & -2 \\ -1 & 3 \end{bmatrix}$

$= \begin{bmatrix} 1 & -2 \\ -1 & 3 \end{bmatrix}$

Then $X = A^{-1} B$

$$= \begin{bmatrix} 1 & -2 \\ -1 & 3 \end{bmatrix} \begin{bmatrix} 360 \\ 150 \end{bmatrix}$$

$$= \begin{bmatrix} 1 \times 360 & + & (-2) \times 150 \\ -1 \times 360 & + & 3 \times 150 \end{bmatrix}$$

$$= \begin{bmatrix} 360 & - & 300 \\ -360 & + & 450 \end{bmatrix}$$

$$= \begin{bmatrix} 60 \\ 90 \end{bmatrix}$$

$\therefore x = 60, \quad y = 90$

Verification: take the firs equation

$3x + 2y = 360$

$3(60) + 2(90) = 360$

$180 + 180$

$360 = 360$

Example-4: The equilibrium condition for three related markets is given by

$11P_1 - P_2 - P_3 = 31$

$-P_1 + 6P_2 - 2P_3 = 26$

$-P_1 - 2P_2 + 7P_3 = 24$

Find the equilibrium price for each market.

Solution: The given system of equations can be written in the matrix form as

$AX = B$

$$\text{Where } A = \begin{bmatrix} 11 & -1 & -1 \\ -1 & 6 & -2 \\ -1 & -2 & 7 \end{bmatrix} \quad X = \begin{bmatrix} P_1 \\ P_2 \\ P_3 \end{bmatrix} \text{ and } B = \begin{bmatrix} 31 \\ 26 \\ 24 \end{bmatrix}$$

$X = A^{-1}.B$

$\therefore A^{-1} = \frac{1}{|A|} \; adj.\, A$

$$\begin{matrix} + & - & + \end{matrix}$$

$$|A| = \begin{bmatrix} 11 & -1 & -1 \\ -1 & 6 & -2 \\ -1 & -2 & 7 \end{bmatrix}$$

$$+11 \begin{vmatrix} 6 & -2 \\ -2 & 7 \end{vmatrix} - (-1) \begin{vmatrix} -1 & -2 \\ -1 & 7 \end{vmatrix} - 1 \begin{vmatrix} -1 & 6 \\ -1 & -2 \end{vmatrix}$$

$= 11\,(42 - 4) + 1\,(-7 - 2) - 1\,(+2 + 6)$

$= 11\,(38) + 1\,(-9) - 1(8)$

$= 418 - 9 - 8$

$|A| = 401$

$\therefore |A| \neq 0$ Thus A^{-1} exists

Then we have to find out ajd. A.

$$\text{Let } A = \begin{bmatrix} A_1 & A_2 & A_3 \\ B_1 & B_2 & B_3 \\ C_1 & C_2 & C_3 \end{bmatrix} = \begin{bmatrix} + & - & + \\ 11 & -1 & -1 \\ - & + & - \\ -1 & 6 & -2 \\ + & - & + \\ -1 & -2 & 7 \end{bmatrix}$$

The co-factors of $A_1 = +\begin{vmatrix} 6 & -2 \\ -2 & 7 \end{vmatrix} = +(42-4) = 38$

The co-factors of $A_2 = -\begin{vmatrix} -1 & -2 \\ -1 & 7 \end{vmatrix} = -(-7-2) = 9$

The co-factors of $A_3 = +\begin{vmatrix} -1 & 6 \\ -1 & -2 \end{vmatrix} = +(2+6) = 8$

The co-factors of $B_1 = -\begin{vmatrix} -1 & 6 \\ -2 & -2 \end{vmatrix} = -(-7-2) = 9$

The co-factors of $B_2 = +\begin{vmatrix} -1 & -1 \\ -2 & -2 \end{vmatrix} = +(77-1) = 76$

The co-factors of $B_3 = -\begin{vmatrix} 11 & -1 \\ -1 & -2 \end{vmatrix} = -(-22-1) = 23$

The co-factors of $C_1 = +\begin{vmatrix} -1 & -1 \\ 6 & -2 \end{vmatrix} = +(+2+6) = 8$

The co-factors of $C_2 = -\begin{vmatrix} 11 & -1 \\ -1 & -2 \end{vmatrix} = -(-22-1) = 23$

The co-factors of $C_3 = +\begin{vmatrix} 11 & -1 \\ -1 & 6 \end{vmatrix} = +(66-1) = 65$

$$\therefore \text{ The Co-factors of } A = \begin{bmatrix} 38 & 9 & 8 \\ 9 & 76 & 23 \\ 8 & 23 & 65 \end{bmatrix}$$

The transpose of co-factors of A is

$$\text{Adj. } A = \begin{bmatrix} 38 & 9 & 8 \\ 9 & 76 & 23 \\ 8 & 23 & 65 \end{bmatrix}$$

$$\therefore X = A^{-1}.B$$

$$X = \frac{1}{401}\begin{bmatrix} 38 & 9 & 8 \\ 9 & 76 & 23 \\ 8 & 23 & 65 \end{bmatrix}\begin{bmatrix} 31 \\ 26 \\ 24 \end{bmatrix}$$

$$= \frac{1}{401}\begin{bmatrix} 38\times 31 + 9\times 26 + 8\times 24 \\ 9\times 31 + 76\times 26 + 23\times 24 \\ 8\times 31 + 23\times 26 + 65\times 24 \end{bmatrix}$$

$$= \frac{1}{401}\begin{bmatrix} 1178 + 234 + 192 \\ 279 + 1976 + 552 \\ 248 + 598 + 1560 \end{bmatrix}$$

$$= \frac{1}{401}\begin{bmatrix} 1604 \\ 2807 \\ 2406 \end{bmatrix}$$

$$\therefore X = \begin{bmatrix} 4 \\ 7 \\ 6 \end{bmatrix}$$

$$\therefore P_1 = 4, \quad P_2 = 7, \quad P_3 = 6$$

Verification: we take the first equation

$$11P_1 - P_2 - P_3 = 31$$

$$11(4) - 7 - 6 = 31$$

$$44 - 13 = 31$$

$$31 = 31$$

Example-5: The equilibrium condition for two substitute goods is given by

$$5P_1 - 2P_2 = 15$$

$$-P_1 + 8P_2 = 16$$

Find the equilibrium prices

Solution: The given system of equations can be written in the matrix as

$$AX = B$$

Where $A = \begin{bmatrix} 5 & -2 \\ -1 & 8 \end{bmatrix}$ $X = \begin{bmatrix} P_1 \\ P_2 \end{bmatrix}$ and B $\begin{bmatrix} 15 \\ 16 \end{bmatrix}$

$$A^{-1} = \frac{1}{|A|} \; adj.\, A$$

Here $|A| = ad - bc = (5)(8) - (-2)(-1)$

$$= 40 - 2$$

$$= 38$$

The adjoint Matrix A is $\begin{bmatrix} d & -b \\ -c & a \end{bmatrix}$

$$= \begin{bmatrix} 8 & 2 \\ 1 & 5 \end{bmatrix}$$

$$A^{-1} = \frac{1}{38}\begin{bmatrix} 8 & 2 \\ 1 & 5 \end{bmatrix}$$

$$= \begin{bmatrix} 8/38 & 2/38 \\ 1/3 & 5/38 \end{bmatrix} = \begin{bmatrix} 4/19 & 1/19 \\ 1/38 & 5/38 \end{bmatrix}$$

The $X = A^{-1}.B$

$$\begin{bmatrix} 4/19 & 1/19 \\ 1/38 & 5/38 \end{bmatrix}\begin{bmatrix} 15 \\ 16 \end{bmatrix}$$

$$= \begin{bmatrix} \frac{60}{19} + \frac{16}{19} \\ \frac{15}{38} + \frac{80}{38} \end{bmatrix}$$

$$= \begin{bmatrix} \frac{76}{19} \\ \frac{95}{38} \end{bmatrix} = \begin{bmatrix} 4 \\ 2.5 \end{bmatrix}$$

The equilibrium prices are $P_1 = 4$ $P_2 = 2.5$

Verification: Take the fist equation

$5P_1 - 2P_2 = 15$

$5(4) - 2(2.5) = 15$

$20 - 5 = 15$

$15 = 15$

Exercise-6

1. Solve the following system of equations by using matrix inversion method

$2x + 4y - z = 9$

$3x + y + 2z = 7$

$x + 3y - 3z = 4$

2. Using matrix inversion method solve the following system of equations

$2x + 3y - z = 9$

$x + y + z = 9$

$3x - y - z = -1$

3. Using matrix inversion method solve the following system of equations

$2x - y + 3z = 1$

$x + y + z = 2$

$x - y + 3z = 4$

4. Using matrix inversion method solve the following system of equations

$2x - y + 2z = 6$

$x - 2y + 3z = 6$

$3x - 3y - z = -6$

5. Using matrix inversion method solve the following system of equations

$x + 2y + 3z = -4$

$2x + 3y + 2z = 2$

$3x - 3y - 4z = 11$

6. Using matrix inversion method solve the following system of equations

$5x - 7y + z = 11$

$6x - 8y - z = 15$

$3x + 2y - 6z = 7$

7. Solve the following system of equations by using matrix inversion method

$$3x + y + z = 2$$

$$2x - 4y + 3z = -1$$

$$4x + y - 3z = -11$$

8. Solve the following system of equations by using matrix inversion method

$$6x + y - 3z = 5$$

$$x + 3y - 2z = 5$$

$$2x + y + 4z = 8$$

9. Solve the following system of equations by using matrix inversion method

$$x + y + z = -1$$

$$x + 2y + 3z = -4$$

$$x + 3y + 4z = 8$$

10. Solve the following system of equations by using matrix inversion method

$$x - 4y - z = 11$$

$$2x - 5y + 2z = 39$$

$$-3x + 2y + z = 1$$

3

Differentiation

The rate at which a function changes with respect to its independent variable is called the derivative of a function.

Definition: Let y = f(x) be a function defined in a certain interval and x be a fixed interior point of this interval. Let Δx (or h) be an increment of x such that x + Δx (or x + h) lies within the stated interval. Let Δy are f(x+h) - f(x) be the corresponding increment of y = f(x). Then the increment ratio is a function of Δx (or h).

$$\frac{\Delta y}{\Delta x} = \frac{f(x+\Delta x) - f(x)}{\Delta x} \ (or) \ \frac{f(x+h) - f(x)}{h}$$

If this ratio $\frac{\Delta y}{\Delta x}$ *or* $\frac{f(x+h) - f(x)}{n}$ tends to a definite finite quantity as Δx tends to zero, from either side, then this finite quantity is called the derivative or the differential coefficient of f(x) with respect to x 'at the point x' and is denoted by f¹(x) or $\frac{d}{dx}[f(x)]$, or $\frac{dy}{dx}$.

Some standards formulae results:

1. $\frac{d}{dx}$ (constant) = 0

2. $\frac{d}{dx}(x) = 1$

3. $\frac{d}{dx}\left(x^{n}\right) = n \cdot x^{n-1}$

4. $\frac{d}{dx}\left(e^{x}\right) = e^{x}$

5. $\frac{d}{dx}(a^{x}) = a^{x} \log a$

6. $\frac{d}{dx}(\log x) = \frac{1}{x}$

7. $\frac{d}{dx}\left(\sqrt{x}\right) = \frac{1}{2\sqrt{x}}$

8. $\frac{d}{dx}\left(e^{-x}\right) = -e^{-x}$

The above stated standard formulae results are very useful for further applications in Economics and Business.

Rules of Differentiation

If u and v are any two functions of x then the following results are true.

Let 'u' is the first term and 'v' is the second term. Then,

1. $\frac{d}{dx}[u \pm v] = \frac{d}{dx}(u) \pm \frac{d}{dx}(v)$

2. $\frac{d}{dx}[uv] = u \cdot \frac{d}{dx}(v) + v \cdot \frac{d}{dx}(u)$

3. $$\frac{d}{dx}\left[\frac{u}{v}\right] = \frac{v \cdot \frac{d}{dx}(u) - u \cdot \frac{d}{dx}(v)}{v^2}$$

4. $$\frac{dy}{dx} = \frac{dy}{du} \cdot \frac{du}{dx} \text{ (chain rule)}$$

5. $\frac{d}{dx}[cu] = c \cdot \frac{d}{dx}(u)$, when 'c' is a constant.

Examples

Example-1: Find the derivative of $x^4 + 3x^2 - 4$

Solution: Let $y = x^4 + 3x^2 - 4$

$$\text{Then } \frac{dy}{dx} = \frac{d}{dx}(y) = \frac{d}{dx}(x^4 + 3x^2 - 4)$$

$$= \frac{d}{dx}(x^4) + \frac{d}{dx}(3x^2) - \frac{d}{dx}(4)$$

$$= 4x^3 + 6x - 0$$

$$\therefore \frac{dy}{dx} = 4x^3 + 6x = 2(2x^3 + 3x)$$

Example-2: Find the derivative of $ax^2 + bx + c$

Solution: Let $y = ax^2 + bx + c$

$$\text{Then } \frac{dy}{dx} = \frac{d}{dx}(y) = \frac{d}{dx}\left(ax^2 + bx + c\right)$$

$$= \frac{d}{dx}\left(ax^2\right)+\frac{d}{dx}\left(bx\right)+\frac{d}{dx}(c)$$

$$= a(2x)+b(1)+0$$

$$\therefore \frac{dy}{dx} = 2ax+b$$

Example-3: Find the derivative of $ax^4+bx^3+cx^2+dx+e$

Solution: Let y = $ax^4+bx^3+cx^2+dx+e$

Then $\frac{dy}{dx} = \frac{d}{dx}(y) = \frac{d}{dx}\left(ax^4+bx^3+cx^2+dx+e\right)$

$$= \frac{d}{dx}\left(ax^4\right)+\frac{d}{dx}\left(bx^3\right)+\frac{d}{dx}\left(cx^2\right)+\frac{d}{dx}(dx)+\frac{d}{dx}(e)$$

$$= a\frac{d}{dx}\left(x^4\right)+b\frac{d}{dx}\left(x^3\right)+c\frac{d}{dx}\left(x^2\right)+d\frac{d}{dx}(x)+\frac{d}{dx}(e)$$

$$= a\,(4x^3) + b\,(3x^2) + c\,(2x) + d\,(1) + 0$$

$$\therefore \frac{dy}{dx} = 4ax^3+3bx^2+2cx+d$$

Example-4: Find the derivative of $\sqrt{x}+x^3$

Solution: Let $y = \sqrt{x}+x^3$

Then, $\frac{dy}{dx} = \frac{d}{dx}(y) = \frac{d}{dx}\left(\sqrt{x}+x^3\right)$ Where $y = \sqrt{x}+x^3$

$$= \frac{d}{dx}\left(\sqrt{x}\right) + \frac{d}{dx}\left(x^3\right)$$

$$\therefore \frac{dy}{dx} = \frac{1}{2\sqrt{x}} + 3x^2$$

Example-5: Find the derivative of $2x^3 + 3x^2 - 6x + 4$

Solution: Let $y = 2x^3 + 3x^2 - 6x + 4$

$$\text{Then } \frac{dy}{dx} = \frac{d}{dx}(y) = \frac{d}{dx}\left(2x^3 + 3x^2 - 6x + 4\right)$$

$$= \frac{d}{dx}\left(2x^3\right) + \frac{d}{dx}\left(3x^2\right) - \frac{d}{dx}(6x) + \frac{d}{dx}(4)$$

$$= 2\frac{d}{dx}\left(x^3\right) + 3\frac{d}{dx}\left(x^2\right) - 6\frac{d}{dx}(x) + \frac{d}{dx}(4)$$

$$= 2\left(3x^2\right) + 3(2x) - 6(1) + 0$$

$$= 6x^2 + 6x - 6$$

$$\therefore \frac{dy}{dx} = 6\left(x^2 + x - 1\right)$$

Example-6: Find the derivative of $\left(x^2 - 2x\right)^2$

Solution: Let $y = \left(x^2 - 2x\right)^2$

$$\text{Then } \frac{dy}{dx} = \frac{d}{dx}\left(x^2 - 2x\right)^2$$

$$= 2\left(x^2 - 2x\right)^1 (2x - 2)$$

Example-7: Find the derivative of xe^x

Solution: Let $y = x\,e^x$

Let $u = x,$ $\qquad v = e^x$

$$\frac{d}{dx}(uv) = u\cdot\frac{d}{dx}(v) + v\cdot\frac{d}{dx}(u)$$

$$\frac{d}{dx}\left(x e^x\right) = x\cdot\frac{d}{dx}\left(e^x\right) + e^x\,\frac{d}{dx}(x)$$

$$= x\cdot e^x + e^x\,(1)$$

$$= x\cdot e^x + e^e$$

$$\frac{dy}{dx} = e^x\,(x+1)$$

Example-8: Find the derivative of $(x^2 - 4x + 5)(x^3 - 2)$

Solution: Let y = $(x^2 - 4x + 5)(x^3 - 2)$

Let u = $x^2 - 4x + 5$

v = $x^3 - 2$

$$\frac{d}{dx}(uv) = u\cdot\frac{d}{dx}(v) + v\cdot\frac{d}{dx}(u)$$

$$\frac{dy}{dx} = (x^2 - 4x + 5)\frac{d}{dx}(x^3 - 2) + (x^3 - 2)\frac{d}{dx}(x^2 - 4x + 5)$$

$$= (x^2 - 4x + 5)(3x^2 - 0) + (x^3 - 2)(2x - 4)$$

$$= (x^2 - 4x + 5)(3x^2) + (x^3 - 2)(2x - 4)$$

$$\therefore \frac{dy}{dx} = 5x^4 - 16x^2 + 15x^2 - 4x + 8$$

Example-9: Find the derivative of $x^2 \log x$

Solution: Let $y = x^2 \log x$

Let $u = x^2$

$v = \log x$

Then $= \frac{d}{dx}(uv) = u \cdot \frac{d}{dx}(v) + v \cdot \frac{d}{dx}(u)$

$$= x^2 \cdot \frac{d}{dx}(\log x) + \log x \frac{d}{dx}(x^2)$$

$$= x^2 \cdot \frac{1}{x} + \log x\,(2x)$$

$$= x + 2x \log x$$

$$= x\,(1 + 2 \log x)$$

$$\therefore \frac{dy}{dx} = x(1 + 2\log x)$$

Example-10: Find the derivative of $x^3 e^{2x}$

Solution: Let $y = x^3 e^{2x}$

Let $u = x^3$

$v = e^{2x}$

Then $\frac{d}{dx}(uv) = u.\frac{d}{dx}(v) + v\frac{d}{dx}(u)$

$$= x^3 \frac{d}{dx}\left(e^{2x}\right) + e^{2x} \cdot \frac{d}{dx}\left(x^3\right)$$

$$= x^3 e^{2x}(2) + e^{2x}\left(3x^2\right)$$

$$= 2x^3 e^{2x} + 3x^2 e^{2x}$$

$$\therefore \quad \frac{dy}{dx} = x^2 e^{2x}(2x+3)$$

Example-11: Find the derivative of $\frac{1}{\left(x^2+3x-5\right)^3}$

Solution: Let y = $\frac{1}{\left(x^2+3x-5\right)^3}$

$$y = \left(x^2+3x-5\right)^{-3}$$

Then $\frac{dy}{dx} = \frac{d}{dx}(y) = \frac{d}{dx}\left(x^2+3x-5\right)^{-3}$

$$= -3\left(x^2+3x-5\right)^{-3-1} \cdot (2x+3)$$

$$= -3\left(x^2+3x-5\right)^{-4} (2x+3)$$

$$= \frac{-3}{\left(x^2+3x-5\right)^4} \cdot (2x+3)$$

$$\frac{dy}{dx} = \frac{-3(2x+3)}{\left(x^2+3x-5\right)^4}$$

Example-12: Find the derivative of $\left(2x^2-5x+3\right)^4$

Solution: Let y = $(2x^2 - 5x + 3)^4$

Then $\frac{dy}{dx} = \frac{d}{dx}(y) = \frac{d}{dx}(2x^2 - 5x + 3)^4$

$$= 4(2x^2 - 5x + 3)^{4-1}(4x - 5)$$

$$\therefore \frac{dy}{dx} = 4(2x^2 - 5x + 3)^3 (4x - 5)$$

Example-13: Differentiate the following functions;

i. $\sqrt{a + \sqrt{a + x}}$

ii. $\log\left[x + \sqrt{x^2 + 1}\right]$

iii. $\log\left[\log(\log x)\right]$

Solution: i. Let y = $\sqrt{a + \sqrt{a + x}}$

$$y = \left(a + \sqrt{a + x}\right)^{1/2}$$

$$\therefore \frac{dy}{dx} = \frac{1}{2}\left(a + \sqrt{a + x}\right)^{-1/2} \times \frac{d}{dx}\left(a + \sqrt{a + x}\right)$$

$$= \frac{1}{2\sqrt{a + \sqrt{a + x}}}\left(0 + \frac{1}{2\sqrt{a + x}}(1)\right)$$

$$= \frac{1}{2\sqrt{a + \sqrt{a + x}}}\left(\frac{1}{2}(a + x)\right)^{-\frac{1}{2}}$$

$$= \frac{1}{2\sqrt{a+\sqrt{a+x}}} \cdot \frac{1}{2\sqrt{a+x}}$$

$$\frac{dy}{dx} = \frac{1}{4\sqrt{a+x} \cdot \sqrt{a+\sqrt{a+x}}}$$

ii. Let $y = \log\left[x + \sqrt{x^2+1}\right]$

Then $\frac{dy}{dx} = \frac{1}{x+\sqrt{x^2+1}} \frac{d}{dx}\left(x+\sqrt{x^2+1}\right)$

$$= \frac{1}{x+\sqrt{x^2+1}}\left(1+\frac{1}{2\sqrt{x^2+1}} \times 2x\right)$$

$$= \frac{1}{x+\sqrt{x^2+1}} \times \left(1+\frac{x}{\sqrt{x^2+1}}\right)$$

$$= \frac{1}{x+\sqrt{x^2+1}} \times \frac{\sqrt{x^2+1}+x}{\sqrt{x^2+1}}$$

$$\therefore \frac{dy}{dx} = \frac{1}{\sqrt{x^2+1}}$$

iii Let $y = \log[\log(\log x)]$

Then $\frac{dy}{dx} = \frac{1}{\log(\log x)} \times \frac{d}{dx}(\log(\log x))$

$$= \frac{1}{\log(\log x)} \cdot \frac{1}{\log x} \cdot \frac{1}{x}$$

$$\therefore \frac{dy}{dx} = \frac{1}{x\log x \ \log(\log x)}$$

Example-14: Find the derivative of $\dfrac{ax+b}{cx+d}$

Solution: Let y = $\dfrac{ax+b}{cx+d}$

Let u = $ax+b$

v = $cx+d$

$$\frac{d}{dx}\left[\frac{u}{v}\right] = \frac{v \cdot \frac{d}{dx}(u) - u \cdot \frac{d}{dx}(v)}{v^2}$$

$$= \frac{(cx+d)\frac{d}{dx}(ax+b) - (ax+b) \cdot \frac{d}{dx}(cx+d)}{(cx+d)^2}$$

$$= \frac{(cx+d)(a(1)+0) - (ax+b)(c(1)+d)}{(cx+d)^2}$$

$$= \frac{(cx+d)(a) - (ax+b)(c)}{(cx+d)^2}$$

$$= \frac{(acx+ad-acx-bc)}{(cx+d)^2}$$

$$\therefore \frac{dy}{dx} = \frac{ad-bc}{(cx+d)^2}$$

Example-15: Find he derivative of $\frac{2x^2-4}{3x^2+7}$

Solution: Let $y=\frac{2x^2-4}{3x^2+7}$

Let u = $2x^2-4$

v = $3x^2+7$

$$\frac{d}{dx}\left(\frac{u}{v}\right)=\frac{v.\frac{d}{dx}(u)-u\cdot\frac{d}{dx}(v)}{v^2}$$

$$=\frac{(3x^2+7)\cdot\frac{d}{dx}(2x^2-4)-(2x^2-4)\frac{d}{dx}(3x^2+7)}{(3x^2+7)^2}$$

$$=\frac{(3x^2+7)(4x)-(2x^2-4)(6x)}{(3x^2+7)^2}$$

$$=\frac{12x^3+28x-12x^3+24x}{(3x^2+7)^2}$$

$$\therefore\frac{dy}{dx}=\frac{52x}{(3x^2+7)^2}$$

Example-16: Find he derivative of $\frac{e^{3x}-e^{2x}}{e^{3x}+e^{2x}}$

Solution: Let y = $\frac{e^{3x}-e^{2x}}{e^{3x}+e^{2x}}$

$$\frac{d}{dx}\left(\frac{u}{v}\right)=\frac{v.\frac{d}{dx}(u)-u\cdot\frac{d}{dx}(v)}{v^2}$$

$$=\frac{\left(e^{3x}+e^{2x}\right)\frac{d}{dx}\left(e^{3x}-e^{2x}\right)-\left(e^{3x}-e^{2x}\right)\frac{d}{dx}\left(e^{3x}+e^{2x}\right)}{\left(e^{3x}+e^{2x}\right)^2}$$

$$=\frac{\left(e^{3x}+e^{2x}\right)\left(3e^{3x}-2e^{2x}\right)-\left(e^{3x}-e^{2x}\right)\left(3e^{3x}+2e^{2x}\right)}{\left(e^{3x}+e^{2x}\right)^2}$$

$$\frac{3e^{3x}.e^{3x}-2e^{3x}e^{2x}+3e^{2x}.e^{2x}-2e^{2x}\cdot e^{2x}-3e^{3x}e^{3x}-2e^{3x}\cdot e^{2x}+3e^{2x}.e^{3x}+2e^{2x}.3e^{2x}}{\left(e^{3x}+e^{2x}\right)^2}$$

$$=\frac{3e^{5x}+3e^{5x}}{\left(e^{3x}+e^{2x}\right)^2}$$

$$=\frac{e^{5x}(6)}{\left(e^{3x}+e^{2x}\right)^2}$$

$$\therefore\ \frac{dy}{dx}=\frac{6\,e^{5x}}{\left(e^{3x}+e^{2x}\right)^2}$$

Exercise – 1

1. Find the derivative of x^2-3x+5

2. Find the derivative of $e^x+e^{-x}-5$

3. Find the derivative of $\frac{6}{x^3}$

4. Differentiate with respect to for the following functions;

   a) e^{3x} b) $2\log x$ c) 3^x

   d) $e^{\frac{-3}{2}x}$ e) $e^{5x}+x$ f) x^a+a^x+3

5. Find the derivative of $x^5\log x + x^2\cdot 3^x$

6. Find the derivative of $\log\left(x+\frac{1}{x}\right)$

7. Find the derivative of $(2x^2+5x-7)^{5/2}$

8. Find the derivative of $3x^{-2/3}+4x^{-1/2}-2$

9. Find the derivative of $y = e^{x^2}$

10. Find the derivative of $(5-2x)(2x^3+3)$

11. Find the derivative of $y=\dfrac{6x^2}{2x+1}$

12. Find the derivative of $y=\dfrac{e^{2x}+e^{-2x}}{e^{2x}-e^{-2x}}$

Differentiation of Implicit function

Sometimes the relation between two variables x and y is given by an equation of the form $f(x,y)=0$ and in such a case, none of the variables is directly expressed in terms of other. But the equation may define y as a function of x. In this case y is called an implicit function of x, the relation being the implicit function of x and y.

Example: Find if $\dfrac{dy}{dx}$ if $x^2-2xy+y^2-2x=0$

Solution: we have $x^2 - 2xy + y^2 - 2x = 0$

Differentiating with respect to 'x', we get

$$2x - 2 - \left(1(y) + x.\frac{dy}{dx}\right) + 2y\frac{dy}{dx} - 2(1) = 0$$

or, $x - y - x\dfrac{dy}{dx} + y\dfrac{dy}{dx} - 1 = 0$

or, $y\dfrac{dy}{dx} - x \cdot \dfrac{dy}{dx} = y - x + 1$

or, $\dfrac{dy}{dx}(y - x) = y - x + 1$

$\therefore \dfrac{dy}{dx} = \dfrac{y - x + 1}{y - x}$

Logarithmic differentiation

The process of taking logarithms before differentiation is called logarithmic differentiation. When the function to be differentiated involves a function in its power or when the function is the product or quotient of a number of functions, first we take logarithms and then differentiate. In such situations the following properties are used.

1. Log mn = log m + log n
2. Log $\dfrac{m}{n}$ = log m – log n
3. Log m^n = n log m
4. log e = 1

Example: Differentiate $x^{\sqrt{x}}$ with respect to x

Solution: Let y = $x^{\sqrt{x}}$

Taking log on both sides

Log y = $\sqrt{x}$ log x

Differentiate with respect to 'x'

$$\frac{1}{y}\cdot\frac{dy}{dx}=\sqrt{x}\cdot\frac{1}{x}+\log x\,\frac{1}{2\sqrt{x}}$$

$$=\frac{1}{\sqrt{x}}+\frac{1}{2\sqrt{x}}\log x$$

$$=\frac{2+\log x}{2\sqrt{x}}$$

$$\therefore\ \frac{dy}{dx}=y\left(\frac{2+\log x}{2\sqrt{x}}\right)$$

$$\frac{dy}{dx}=x^{\sqrt{x}}\left(\frac{2+\log x}{2\sqrt{x}}\right)$$

Differentiation of Parametric forms

In some cases, both the variables x and y concerning the equation of a curve are expressed in terms of a third variable't'. The two relations which express x and y in terms of t are together called the parametric equation of the curve. The third variable't' is called a parameter.

$$\therefore\ \frac{dy}{dx}=\frac{dy}{dt}\Big/\frac{dx}{dt}\ =\frac{dy}{dt}\times\frac{dt}{dx}$$

Where $\frac{dt}{dx}\neq 0$

Example: For the parabola x = at2², y = 2at

Solution: Given x = at²

y = 2 at

Then $\frac{dx}{dy} = 2at$ and $\frac{dy}{dt} = 2a$

$$\therefore \frac{dy}{dx} = \frac{dy}{dt} \Big| \frac{dx}{dt}$$

$$= \frac{2a}{2at} = \frac{1}{t}, \text{ where } t \neq 0$$

Exercise – 2

1. Find the derivative of $y = e^{\frac{x^2}{1+x^3}}$

2. Find the derivative of $x^3 + y^3 = 3axy$

3. Find at $\frac{dy}{dx}$ $x = 1$, $y = 1$ if $x^3 - 2x^2y^2 + 5x + y - 5 = 0$

4. Find $\frac{dy}{dx}$ if $e^{xy} - 4xy = 4$

5. If $x = \frac{2t}{1+t^2}$, $y = \frac{1-t^2}{1+t^2}$, prove that $\frac{dy}{dx} + \frac{x}{y} = 0$

6. Find $\frac{dy}{dx}$ if $x^2 + y^2 = 4$

7. Find $\frac{dy}{dx}$ if $x^2 - 2xy + y^2 = 9$

8. Find $\frac{dy}{dx}$ if $3x^4 - x^2y + 2y^3 = 0$

9. Find the derivative of $x^4 + x^2y^2 + y^4 = 0$

10. Find $\frac{dy}{dx}$ if $3x = t^3, 2y = t^2$

11. Find $\frac{dy}{dx}$ if $x = t^3$, $y = 3t$ *at* $t = 2$

12. Find $\frac{dy}{dx}$ if $x = 6t - t^2$, $y = 2t + 3$ *at* $t = 0$

13. Find $\frac{dy}{dx}$ if $x = \frac{2t}{1+t^2}$, $y = \frac{1-t^2}{1+t^2}$

14. Find $\frac{dy}{dx}$ when

i. $x^y = y^x$

ii. $x = y\log(xy)$

iii. $x = y\log\left(\frac{x}{y}\right)$

15. Find $\frac{dx}{dy}$ when

i. $x^y + y^x = 1$

ii. $x^y + xy = 8$

16. For the equation $ax^2 + 2h\,xy + by^2 = 1$ verify that

$$\frac{dy}{dx} \cdot \frac{dx}{dy} = 1$$

17. Differentiate $x^{\sqrt{x}}$ with respect to 'x'

18. If $x^y = e^{x-y}$, show that $\frac{dy}{dx} = \frac{\log x}{(1+\log x)^2}$

19. If $x^y = y^x$, show that $\frac{dy}{dx} = \frac{y(y-x\log y)}{x(x-y\log x)}$

20. If $x = t\,e^t,\ y = 1+\log t$, find $\frac{dy}{dx}$

Second and higher order derivatives

Let $y=f(x)$ then $\frac{dy}{dx}$ is a function of and is called the fist derivative of 'y' with respect to 'x'. If the first derivative is differentiable its derivative is called second derivative of the original function and is denoted by $\frac{d^2y}{dx^2}$ or y^{11}. If second derivative is differentiate its derivative is called the third derivative of the original function and is denoted by $\frac{d^3y}{dx^3}$ *or* y^{111} and so on. This process of differentiating a function more than once is called successive differentiation.

Example-1: if $y = ae^{mx} + b\,e^{-mx}$, show that $\frac{d^2y}{dx^2} = m^2y$

Solution: we have $y = ae^{mx} + b\,e^{-mx}$

Differentiating with respect to 'x', we get

$$\frac{dy}{dx} = am\ e^{mx} + b(-m)\ e^{-mx}$$

$$\frac{dy}{dx} = ame^{mx} - bme^{-mx}$$

Differentiating again with respect to 'x', we get

$$\frac{d^2y}{dx^2} = \frac{d}{dx}\left(\frac{dy}{dx}\right) = ame^{mx}(m) - bm(-m)e^{-mx}$$

$$= am^2e^{mx} + bm^2e^{-mx}$$

$$= m^2\left(ae^{mx} + be^{-mx}\right)$$

Hence $\frac{d^2y}{dx^2} = m^2y$

Example-2: If $y = \left(x+\sqrt{1+x^2}\right)^m$, prove that

Solution: we have $y = \left(x+\sqrt{1+x^2}\right)^m$

$$\frac{dy}{dx} = m\left(x+\sqrt{1+x^2}\right)^{m-1} \times \left(1+\frac{1}{2}\left(1+x^2\right)\right)^{\frac{1}{2}-1} \times (0+2x)$$

$$= m\left(x+\sqrt{1+x^2}\right)^{m-1} \times \left(1+\frac{x}{\sqrt{1+x^2}}\right)$$

$$= m\left(x+\sqrt{1+x^2}\right)^{m-1} \times \left(\frac{\sqrt{1+x^2}+x}{\sqrt{1+x^2}}\right)$$

$$= \frac{m\left(x+\sqrt{1+x^2}\right)^m}{\sqrt{1+x^2}} = \frac{my}{\sqrt{1+x^2}}$$

(or) $\left(\frac{dy}{dx}\right)^2 = \frac{m^2y^2}{1+x^2}$

(or) $(1+x^2)\left(\frac{dy}{dx}\right)^2 = m^2y^2$

Differentiating both sides with respect to 'x' we get

$$(1+x^2).2\frac{dy}{dx}\cdot\frac{d^2y}{dx^2}+2x\left(\frac{dy}{dx}\right)^2 = m^2\cdot 2y\frac{dy}{dx}$$

Dividing both sides by $2\cdot\frac{dy}{dx}$, then we get

$$(1+x^2)\frac{d^2y}{dx^2}+x\frac{dy}{dx}=m^2y$$

(or) $(1+x^2)\frac{d^2y}{dx^2}+x\frac{dy}{dx}-m^2y=0$

Example-3: Find $\frac{d^2y}{dx^2}$ from the equation $x^2+y^2=a^2$

Solution: we have $x^2+y^2=a^2$

Differentiating both sides with respect to 'x', we get

$$2x+2y\frac{dy}{dx}=0$$

(or) $\frac{dy}{dx}=\frac{-x}{y}$

Differentiating again with respect to 'x'

$$\frac{d^2y}{dx^2}=-\frac{d}{dx}\left(\frac{x}{y}\right)=\frac{y(1)-x\cdot\frac{dy}{dx}}{y^2}$$

$$=\frac{y-x\times(-\frac{x}{y})}{y^2}$$

$$=-\frac{y+\frac{x^2}{y}}{y^2}$$

$$=-\frac{y^2+x^2}{y^3}$$

Hence $\frac{d^2y}{dx^2}=-\frac{a^2}{y^3}$

Exercise – 3

1. Find $\frac{d^3y}{dx^3}$ if $y = e^{3x}$

2. Find $\frac{d^2y}{dx^2}$ if $y = \log x$

3. *If* $y = 2x+\frac{4}{x}$, Prove that $x^2\frac{d^2y}{dx^2}+x\frac{dy}{dx}-y=0$

4. If $y=x^4-3x^3+4x^2-7x$, find $\frac{d^2y}{dx^2}$ and $\frac{d^3y}{dx^3}$

5. If $y = \sqrt{x} + \frac{1}{\sqrt{x}}$ find $\frac{d^2y}{dx^2}$

6. If $y = \frac{1+x}{1-x}$, prove that $\frac{d^2y}{dx^2} = \frac{4}{(1-x)^3}$

7. Find $\frac{d^2y}{dx^2}$ if $y = \frac{x^2}{a^2} + \frac{y^2}{b^2} = 1$

8. If $y = x\sqrt{x^2+9}$, find $\frac{d^2y}{dx^2}$ at $x = 4$

9. If $y = \frac{x}{x^2+a^2}$, prove that $\frac{d^2y}{dx^2} = \frac{2x(x^2-3a^2)}{(x^2+a^2)^3}$

10. If $x^2 + xy + 2y^2 = 1$, show that $(x+2y)^3 \frac{d^2y}{dx^2} + 6 = 0$

Maxima and Minima

Maxima and Minima

A function $f(x)$ is said to have a maximum at a point $x = C$ if $f(x) < f(c)$ for all x near c. In the case, $f(c)$ is called a maximum value of $f(x)$.

Similarly, a function $f(x)$ is said to have a minimum at a point x = c if f(x) > f(c) for all x near 'c'. Then $f(c)$ in this case is called a minimum value of $f(c)$.

Working rule for the determination of Maxima and Minima in a single variable case:

1) Find $f'(x)$

2) Put $f'(x) = 0$, calculate the stationary points

3) Compute $f''(x)$ a these stationary points

In case $f''(x) > 0$, the stationary point is a Minimum point

In case $f''(x) < 0$, the stationary point is a Maximum point

If $f''(x) = 0$ then compute $f'''(x)$

If $f'''(x) \neq 0$ for a stationary point, there is neither a Maximum nor Minimum at that point.

If $f'''(x) = 0$ find $f^{iv}(x)$. If the fourth derivative is negative at that point then there is a Maximum and if it is positive then there is a Minimum.

Again incase $f^{iv}(x) = 0$, find the fifth derivative and proceed as above till we get a definite answer.

Examples

Example-1 Show that $y = x + \frac{1}{x}$ has one maximum and one minimum value and that the latter is larger than the former.

Solution: Here we have $y = x + \frac{1}{x}$

Then $\frac{dy}{dx} = 1 - \frac{1}{x^2}$

For maxima and minima, $\frac{dy}{dx} = 0$

$$1 - \frac{1}{x^2} = 0$$

$$-\frac{1}{x^2}=-1$$

$$\frac{1}{x^2}=1$$

$$x^2=1$$

$$x=\pm 1$$

Now the second order condition is $\frac{d^2y}{dx^2}=\frac{2}{x^3}$

At $x=1$, $\frac{d^2y}{dx^2}=\frac{2}{1^3}=\frac{2}{1}=2>0$ minimum

$x=-1$, $\frac{d^2y}{dx^2}=\frac{2}{-1}=-2<0$ Maximum

We observe that the minimum value 2 of y is larger than the maximum value -2.

Example-2: Find the Maximum and Minimum values of $x^4-62x^2+120x+9$

Solution: Let $y=x^4-62x^2+120x+9$

Then $\frac{dy}{dx}=4x^3-124x+120$

$$=4(x^3-31x+30)$$

Now we have to find out the factors of $4(x^3-31x+30)$.

By using Horner method

	1	0	−31	30
	0	1	1	−30
x = 1	1	1	−30	|0

$$(x-1)\left(x^2+x-30\right)$$

$$x^2+6x-5x-30$$

$$x(x+6)-5(x+6)$$

$$(x+6)(x-5)$$

$$\therefore\ 4(x-1)(x-5)(x+6)$$

For Maxima and Minima, $\frac{dy}{dx}=0$

$$(x-1)(x-5)(x-6)=0$$

x = *1*, 5, -6.

Now we have to find out the second order condition

$$\frac{d^2y}{dx^2}=4\left(3x^2-31\right)$$

At $x=1,\ \frac{d^2y}{dx^2}=-112\prec 0$

Thus y has a Maximum at x = 1 and the maximum value is

$$(1)^4-62(1)^2+120(1)+9=68$$

At $x=5,\ \frac{d^2y}{dx^2}=-176>0$

Thus y has a minimum at $x=5$ and the minimum value is

$(5)^4 - 62\ (5)^2 - 120(5) + 9 = -316.$

At $x = -6$, $\frac{d^2y}{dx^2} = 308 > 0$

Thus y has a minimum at $x = -6$ and the minimum value is

$$(-6)^4 - 62(-6)^2 + 120(-6) + 9 = -1647$$

Example-3: Show that the function $y = x^3 - 6x^2 + 9x - 8$ has a maximum value at x =1 and a minimum value at x =3.

Solution: Given $y = x^3 - 6x^2 + 9x - 8$

Then $\frac{dy}{dx} = 3x^2 - 12x + 9$

$= 3(x^2 - 4x + 3)$

The factors for $(x^2 - 4x + 3)$ is

$= x^2 - 4x + 3$

$= x^2 - 3x - x + 3$

$= x(x-3) - 1(x-3)$

$= (x-1)\ (x-3)$

For a maxima and minima,

The necessary condition is $\frac{dy}{dx} = 0$

$3(x-1)(x-3) = 0$

$(x-1)(x-3) = 0$

$x = 1, 3$

Now we have to find out the sufficient condition for maxima and minima

$$\frac{d^2y}{dx^2} = 2x-4$$

At $x=1$, $\frac{d^{2y}}{dx^2} = -2<0$

Thus y has a maximum at x = 1 and the maximum value is

$$= (1)^3 - 6(1)^2 + 9(1) - 8$$

$$1-6+9-8=-4$$

At $x=3$, $\frac{d^2y}{dx} = 2 > 0$ thus 'y' has a minimum at x=3 and the minimum value is $(3)^3 - 6(3)^2 + 9(3) - 8 = -8$

Example-4: Find the maxima and minima of the function

$$8x^5 - 15x^4 + 10x^2$$

Solution: Let $y = 8x^5 - 15x^4 + 10x^2$

Then $= \frac{dy}{dx} = 40x^4 - 60x^3 + 20x$

For a Maxima and Minima i.e., $\frac{dy}{dx} = 0$

$$40x^4 - 60x^3 + 20x = 0$$

$$20x(2x^3 - 3x^2 + 1) = 0$$

Then factors of $2x^3 - 3x^2 + 1$ is

$$\begin{array}{c|cccc} & 2 & -3 & 0 & 1 \\ x=1 & 0 & 2 & -1 & -1 \\ \hline & 2 & -1 & -1 & 0 \end{array}$$

$$(x-1)(2x^2-x-1)$$

$$2x^2-x-1=0$$

$$2x^2-2x+x-1=0$$

$$(2x+1)(x-1)=0$$

The factors are $x = 0$, $x = 1$, $x = -1/2$ and $x = 1$

$$\frac{dy^2}{dx^2} = \frac{d}{dx}\left(40x^4 - 60x^3 + 20x\right)$$

$$= 160x^3 - 180x^2 + 20$$

At $x = 0 \Rightarrow \frac{d^2y}{dx^2} = 20 > 0$ minimum

At $x = 1 \Rightarrow \frac{d^2y}{dx^2} = 0$

At $\Rightarrow \frac{d^2y}{dx^2} = -5 < 0$ maximum

Thus at $x = \frac{-1}{2}$ then y has maximum

Example-5: Find the maximum and minimum values of

$$y = x^3 - 3x^2 - 9x + 27$$

Solution we have $y = x^3 - 3x^2 - 9x + 27$

Then $\frac{dy}{dx} = 3x^2 - 6x - 9$

$= 3(x^2 - 2x - 3)$

The factors of $x^2 - 2x - 3$ is

$x^2 - 3x + x - 3$

$x(x-3) + 1(x-3)$

$(x-3)(x+1)$

For a maxima and minima i.e., $\frac{dy}{dx} = 0$

$3(x-3)\ (x+1) = 0$

Therefore $3(x-3)\ (x+1) = 0$

Now we have to apply the sufficient condition is

$\frac{d^2y}{dx^2} = 2x - 2$

At $x = -1$, $\frac{d^2y}{dx^2} = 2(-1) - 2 = -2 - 2 = -4 < 0$

Thus y has a maximum point at $x = -1$ and the Maximum value is

$(-1)^3 - 3(-1)^2 - 9(1) + 27$

$= -1 - 3 - 9 + 27$

$= 14$

At $x = 3$, $\frac{d^2y}{dx^2} = 2(3) - 2 = 6 - 2 = 4 > 0$

Thus y has a minimum point at x = 3 and the Minimum value is

$(3)^3 - 3(3)^2 - 9(3) + 27$

$= 27\text{-}27\text{-}27\text{+}27$

$= 0$

Example-6: Find the Maximum and Minimum value of

$x^3 - 3x - 1$

Solution: Let $y = x^3 - 3x - 1$

Then $\frac{dy}{dx} = 3x^2 - 3$

For a Maxima or Minima

$\frac{dy}{dx} = 0$

$3x^2 - 3 = 0$

$3x^2 = 3$

$x^2 = \frac{3}{3}$

$x^2 = 1$

$x = \pm 1$

Then we have to apply the sufficient condition for Maxima and Minima

$\frac{d^2y}{dx^2} = 3x$

At $x=-1$, $\frac{d^2y}{dx^2}=-3<0$

Thus y has a Maximum point at $x=-1$

And maximum value is $(-1)^3-3(-1)-1$

$-1+3-1=1$

At $x=+1$, $\frac{d^2y}{dx^2}=3>0$

Thus y has a minimum point at $x=1$ and the Minimum value is $(1)^3-3(-1)-1=1-3-1=-3$

Example-7: Find the values of Maximum and Minimum of $y=2x^3+3x^2-36x+10$

Solution: We have $y=2x^3+3x^2-36x+10$

Then $\frac{dy}{dx}=6x^2+6x-36$

$=6(x^2+x-6)$

The factors of x^2+x-6 is $x^2+3x-2x-6$

$x(x+3)-2(x+3)$

$(x+3)(x-2)$

For a maxima or minima

$\frac{dy}{dx}=0$

$6(x+3)(x-2)=0$

$(x+3)(x-2)=0$

$x=2$ and -3

Then sufficient condition is that $\frac{d^2y}{dx^2} = 12x + 6$

At, $\frac{d^2y}{dx^2} = 12(2) + 6 = 24 + 6 = 30 > 0$

Thus y has a minimum point at $x = 2$ and the minimum value is

$$2x^3 + 3x^2 - 36x + 10$$

$$2(2)^3 + 3(2)^2 - 36(2) + 10$$

$$16 + 12 - 72 + 10 = -38$$

At $x = -3$, $\frac{d^2y}{dx^2} = 12(-3) + 6$

$$= -36 + 6$$

$$= -30 < 0$$

Thus y has a maximum point at x = –3 and the maximum value is $2(-3)^3 + 3(-3)^2 - 36(-3) + 10$

$$= -52 + 27 + 108 + 10$$
$$= 93$$

Example-8: Find the maximum and minimum value of $x + \frac{1}{x+1}$

Solution: Let $y = x + \frac{1}{x+1}$

$$y = x + (x+1)^{-1}$$

Then $\frac{dy}{dx} = 1 + (-1)(x+1)^{-1-1}(1)$

$$= 1 - (x+1)^{-2}$$

$$= 1 - \frac{1}{(x+1)^2}$$

For a maxima or minima, $\frac{dy}{dx} = 0$

$$1 - \frac{1}{(x+1)^2} = 0$$

$$\frac{(x+1)^2 - 1}{(x+1)^2} = 0$$

$$(x+1)^2 - 1 = 0$$

$$x^2 + 2x + 1 - 1 = 0$$

$$x^2 + 2x = 0$$

$$x(x+2) = 0$$

$$x = -2$$

$\therefore\ x = 0$ and -2

By applying the sufficient condition for maxima and minima

$$\frac{d^2y}{dx^2} = \frac{d}{dx}\left[1 - (x+1)^{-2}\right]$$

$$= 0 - (-2)(x+1)^{-2-1}(1)$$

$$= 2(x+1)^{-3}$$

$$\frac{d^2y}{dx^2} = \frac{2}{(x+1)^3}$$

At $x = 0$, $\frac{d^2y}{dx^2} = \frac{2}{(0+1)^3} = \frac{2}{1} = 2 > 0$

Thus y has a minimum point at $x = 0$ and the minimum value is

$$0+\frac{1}{0+1}=0+1=1$$

and At $x = -2$, $\frac{d^2y}{dx^2}=\frac{2}{(-2+1)^3}$

$$=\frac{2}{(-1)^3}$$

$$=\frac{2}{-1}=-2<0$$

Thus y has a maximum point at $x = -2$ and the maximum value is

$$-2+\frac{1}{-2+1}=\frac{-2}{1}+\frac{1}{-1}=-2-1=-3$$

Exercise – 1

1. Find the maximum and minimum values of $y = x^4 - 8x^3 + 22x^2 - 24x + 1$
2. Find the maximum and minimum values of $y = 4x + 10 + \frac{16}{x}$
3. Find the maximum and minimum values of $\frac{1}{3}x^3 - x^2 + 5x + 3$
4. Find the maximum and minimum values of $2x^3 - 21x^2 + 36x - 20$
5. Show that the function $x^3 - 6x^2 + 12x + 30$ is neither a maximum nor a minimum at $x = 2$.

6. Find for what values of x the expression $2x^3 - 15x^2 + 24x - 15$ is maximum and minimum respectively. Find also the maximum and minimum values.

7. Find the maximum and minimum values of $y = \frac{1}{2}x^4 - x^2 + 1$

8. Show that the function $y = x^3 - 3x^2 + 15$ has a maximum value at $x = 0$ and a minimum value at $x = 2$

9. Show that the local maximum value of $x + \frac{1}{x}$ is less than its local minimum value.

10. Show that the function $y = x^2 + \frac{250}{x}$ has a minimum value at $x = 5$

11. Investigate the following function for maximum :

$$y = \frac{1}{3}x^3 - 2x^2 + 3x + 1$$

12. Find the maximum and minimum values of the function. $x^5 - 5x^4 + 5x^3 - 1$ Discuss its nature at $x = 0$

Applications

Demand function

In term 'Demand' refers to the relationship between the quantity of product, or, service that customer's desire, or, are able to purchase during a given period of time might be an hour, a day, or, a year. Majority of the economists assess "consumer demand" on the basis of utility, which is the level of satisfaction of consumers and is related to the quantities of goods purchased by the consumers.

The demand function is the relationship between the price per unit and quantity demand at that price of a commodity. Suppose if 'P' is the price per unit and 'x' is the quantity demand at that price of a certain commodity, then we can express the demand function mathematically as $x = f(P)$. It usually slopes downwards as demand decreases when the price are increased.

Supply function

The relationship between the price per unit and the quantity supplied at the price. If P is the price per unit and x is the quantity supplied at that price of certain product, then we can express the supply function mathematically as

$$x = g(P)$$

It is often noted that when supply is increased, the profiteers increase prices, so a supply curve frequently slopes upwards.

Cost function: cost function is a symbolic statement of the technological relationship between cost and output. In its general form, it is expressed by an equation TC = f (Q)

Generally there are three kinds of cost functions;

1. Linear cost function

   $$TC = a + b Q$$

2. Quadratic cost function

   $$TC = a + bQ + Q^2$$

3. Cubic cost function

   $$TC = a + bQ - Q^2 + Q^3$$

Total cost: Total Cost (TC) is the total expenditure incurred on the production of goods and services. It refers to the total outlays of money expenditure, both explicit and implicit on the inputs used to produce a given level of output.

Average Cost

If TC = $f(x)$ be the total cost of producing x unit of output, Then the average cost is defined as the ratio of the total cost to the output and is denoted by AC.

$$\therefore \ AC = \frac{TC}{x}$$

$$TC = AC \times x$$

Therefore TC = VC + FC

$$AC = \frac{TC}{x}$$

Where x – output

$$AVC = \frac{VC}{x}$$

$$AFC = \frac{FC}{x}$$

Marginal Cost

Marginal cost at a certain level of output is the change in cost that results when the output is increased by a unit of amount from this level, i.e. if the total cost is known then the extra cost of producing one additional unit is called marginal cost and it is denoted by MC.

$$\therefore \ MC = \frac{d}{dx}(TC)$$

Revenue function

It is the revenue obtained by selling the output produced.

$$TR = P.\, x$$

Where P is the demand function

x is the output

Profit function

The excess of total revenue over the total cost of production is called the profit.

$$\therefore \Pi = TR - TC$$

Where Π is the Profit

TR is the Total Revenue

TC is the Total Cost

Market equilibrium

If the quantity supplied of a certain product is equal to the quantity demanded, the market is said to be in equilibrium. The point of intersection of demand and supply curve is called the equilibrium point. The price at which the demand is equal to the supply is called equilibrium price and the quantity at which the demand is equal to the supply is called the equilibrium quantity.

Relationship between MC and AC

Sol: We have MC = $\frac{d}{dx}(TC)$

$$AC = \frac{TC}{x} \rightarrow (1)$$

Differentiating both sides of eq(1) with respect to 'x', then we get

$$\frac{d}{dx}(AC) = \frac{d}{dx}\left[\frac{TC}{x}\right]$$

$$= \frac{x \cdot \frac{d}{dx}(TC) - TC \cdot \frac{d}{dx}(x)}{x^2}$$

$$= \frac{x \,.\, MC - TC(1)}{x^2}$$

$$= \frac{x.\, MC - TC}{x^2}$$

$$= \frac{x\left[MC - \frac{TC}{x}\right]}{x^2}$$

$$= \frac{1}{x}\left[MC - \frac{TC}{x}\right] \quad \therefore \frac{TC}{x} = AC$$

$$\frac{d}{dx}[AC] = \frac{1}{x}[MC - AC]$$

When AC is increasing function

$$\frac{d}{dx}(AC) > 0$$

$$\frac{1}{x}[MC - AC] > 0$$

$\therefore$ MC > AC

When AC is decreasing function

$$\frac{d}{dx}[AC] < 0$$

i.e $\frac{1}{x}[MC - AC] < 0$

MC < AC

When AC is Minimum

$$\frac{d}{dx}[AC] = 0$$

i.e $\frac{1}{x}[MC - AC] = 0$

MC − AC = 0

MC = AC

Examples

Example-1: Find the equilibrium price and quantity for the following demand and supply functions

$P_d = 200 - 2x^2$ and $P_s = 2x + 20$

Solution: At the equilibrium point, the demand equals to supply i.e $P_d = P_s$

$$\therefore 200-2x^2=2x+20$$

$$200-2x^2-2x-20=0$$

$$-2x^2-2x+180=0$$

$$2x^2+2x-180=0$$

$$x^2+x-90=0$$

$$x^2+10x-9x-90=0$$

$$x(x+10)-9(x+10)=0$$

$$(x+10)(x-9)=0$$

$x = 9$ and -10

We disregard $x = -10$, since price cannot be negative substituting this value of x into the demand or supply function, then we get

$$P_d = 200 - 2(9)^2$$

$$= 200 - 2(81)$$

$$= 200 - 162$$

$$= 38$$

$\therefore$ Equilibrium price $= 9$

Equilibrium quantity $= 38$.

Example-2: In a perfect competition, the demand curve of a commodity is $x_d = 20 - 3p - p^2$ and the supply curve is $x_s = P - 1$. Where 'P' represents the price per unit and 'x' represents the number of units per time period. Find the equilibrium price and quantity.

Solution: At the equilibrium price

$$x_d = x_s$$

$$20 - 3p - p^2 = p - 1$$

$$p^2 + 4p - 21 = 0$$

$$p^2 + 7p - 3p - 21 = 0$$

$$p(p+7) - 3(p+7) = 0$$

$$(p+7)(p-3) = 0$$

We disregard p = -7, since price cannot be negative $\therefore$ p= 3

Substituting the price value in quantity demanded equation

$$x_d = 20 - 3p - p^2$$

$$= 20 - 3(3) - (3)^2$$

$$= 2$$

Therefore equilibrium price = 3 and quantity = 2.

Example-3: The demand and supply equations of commodity are given by $P_d = 3(6\text{-}x)$ and $P_s = \frac{1}{3}(x+4)$ respectively. Find the equilibrium price and quantity. If a tax of Re. 10/3 per unit is imposed. Find the new equilibrium price and quantity.

Solution: At the equilibrium price, we have

$$3(6 - x) = \frac{1}{3}(x + 4)$$

$$54 - 9x = x + 4$$

(or)

$$10x = 50$$

$$x = 5$$

For $p = 5$ then $P_d = 3(6\text{-}5) = 3$

Thus P = 3 and x= 5 are equilibrium price and quantity respectively.

When a tax of Re.$\frac{10}{3}$ per unit is imposed on the commodity, the supply function becomes;

$$P - \frac{10}{3} = \frac{1}{3}(x+4)$$

(or)

$$P = \frac{1}{3}(x+14)$$

The new equilibrium price and quantity are given by: $x_d = x_s$

$$\text{i.e. } 3(6-x)) = \frac{1}{3}(x+14)$$

$$\text{or } 54-9x = x+14$$

$$\Rightarrow 10x = 40$$

$$x = 4$$

And $P_d = 3(6-4) = 6$

Thus after the imposition of tax, equilibrium price = 6 and the equilibrium quantity = 4.

Example-4: If the total cost function is $TC = 2x^2 + 3x + 4$ then find out Average Cost (AC)?

Solution: Given $TC = 2x^2 + 3x + 4$

$$\therefore AC = \frac{TC}{x}$$

$$= \frac{2x^2 + 3x + 4}{x}$$

$$= \frac{2x^2}{x} + \frac{3x}{x} + \frac{4}{x}$$

$$AC = 2x + 3 + \frac{4}{x}$$

Example-5: If the total cost function is $TC = 3x^2 + 7x + 12$ find out Average cost and Marginal cost at $x = 3$

Solution: Given $TC = 3x^2 + 7x + 12$

$$\therefore AC = \frac{TC}{x}$$

$$= \frac{3x^2 + 7x + 12}{x}$$

$$= 3x + 7 + \frac{12}{x}$$

At $x = 3$, the AC $= 3(3) + 7 + \frac{12}{3}$

$= 9 + 7 + 4$

$\therefore$ AC = 20

$$\text{Marginal cost} = \frac{d}{dx}(TC)$$

$$= \frac{d}{dx}\left(3x^2 + 7x + 12\right)$$

$\therefore$ MC = $6x + 7$

At $x = 3$, then MC = 6(3) + 7

= 18 +7

= 25.

Example-6: If then find out MR and AR at $x = 5$

Solution: Given $TR = 12x - x^2$

$$MR = \frac{d}{dx}(TR)$$

$$= \frac{d}{dx}\left(12x - x^2\right)$$

MR = $12 - 2x$

At $x = 5$, MR = 12 – 2 (5)

= 12 - 10

= 2

$$AR = \frac{TR}{x}$$

$$AR = \frac{12x - x^2}{x}$$

$= 12 - x$

$AR = 12 - x$

At $x = 2$, AR = 12-2 = 10.

Example-7: If then find out TR and MR at $x = 4$ and 10.

Solution: Given $x = 36 - 2P$

$$P = 18 - 0.5x$$

$$TR = P.x$$

$$= (18 - 0.5x)x$$

$$TR = 18x - 0.5x^2$$

At $x = 4$

$$TR = 18(4) - 0.5\,(4)^2$$

$$= 72 - 8.0$$

$$TR = 64$$

At $x = 10$

$$TR = 18(10) - 0.5\,(10)^2$$

$$= 180\text{-}50$$

$$TR = 130$$

Then we have to find out

$$MR = \frac{d}{dx}(TR)$$

$$MR = \frac{d}{dx}\left(18x - 0.5x^2\right)$$

$$MR = 18 - x$$

At $x = 4 \Rightarrow MR = 18 - (4) = 18 - 4 = 14$

At $x = 10 \Rightarrow MR = 18 - (10) = 18 - 10 = 8$

Example-8: The total revenue from the sale of x items is given by

$TR = 200x + \frac{x^2}{5}$ Find the average revenue and marginal revenue when $x = 25$

Solution: Given $TR = 200x + \frac{x^2}{5}$

$$AR = \frac{TR}{x} = \frac{200x + \frac{x^2}{5}}{x}$$

$$= \frac{200x}{x} + \frac{x^2}{5} \bigg/ x$$

$$AR = 200 + \frac{x^2}{5x} = 200 + \frac{x}{5}$$

Then $MR = \frac{d}{dx}(TR)$

$$= \frac{d}{dx}\left(200x + \frac{x^2}{5}\right)$$

$$= 200 + \frac{1}{5}(2x)$$

When $x = 25 \Rightarrow MR = 200 + \frac{2}{5}(25)$

$$= 200 + 2(5)$$

$$MR = 210$$

Example-9: The cost function of firm is given by $TC = 300x - 10x^2 + \frac{x^3}{3}$ calculate the output at which the marginal cost is minimum. Will it be the same for the output at which the average cost is minimum?

Solution: We have $TC = 300x - 10x^2 + \frac{x^3}{3}$

$$MC = 300 - 20x + x^2$$

For maxima or minima, $\frac{d}{dx}(MC) = 0$

$$-20 + 2x = 0$$

$$x = 10$$

Then apply the sufficient condition;

$$\frac{d^2}{dx^2}(MC) = 2 > 0$$

At $x = 10$, then MC is minimum

Now AC = $\frac{TC}{x} = 300 - 10 + \frac{x^2}{3}$

For the AC to be minimum

$$\frac{d}{dx}(AC) = 0$$

$$-10 + \frac{2}{3}x = 0 \qquad x = 15$$

Again, $\frac{d^2}{dx^2}(AC) = \frac{2}{3} > 0$

i.e. at $x = 15$, the AC is minimum

Example-10: At Neha's toy store, the revenue R, in rupees, derived from selling 'x' electric trucks is TR $= -0.005x^2 + 20x$

i. What is the average rate of change in revenue due to selling 10 additional trucks after 1000 have been sold.

ii. What is the Marginal Revenue?

iii. What is the Marginal Revenue a $x = 1000$

Solution

i. Given TR = – 0.005x^2 + 20x

$$AR = \frac{TR}{x} = \frac{-0.005x^2 + 20x}{x} = \frac{-0.005x^2}{x} + \frac{20x}{x}$$

AR = – 0.005x + 20

The average revenue of 1000 trucks have been sold is

At x = 1000 ⇒ AR = – 0.005 (1000) + 20 = – 5 + 20 = 15

and in addition of 10 trucks i.e. x = 1010 (1000 + 10)

Then AR is – 0.005 (1010) + 20 = –5.05 + 20 = 14.95

∴ The average rate of change in Revenue due to selling 10 additional trucks after 1000 trucks have been sold i.e. 15 – 14.95 = 0.05

ii. $MR = \frac{d}{dx}(TR)$

$$= \frac{d}{dx}\left(-0.005x^2 + 20x\right)$$

MR = –0.01x + 20

iii. When x = 1000, MR = –0.01 (1000) + 20

= –10 + 20 = 10

∴ Rs. 10 per truck

Exercise-2

1. The demand and supply functions of a commodity are $P_d = 5 - 2x$ and $P_s = \frac{1}{2}(x+5)$ respectively. Find the equilibrium price and quantity.

2. The total cost (TC) of a form is $0.0005x^3 - 0.7x^2 - 30x + 3000$ where x is the output. Determine Average cost (AC) and Marginal Cost (MC).

3. Let the demand function be $x_d = 25 - 2P$ and the supply function be $x = 3P$ what amount of tax per unit would have to be imposed to double the equilibrium Price without tax?

4. The total cost function (TC) is given by $TC = 5000 + 1000x - 500x^2 + \frac{2}{3}x^3$ find the Marginal cost and Average cost.

5. Determine whether equilibrium solutions exist for markets with the following demand and supply functions:

   a) $P_d = 12 - 3p$; $P_s = -10 + 2p$

   b) $P_d = 16 - 2p$; $P_s = 20 - 2p$

   c) $P_d = 50 - 4p$; $P_s = 10 + 10p - p^2$

   d) $P_d = 50 - 4p$; $P_s = 2 + 10p - p^2$

6. Determine equilibrium price and quantity for a market with the following demand and supply factors $P_d = 20 - 2p$ and $P_s = 40 - 6p$. Assume that a specific tax of 1 dollar per unit is imposed. Compute the changes in equilibrium price and quantity.

7. A certain item can be produced at a cost of Rs. 10 per unit. The demand equation for this item is $P = 90 - 0.02x$, where P is the price in rupees and x is the number of units.

   Find a) The Revenue function

   b) The Marginal Revenue

   c) The Marginal cost

Profit Maximization under Monopoly:

Monopoly is a market situation in which there is a single seller of a product for which there are no good substitutes. Good examples are public utilities such as electric, water and telephone undertakings.

It would always be remembered that the monopolist producer cannot fix both the quantity to be sold and the price to be charged. He can only fix one of them at a time.

If he fixes the output, then the profits

$\Pi = TR - TC$ will be maximized when

$$\frac{d\Pi}{dx} = 0 \text{ and } \frac{d^2\Pi}{dx^2} < 0$$

If he fixed the price, the profit will be maximized when $\frac{d\Pi}{dx} = 0$

and $\frac{d^2\Pi}{dx^2} < 0$

Examples

Example-1: A sitar manufacturer can sell sitars per week at 'p' rupees each, when $5x = 375 - 3p$. The cost of production is $500 + 13x + \frac{1}{5}x^2$ rupees. Find how many sitars he should manufacture from Maximum profit and what is that profit.

Solution: The demand function is

$$5x = 375 - 3p$$

$$p = \frac{1}{3}(375 - 5x).$$

$$TR = p.x = \frac{1}{3}(375 - 5x) \cdot$$

$$= \frac{1}{3}(375x - 5x^2)$$

$$\text{And } TC = 500 + 13x + \frac{1}{5}x^2$$

$$\therefore \Pi = TR - TC$$

$$= \frac{1}{3}(375x - 5x^2) - \left(500 + 13x + \frac{1}{5}x^2\right)$$

$$\Pi = 112x - \frac{28}{15}x^2 - 500$$

For maximum profit $\frac{d\Pi}{dx} = 0$

$$\frac{d}{dx}\left(112x - \frac{28}{15}x^2 - 500\right) = 0$$

$$112 - \frac{56}{15}x = 0$$

$$x = 30$$

and the sufficient conditions is

$$\frac{d^2\Pi}{dx^2} = \frac{-56}{15} < 0$$

Hence, the profit is Maximum when x = 30 sitars are manufactured. Then the maximum profit is

$$112(30) - \frac{28}{15}(30)^2 - 500 = \text{Rs. } 1180$$

Example-2: A radio manufacture producers x sets per week at a total cost of Re. $x^2 + 78x + 2500$. He is a monopolist and the demand function for his product is $x = \frac{600 - P}{8}$, when the price is Re. P per set. Show that the Maximum net revenue is obtained when 29 sets are produced per week. What is the Monopoly Price?

Solution: Given TC = $x^2 + 78x + 2500$

$$x = \frac{600 - P}{8}$$

And TR = P . x

$= (600 - 8x)\,x$

$\therefore$ TR = $600x - 8x^2$

If Π be the net revenue or profit, then

$\Pi = TR - TC$

$= \left(600x - 8x^2\right) - \left(x^2 + 78x + 2500\right)$

$= 600x - 8x^2 - x^2 - 78x + 2500$

$\Pi = 522x - 9x^2 - 2500$

For maximum Profit, $\frac{d\Pi}{dx} = 0$

$$\frac{d}{dx}(\Pi) = \frac{d}{dx}\left(522x - 9x^2 - 2500\right)$$

$$\frac{d\Pi}{dx} = 522 - 18x = 0$$

$18x = 522$

$$x = \frac{522}{18} = 29$$

and the sufficient condition is

$$\frac{d^2\Pi}{dx^2} = -18 < 0$$

Hence the profit is maximum when $x = 29$ i.e. when 29 sets are produced per week.

At Price 'p' at $x = 29$

$$P = 600 - 8 \times 29$$

$$= 600 - 232$$

$$= \text{Re. } 368$$

$\therefore$ The Monopoly price is Re. 368

Example-3: The total cost function of a firm is $\frac{1}{3}x^3 - 5x^2 + 28x + 10$, where 'C' is the total cost and x is the output. A tax at the rate of Re. 2 per unit of output is imposed and the producer adds it to his cost. If the demand function is given by p = 2530-5x, where Re.p is the price per unit of output, find the profit maximizing output and the price at the level.

Solution: Given $TC = \frac{1}{3}x^3 - 5x^2 + 28x + 10$

After imposition tax, the new total cost function is

$$TC = \frac{1}{3}x^3 - 5x^2 + 30x + 10$$

and the total revenue: $TR = P.\ x$

$$TR = (2530\text{-}5x)x$$

$$TR = 2530x - 5x^2$$

If Π be the profit on sale of x units, then

$$\Pi = TR - TC$$

$$\Pi = (2530x - 5x^2) - (\frac{1}{3}x^3 - 5x^2 + 28x + 10)$$

$$\Pi = 2500 - \frac{1}{3}x^3 - 10$$

The necessary condition for maximum profit is $\frac{d\Pi}{dx} = 0$

$$\frac{d}{dx}(\Pi) = \frac{d}{dx}\left(2500x - \frac{1}{3}x^3 - 10\right) = 0$$

$$2500 - x^2 = 0$$

$$x^2 = 2500$$

$$x = 50$$

and the sufficient condition is

$$\frac{d^2\Pi}{dx^2} = -2x$$

At $x = 50$, $\frac{d^2\Pi}{dx^2} = -2(50) = -100 < 0$

Hence, the profit 'Π' is maximum at $x = 50$

and the price is P = 2530 – 5 × 50

= Re. 2, 280

Example-4: A company has for x items produced the total cost 'C' and the total revenue 'R' gives by equation TR = $3x$ and TC = 100 + $0.015x^2$. Find how many items be produced to maximize the profit. What is the profit?

Solution: Given TR = $3x$

$$TC = 100 + 0.015\,x^2$$

$$\Pi = 3x - 100 - 0.015x^2$$

For profit maximization, the necessary condition is $\frac{d\Pi}{dx} = 0$

$$\frac{d}{dx}(\Pi) = \frac{d}{dx}\left(3x - 100 - 0.015x^2\right)$$

$$3 - 0.03x = 0$$

$$x = \frac{3}{0.03} = 100$$

and the sufficient condition is

$$\text{At } x = 100, \ \frac{d^2\Pi}{dx^2} = -0.03 < 0$$

Hence, 100 units should be the output for profit maximization

$$\Pi = -0.015\,(100)^2 + 3(100) - 100$$

$$\therefore \ \Pi = 50$$

Example-5: Let the average cost be $Ac = 10 + \frac{x}{25}$ and the demand function $x = 200 - 10p$, where x represent the units of output and 'p' represents price. Find the profit maximizing output level.

Solution: We have $x = 200 - 10P$

$$P = 20 - \frac{x}{10}$$

$$\text{and } AC = 10 + \frac{x}{25}$$

$$TC = x \times AC = x\left(10 + \frac{x}{25}\right)$$

$$TC = 10x + \frac{x^2}{25}$$

Then the total revenue is

$$TR = P.\,x$$

$$= \left(20 - \frac{x}{10}\right) \cdot x$$

$$= 20x - \frac{x^2}{10}$$

The profit Π = TR – TC

$$\Pi = \left(20x - \frac{x^2}{10}\right) - \left(10x + \frac{x^2}{25}\right)$$

$$= 20x - \frac{x^2}{10} - 10x - \frac{x^2}{25}$$

$$\Pi = 10x - \frac{7}{50}x^2$$

For profit maximization, the necessary condition is

$$\frac{d\Pi}{dx} = 0$$

$$\frac{d}{dx}\left(10x - \frac{7}{50}x^2\right)$$

$$10 - \frac{14}{50}x = 0$$

$$\therefore x = \frac{250}{7}$$

and the sufficient condition is for, $x = \frac{250}{7}$, $\frac{d^2\Pi}{dx^2} = -\frac{14}{50}$

Hence, the maximization profit is obtained where $x = \frac{250}{7}$

Profit maximization under perfect competition:

Perfect competition is a market situation in which there is a large number of buyers and sellers and the sellers sell a homogeneous product under perfect competition price is determined by the joint efforts of all the buyers and sellers or by the whole industry.

The total revenue is TR = P. x

$$MR = \frac{d}{dx}(TR)$$

$$= \frac{d}{dx}(P \cdot x)$$

$$= P \cdot \frac{d}{dx}(x) + x\,\frac{d}{dx}(P)$$

$$= P \cdot (1) + x \cdot \frac{dP}{dx}$$

$$\therefore\ \text{MR} = P + x\frac{dP}{dx}$$

Under perfect competition, $\frac{dP}{dx} = 0$

Where P is a constant

$\therefore \text{MR} = \text{P}$

Assuming that the cost function is

TC = c(x)

Then Π = TR – TC

= P.x - c(x)

The necessary condition for the profit maximization is $\frac{d\Pi}{dx} = 0$

$$\frac{d}{dx}(TR) - \frac{d}{dx}(TC) = 0$$

MR – MC = 0

MR = MC

Since MR = P, therefore MR = P is the necessary condition for maximum profits.

The sufficient condition for the maximum profit $\frac{d^2\pi}{dx^2} < 0$

$$\frac{d^2TR}{dx^2} - \frac{d^2TC}{dx^2} < 0$$

$$0 - \frac{d^2TC}{dx^2} < 0$$

$$\frac{d^2C}{dx^2} > 0$$

$$\frac{d^2TR}{dx^2} = \frac{d}{dx}\left(\frac{dTR}{dx}\right) = \frac{d}{dx}(MR) = \frac{d}{dx}(P) = 0$$

i.e. the MC curve must have a positive slope.

Example-1: If the cost function of a firm is

$$TC = \frac{1}{3}x^3 - 5x^2 + 30x + 10$$

Where TC is the total cost and '*x*' is the output, and price under perfect competition is given as 6, find for what value of x the profit will be maximized.

$$\text{TC} = \frac{1}{3}x^3 - 5x^2 + 30x + 10$$

$$\text{MC} = \frac{d}{dx}(TC) = x^2 - 10x + 30$$

Under perfect competition, the necessary condition for profit maximization

$$\text{MC} = \text{p}$$

$$x^2 - 10x + 30 = 6$$

$$x^2 - 10x + 24 = 0$$

$$x^2 - 6x - 4x + 24 = 0$$

$$x(x-6) - 4(x-6) = 0$$

$$(x-6)(x-4) = 0$$

$\therefore x = 4$ and 6

The sufficient condition for profit maximization requires

$$\frac{d^2TC}{dx^2} > 0$$

$$\frac{d^2TC}{dx^2} = 2x - 10$$

At $x = 4$, $\frac{d^2TC}{dx^2} = 2(4) - 10$

$= 8 - 10 = -2 < 0$

And at $x = 6$, $\frac{d^2TC}{dx^2} = 2(6) - 10$

$12 - 10 = 2 > 0$

Therefore, at x = 6 is the level of output where the profit is maximum.

Example-2: For a firm under perfect competition it is given that $TC = \frac{1}{3}x^3 + 2x^2 - 7x + 6$ and $P = 5$, where x stands for level of output, P for price per unit and TC is the total cost. Find the quantity produced at which profit will be maximum.

Solution: We have $TC = \frac{1}{3}x^3 + 2x^2 - 7x + 6$

$$MC = \frac{d}{dx}(TC) = \frac{d}{dx}\left(\frac{1}{3}x^3 + 2x^2 - 7x + 6\right)$$

$$MC = x^2 + 4x - 7$$

Under perfect competition, the necessary condition for profit maximum is MC = P

$$x^2 + 4x - 7 = 5$$

$$x^2 + 4x - 12 = 0$$

$$x^2 + 6x - 2x - 12 = 0$$

$$x(x+6) - 2(x+6) = 0$$

x = -6 and 2

The sufficient condition is

$$\frac{d^2TC}{dx^2} = 2x + 4$$

At $x = 2$, $\quad 4 + 4 = 8 > 0$

Therefore, x = 2 is the level of output where the profit is maximum.

Example-3: The demand function P = 90 – x^2 and the cost function TC = 10 + $2x^2$ + $3x^3$, determine the profit maximizing output of a monopolist firm. What would be the impact of a tax of Re. 10 per unit of output on price and profit?

Solution: Before imposition of Tax

$$\Pi = TR - TC$$

Where P = 90 – x^2, then TR = P. x

$$= (90 - x^2)x$$

$$TR = 90x - x^3$$

$$\text{Then } \Pi = (90x - x^3) - (10 + 2x^2 + 3x^3)$$

$$\Pi = -4x^3 - 2x^2 + 90x - 10$$

Then the necessary condition for maximization is $\frac{d\Pi}{dx} = 0$

$$\frac{d}{dx}\left(-4x^3 - 2x^2 + 9x - 10\right) = 0$$

$$-12x^2 - 4x + 90 = 0$$

$$x = 2.74$$

$$\text{At } x = 2.74, \frac{d^2\Pi}{dx^2} = - < 0$$

∴ The profit maximizing output before the imposition of tax is at $x = 2.74$

After the imposition of tax:

After a tax of Re. 10 per unit is imposed, the cost function can be written as $TC = 10 + 2x^2 + 3x^3 + 10x$

And the profit function is $\Pi_N = TR - TC_N$

$$= 90 - x^3 - (10 + 2x^2 + 3x^3 + 10x)$$

$$= -4x^3 - 2x^2 + 80x - 10$$

$$\text{For a maximum profit } \frac{d\Pi_N}{dx} = -12x^2 - 4x + 80$$

$$= 3x^2 + x - 20 = 0$$

$$x = 2.42$$

$$\text{Also for } x = 2.42, \frac{d\Pi_N}{dx} = -24(2.42) - 4 < 0$$

∴ The profit maximizing level of output after the imposition of tax is $x = 2.42$

∴ Price after tax $= 90 - 2(2.42)^2$

$= \text{Re. } 84.14$

Exercise-3

1. Given that $TR = 4000x - 33x^2$ and $TC = 2x3 - 3x^2 + 400x + 500, x > 0$ find out the profit maximizing level of output.
2. A steel plant produces x tones of steel per week at a total cost of Re. $\frac{1}{2}x^3 - 7x^2 + 111x + 50$. Find the output level at which the marginal cost attains its minimum.

3. A firm produces 'x' tones of output at total cost TC = Re. $\frac{1}{10}x^3 - 5x^2 + 10x + 5$. At what level of output will the marginal and the average variable cost attain their respective minima?

4. If TC $= 300x - 10x^2 + \frac{1}{3}x^3$, where '$x$' is output find the output levels at which the marginal cost and the average cost attain their respective minima?

5. The price 'p' per unit at which a company can sell all that it produces is given by the function P = 300 – 4x. The cost function is TC = 500 + 28x, where 'x' is the number of units produced. Find the profit maximizing level of output.

6. Determine the Maximum profit and the corresponding price and quantity for a monopolist whose demand and cost functions are $P = 20 - 0.5x$ and $TC = 0.04x^3 - 1.94x^2 + 32.96x$ respectively.

7. Determine the maximum profit and the corresponding marginal price and quantity for a perfectly discriminating monopolist whose demand and cost functions are $P = 2200 - 6x$ and $TC = 0.5x^3 - 61.5x^2 + 2740x$ respectively.

4

Partial Differentiation

In the previous chapter, we have considered only one variable function i.e. $y = f(x)$. But in many situations, the demand for a commodity may be regarded as a function of its own price, the price of other commodities, income of the consumer etc. In such situation we used the concept of partial derivatives.

By a partial derivative of a function of two or more variables, we simply mean the limiting value of the ratio of the change in the dependent variable to the change in one of the independent variables. The procedure of finding partial derivatives of a function of two or more variables is exactly the same as that of finding partial derivatives of a function of one variable.

If $z = f(x, y)$ be a function of two variables.

The partial derivative of Z with respect to x and it is denoted by $\frac{\partial z}{\partial x}$ or $f(x, y)$ or fx and is defined by $\frac{\partial z}{\partial x} = \underset{\Delta x \to 0}{Lt} \frac{f(x+\Delta x, y) - f(x, y)}{\Delta x}$, provided the limit exists.

and the partial derivative of 'z' with respect to y and it is denoted by $\frac{\partial z}{\partial y}$ or fy and is defined as $\frac{\partial z}{\partial y} = \underset{\Delta y \to 0}{Lt} \frac{f(x, y+\Delta y) - f(x, y)}{\Delta y}$, provided the limit exists.

Therefore finding partial derivatives of functions of more than one variable reduces to finding derivative of the functions with respect to one independent variable, holding all other independent variables constant.

Examples

Example-1: If $z = x^2y + xy^3$ find out the first order partial derivatives.

Solution: we have $z = x^2y + xy^3$

$$\frac{\partial z}{\partial x} = \frac{\partial}{\partial x}\left(x^2y + xy^3\right)$$

$$= \frac{\partial}{\partial x}\left(x^2y\right) + \frac{\partial}{\partial x}\left(xy^3\right)$$

$$\frac{\partial z}{\partial x} = 2xy + y^3$$

$$\frac{\partial z}{\partial y} = \frac{\partial}{\partial y}\left(x^2y + xy^3\right)$$

$$= \frac{\partial}{\partial y}\left(x^2y\right) + \frac{\partial}{\partial y}\left(xy^3\right)$$

$$\frac{\partial z}{\partial y} = x^2 + 3xy^2$$

Example-2: If $z = e^{x^2y}$, then find out first-order partial derivatives.

Solution: We have $z = e^{x^2y}$

$$\frac{\partial z}{\partial x} = \frac{\partial}{\partial x} e^{x^2y} = e^{x^2y}\, 2xy$$

$$\frac{\partial z}{\partial y} = \frac{\partial}{\partial y}\left(e^{x^2y}\right) = e^{x^2y}\, x^2$$

Example-3: If z = log $\left(x^2+y^2\right)^{1/2}$ then find out $\frac{\partial z}{\partial x}$ and $\frac{\partial z}{\partial y}$

Solution: Given z = log $\left(x^2+y^2\right)^{1/2}$

$$\frac{\partial z}{\partial x}=\frac{\partial}{\partial x}\left(\log\left(x^2+y^2\right)^{1/2}\right)$$

$$=\frac{1}{2\left(x^2+y^2\right)}\cdot 2x$$

$$=\frac{x}{x^2+y^2}$$

$$\frac{\partial z}{\partial y}=\frac{\partial}{\partial z}\left(\log\left(x^2+y^2\right)^{1/2}\right)$$

$$=\frac{1}{2\left(x^2+y^2\right)}\cdot 2y$$

$$=\frac{y}{x^2+y^2}$$

Exercise-1

1. If z = $xy+2$ then find out $\frac{\partial z}{\partial x}$ and $\frac{\partial z}{\partial y}$
2. If z = x^2y+xy^2 then find out $\frac{\partial z}{\partial x}$ and $\frac{\partial z}{\partial y}$
3. If z = x^2y+2y^2 then find out $\frac{\partial z}{\partial x}$ and $\frac{\partial z}{\partial y}$

4. If $z = 3x^2y^2 + x^6 + 3y^3$ then find out $\frac{\partial z}{\partial x}$ and $\frac{\partial z}{\partial y}$

5. If $z = 2L^{0.8}K^{0.2}$ then find out $\frac{\partial z}{\partial L}$ and $\frac{\partial z}{\partial K}$

6. If $z = 2L^{0.75}K^{0.25}$ then find out $\frac{\partial z}{\partial L}$ and $\frac{\partial z}{\partial K}$

7. If $z = y \cdot e^x$ then find out $\frac{\partial z}{\partial x}$ and $\frac{\partial z}{\partial y}$

8. If $z = \left(x^2 + y^2\right)^3$ then find out $\frac{\partial z}{\partial x}$ and $\frac{\partial z}{\partial y}$

9. If $z = \log\left(x^2 + y^2\right)^{1/3}$ then find out $\frac{\partial z}{\partial x}$ and $\frac{\partial z}{\partial y}$

10. If $z = \log\left(x^2 - y^2\right)^{1/8}$ then find out $\frac{\partial z}{\partial x}$ and $\frac{\partial z}{\partial y}$

Higher order partial derivatives

The second partial derivatives are also called 'direct" second order partial derivatives. It is direct in the sense that the second-time partial differentiation is taken with respect to the same independent variable as in the first partial differentiation. However, since $f(x, y)$ is a function of two variables x and y, it will change as y changes when x is held constant. In this case, we speak of the 'cross' second-order partial derivative and denote the rate of change in $f(x, y)$ as y is varied by

$$fxy \text{ or } \frac{\partial^2 z}{\partial y \partial x} = \frac{\partial}{\partial y}\left(\frac{\partial z}{\partial x}\right)$$

In the similar way, we can speak of the cross second-order partial

$$fyx \text{ or } \frac{\partial^2 z}{\partial x \partial y} = \frac{\partial}{\partial x}\left(\frac{\partial z}{\partial y}\right)$$

There is no reason why *fxy* and *fyx* should be equal since *fxy* denotes the change in *fx* due to a change in *y* holding *x* constant, where as *fyx* denote the change in *fy* due to a change in *x* holding y constant.

Example-1: If z = $e^{2x^2+xy+3y^2}$ then find out the first order partial derivations

Solution: We have z = $e^{2x^2+xy+3y^2}$

and then $\frac{\partial z}{\partial x} = \frac{\partial}{\partial x}\left(e^{2x^2+xy+3y^2}\right)$

$$\therefore \frac{\partial z}{\partial x} = e^{2x^2+xy+3y^2} \times (4x+y)$$

and $\frac{\partial z}{\partial y} = \frac{\partial}{\partial y}\left(e^{2x^2+xy+3y^2}\right)$

$$= e^{2x^2+xy+3y^2} \times (x+6y)$$

Example-2: If z = $3x^3y - xy^2 + 4y^4$ find out $\frac{\partial z}{\partial x}$ and $\frac{\partial z}{\partial y}$

Solution: Given z = $3x^3y - xy^2 + 4y^4$

$$\frac{\partial z}{\partial x} = \frac{\partial}{\partial x}\left(3x^3y - xy^2 + 4y^4\right)$$

$$= 9x^2y - y^2$$

and $\frac{\partial z}{\partial y} = \frac{\partial}{\partial y}\left(3x^3y - xy^2 + 4y^4\right)$

$$= 3x^3 - 2yx + 16y^3$$

Example-3: Show that $x\cdot\frac{\partial z}{\partial x} + y\frac{\partial z}{\partial y} = -z, \text{ if } z = \frac{x+y}{x^2+y^2}$

Solution: We have $z = \dfrac{x+y}{x^2+y^2}$

Let $u = x + y$

$v = x^2 + y^2$

$$\frac{\partial}{\partial x}\left(\frac{x+y}{x^2+y^2}\right) = \frac{\left(x^2+y^2\right)\frac{\partial}{\partial x}(x+y)-(x+y)\frac{\partial}{\partial x}\left(x^2+y^2\right)}{\left(x^2+y^2\right)^2}$$

$$= \frac{\left(x^2+y^2\right)(1)-(x+y)(2x)}{\left(x^2+y^2\right)^2}$$

$$\therefore \frac{\partial z}{\partial x} = \frac{-x^2+y^2-2xy}{\left(x^2+y^2\right)^2}$$

And $$\frac{\partial z}{\partial y} = \frac{\partial}{\partial y}\left(\frac{x+y}{x^2+y^2}\right) = \frac{\left(x^2+y^2\right)\frac{\partial}{\partial y}(x+y)-(x+y)\frac{\partial}{\partial y}\left(x^2+y^2\right)}{\left(x^2+y^2\right)^2}$$

$$= \frac{\left(x^2+y^2\right)(1)-(x+y)(2y)}{\left(x^2+y^2\right)^2}$$

$$= \frac{\left(x^2+y^2\right)-\left(2xy+2y^2\right)}{\left(x^2+y^2\right)^2}$$

$$= \frac{\left(x^2+y^2-2xy-2y^2\right)}{\left(x^2+y^2\right)^2}$$

$$\therefore \frac{\partial z}{\partial y} = \frac{x^2-y^2-2xy}{\left(x^2+y^2\right)^2}$$

$$x \cdot \frac{\partial z}{\partial x} = \frac{-x^3 + xy^2 - 2x^2y}{\left(x^2 + y^2\right)^2}$$

$$y \cdot \frac{\partial z}{\partial y} = \frac{x^2y - y^3 - 2xy^2}{\left(x^2 + y^2\right)^2}$$

$$\therefore\ x\frac{\partial z}{\partial x} + y\frac{\partial z}{\partial y} = \frac{-x^3 + xy^2 - 2x^2y}{\left(x^2 + y^2\right)^2} + \frac{x^2y - y^3 - 2xy^2}{\left(x^2 + y^2\right)^2}$$

$$= \frac{-x^3 + xy^2 - 2x^2y + x^2y - y^3 - 2xy^2}{\left(x^2 + y^2\right)^2}$$

$$= \frac{-x^3 - y^3 - xy^2 - x^2y}{\left(x^2 + y^2\right)^2}$$

$$= -\frac{\left(x^2 + y^2\right)\left(x + y\right)}{\left(x^2 + y^2\right)^2}$$

$$= -\frac{x + y}{x^2 + y^2}$$

$$= -Z$$

Example-4: If u = $\log\left(x^2 + y^2 + z^2\right)$, show that

$$x \cdot \frac{\partial u}{\partial x} + y\frac{\partial u}{\partial y} + z\frac{\partial u}{\partial z} = 2$$

Solution: We have u = $\log\left(x^2 + y^2 + z^2\right)$

$$\frac{\partial u}{\partial x} = \frac{1}{x^2 + y^2 + z^2} \times (2x)$$

$$x \cdot \frac{\partial u}{\partial x} = x \cdot \frac{2x}{x^2 + y^2 + z^2} = \frac{2x^2}{x^2 + y^2 + z^2}$$

$$\frac{\partial u}{\partial y} = \frac{1}{x^2 + y^2 + z^2} \times 2y$$

$$= \frac{2y}{x^2 + y^2 + z^2}$$

$$y \cdot \frac{\partial u}{\partial y} = y \cdot \frac{2y}{x^2 + y^2 + z^2} = \frac{2y^2}{x^2 + y^2 + z^2}$$

$$\frac{\partial u}{\partial z} = \frac{1}{x^2 + y^2 + z^2} \times (2z) = \frac{2z}{x^2 + y^2 + z^2}$$

$$z \cdot \frac{\partial u}{\partial z} = \frac{2z^2}{x^2 + y^2 + z^2}$$

$$\therefore\ x \cdot \frac{\partial u}{\partial x} + y \cdot \frac{\partial u}{\partial y} + z \cdot \frac{\partial u}{\partial z} = \frac{2(x^2 + y^2 + z^2)}{(x^2 + y^2 + z^2)} = 2$$

Exercise-2

1. **If $z = 2x^2 - 2y^2 + 4xy - 5$ then find out the second order partial derivatives.**
2. **If $z = x^2 + y^2 - 5xy$ then find out the second order partial derivatives.**
3. **If $z = \frac{1}{\sqrt{x^2 + y^2}}$ then find out the second order partial derivatives.**

4. If $z = \frac{x}{y} + \frac{y}{x}$ then find out the second order partial derivatives.

5. If $u = x^2y + y^2z + z^2x$, show that

$$\frac{\partial u}{\partial x} + \frac{\partial u}{\partial y} + \frac{\partial u}{\partial z} = (x+y+z)^2$$

6. If $u = \log\left(\frac{x^3 + y^3}{x^2 + y^2}\right)$, show that $x . \frac{\partial u}{\partial x} + y . \frac{\partial u}{\partial y} = 1$

7. If $u = \log(x^3 + y^3 + z^3 - 3xyz)$, show that

$$\frac{\partial u}{\partial x} + \frac{\partial u}{\partial y} + \frac{\partial u}{\partial z} = \frac{3}{x+y+z}$$

8. If $z = \sqrt{ax^2 + 2hxy + by^2}$, verify that

$$x^2 \frac{\partial^2 z}{\partial x^2} + 2xy \frac{\partial^2 z}{\partial x \partial y} + y^2 \frac{\partial^2 z}{\partial y^2} = 0$$

9. If $u = \log(x^2 + y^2 + z^2)$, prove that

$$x \frac{\partial^2 u}{\partial y \partial z} = y \frac{\partial^2 u}{\partial z \partial x} = z \frac{\partial^2 u}{\partial x \partial y}$$

10. Find out the second order partial derivatives for the following:
$z = 3x^5y^4 + 2x^3y^2 + x^2 + 3$.

Homogeneous functions

A class of functions widely used in economic analysis is the homogeneous function. A homogenous function has the property that, given a proportionate change in its independent variables, the dependent variable increases by some power of the proportion of change.

More formally, for given z = *f*(x,y) and any constant 'λ', if

f is said to be a homogenous function of degree 'k'

Example: Determine the degree of homogeneity of the following

$$Z = \sqrt{ax^2 + by^2 + 2cxy}$$

Solution: Given $Z = \sqrt{ax^2 + by^2 + 2cxy}$

Then $\sqrt{a(\lambda x)^2 + b(\lambda y)^2 + 2c(\lambda x)(\lambda y)}$

$$= \sqrt{\lambda^2 ax^2 + \lambda^2 by^2 + \lambda^2 2cxy}$$

$$= \sqrt{\lambda^2 \left(ax^2 + by^2 + 2cxy\right)}$$

$$= \lambda\sqrt{ax^2 + by^2 + 2cxy}$$

$$= \lambda Z$$

Therefore 'Z' is a homogeneous function of degree one. This type of homogeneous function is called a linear homogeneous function, and it is frequently used in analysis of production function.

Example: if $z = \dfrac{x^3 + y^3}{x^2 + y^2}$ find the degree of homogeneous

Solution: we have $z = \dfrac{x^3 + y^3}{x^2 + y^2}$

Then $z = \dfrac{(\lambda x)^3 + (\lambda y)^3}{(\lambda x)^2 + (\lambda y)^2}$

$$= \frac{\lambda^3 x^3 + \lambda^3 y^3}{\lambda^2 x^2 + \lambda^2 y^2}$$

$$= \frac{\lambda^3\left(x^3 + y^3\right)}{\lambda^2\left(x^2 + y^2\right)}$$

$$= \lambda z$$

Thus the degree of homogeneity is one.

Euler's theorem

A production function, $Q=f(L,K)$ is homogeneous of degree v if

$$f(\lambda L, \lambda K) = \lambda^v . f(L,K)$$

Differentiating with respect to 'λ' we obtain

$$L.\frac{df}{dL} + K.\frac{df}{dK} = v.\lambda^{v-1}.f(L,K)$$

With constant returns to scale $v = 1$, and we have

$$L.(MPP_L) + K.(MPP_K) = f(L,K)$$

Given that $f(L,K)=Q$ we obtain

$$Q = L.(MPP_L) + K.(MPP_K)$$

Total physical payments to factors would exhaust and total physical output

Multiplying through by P, the price of output we see that in the case of constant returns to scale

$$PQ = L.(MPP_L . P) + K.(MPP_K\ P)$$

i.e. payment of factors according to their VMP exhausts the value of output, and share factors add up to unity.

Example-1: If $z = x^3 - 3x^3y + 2y^2x - 5$ then find out second partial derivatives.

Solution: We have $z = x^3 - 3x^2y + 2y^2x - 5$

$$\frac{\partial z}{\partial x} = \frac{\partial}{\partial x}\left(x^3 - 3x^2y + 2y^2x - 5\right)$$

$= 3x^2 - 6xy + 2y^2$

Then $\dfrac{\partial^2 z}{\partial x^2} = \dfrac{\partial}{\partial x}\left(3x^2y - 6xy + 2y^2\right)$

$= 6x - 6y$

$$\frac{\partial z}{\partial y} = \frac{\partial}{\partial y}\left(x^3 - 3x^2y + 2y^2x - 5\right)$$

$= -3x^2 + 4xy$

Then $\dfrac{\partial^2 z}{\partial y^2} = \dfrac{\partial}{\partial y}\left(-3x^2 + 4xy\right)$

$= 4x$

Then $\dfrac{\partial^2 z}{\partial x \partial y} = \dfrac{\partial}{\partial x}\left(\dfrac{\partial z}{\partial y}\right) = \dfrac{\partial}{\partial x}\left(-3x^2 + 4xy\right)$

$= -6x + 4y$

Then $\dfrac{\partial^2 z}{\partial y \partial x} = \dfrac{\partial}{\partial y}\left(\dfrac{\partial z}{\partial x}\right) = \dfrac{\partial}{\partial y}\left(3x^2 - 6xy + 2y^2\right)$

$= -6x + 4y$

Example-2: If $z = 3x^2 + xy - 2y^2$ then find out the second order partial derivatives?

Solution: we have $z = 3x^2 + xy - 2y^2$

$$\frac{\partial z}{\partial x} = \frac{\partial}{\partial x}\left(3x^2 + xy - 2y^2\right)$$

$= 6x + y$

Then $\frac{\partial^2 z}{\partial x^2} = \frac{\partial}{\partial x}(6x + y))$

$= 6$

$\frac{\partial z}{\partial y} = \frac{\partial}{\partial y}(3x^2 + xy - 2y^2)$

$= x - 4y$

Then $\frac{\partial z}{\partial y} = \frac{\partial}{\partial y}(3x^2 + xy - 2y^2)$

$= -4$

$\frac{\partial^2 z}{\partial x \partial y} = \frac{\partial}{\partial x}\left(\frac{\partial z}{\partial y}\right) = \frac{\partial}{\partial x}(x - 4y)$

$= 1$

$\frac{\partial^2 z}{\partial y \partial x} = \frac{\partial}{\partial y}\left(\frac{\partial z}{\partial x}\right) = \frac{\partial}{\partial y}(x - 4y)$

$= -4$

Example-3: If $z = \log(x^2 + y^2)$, show that $\frac{\partial^2 z}{\partial x^2} + \frac{\partial^2 z}{\partial y^2} = 0$

Solution: Given $z = \log(x^2 + y^2)$

$\frac{\partial z}{\partial x} = \frac{\partial}{\partial x}(\log(x^2 + y^2))$

$= \frac{1}{x^2 + y^2} \times 2x$

$$\frac{\partial z}{\partial x} = \frac{2x}{x^2 + y^2}$$

Then $\dfrac{\partial^2 z}{\partial x^2} = \dfrac{\partial}{\partial x}\left(\dfrac{2x}{x^2 + y^2}\right)$

$$\frac{\left(x^2 + y^2\right)\frac{\partial}{\partial x}(2x) - 2x \, . \, \frac{\partial}{\partial x}\left(x^2 + y^2\right)}{\left(x^2 + y^2\right)^2}$$

$$= \frac{\left(x^2 + y^2\right)(2) - 2x(2x)}{\left(x^2 + y^2\right)^2}$$

$$= \frac{2x^2 + 2y^2 - 4x^2}{\left(x^2 + y^2\right)^2}$$

$$= \frac{2y^2 - 2x^2}{\left(x^2 + y^2\right)^2}$$

Again $\dfrac{\partial z}{\partial y} = \dfrac{\partial}{\partial y}\left(\log\left(x^2 + y^2\right)\right)$

$$= \frac{1}{x^2 + y^2} \times 2y$$

$$\frac{\partial z}{\partial y} = \frac{2y}{x^2 + y^2}$$

Then $\dfrac{\partial^2 z}{\partial y^2} = \dfrac{\partial}{\partial y}\left(\dfrac{2y}{x^2 + y^2}\right)$

$$= \frac{\left(x^2+y^2\right)\frac{\partial}{\partial y}(2y) - 2y \cdot \frac{\partial}{\partial y}\left(x^2+y^2\right)}{\left(x^2+y^2\right)^2}$$

$$= \frac{\left(x^2+y^2\right)(2) - 2y.\,(2y)}{\left(x^2+y^2\right)^2}$$

$$= \frac{2x^2+2y^2-4y^2}{\left(x^2+y^2\right)^2}$$

$$= \frac{2x^2-2y^2}{\left(x^2+y^2\right)^2}$$

$$\therefore \frac{\partial^2 z}{\partial x^2} + \frac{\partial^2}{\partial y^2} = \frac{2y^2-2x^2}{\left(x^2+y^2\right)^2} + \frac{2x^2-2y^2}{\left(x^2+y^2\right)^2}$$

$$= \frac{2y^2-2x^2+2x^2-2y^2}{\left(x^2+y^2\right)^2}$$

$$= 0$$

Hence, $\frac{\partial^2 z}{\partial x^2} + \frac{\partial^2 z}{\partial y^2} = 0$

Example-4: If u = $\sqrt{x^2+y^2+z^2}$, show that

$$\left(\frac{\partial u}{\partial x}\right)^2 + \left(\frac{\partial u}{\partial y}\right)^2 + \left(\frac{\partial u}{\partial z}\right)^2 = 1$$

Solution: We have u = $\sqrt{x^2+y^2+z^2}$

Then $\frac{\partial u}{\partial x} = \frac{\partial}{\partial x}\left(\sqrt{x^2 + y^2 + z^2}\right)$

$$= \frac{1}{2\sqrt{x^2 + y^2 + z^2}} \times 2x$$

$$= \frac{x}{\sqrt{x^2 + y^2 + z^2}}$$

Similarly $\frac{\partial u}{\partial y} = \frac{y}{\sqrt{x^2 + y^2 + z^2}}$

$$\frac{\partial u}{\partial z} = \frac{z}{\sqrt{x^2 + y^2 + z^2}}$$

$$\left(\frac{\partial u}{\partial x}\right)^2 + \left(\frac{\partial u}{\partial y}\right)^2 + \left(\frac{\partial u}{\partial z}\right)^2 = \left(\frac{x}{\sqrt{x^2 + y^2 + z^2}}\right)^2 + \left(\frac{y}{\sqrt{x^2 + y^2 + z^2}}\right)^2$$

$$+ \left(\frac{z}{\sqrt{x^2 + y^2 + z^2}}\right)^2$$

$$= \frac{x^2}{x^2 + y^2 + z^2} + \frac{y^2}{x^2 + y^2 + z^2} + \frac{z^2}{x^2 + y^2 + z^2}$$

$$= \frac{x^2 + y^2 + z^2}{x^2 + y^2 + z^2}$$

$$= 1$$

Example-5: If $u = (x^2 + y^2 + z^2)^{-1/2}$ show that

$$\frac{\partial^2 u}{\partial x^2} + \frac{\partial^2 u}{\partial y^2} + \frac{\partial^2 u}{\partial z^2} = 0$$

Solution: We have $u = (x^2 + y^2 + z^2)^{-1/2}$

$$\frac{\partial u}{\partial x} = -\frac{1}{2}\left(x^2 + y^2 + z^2\right)^{-3/2} \times (2x)$$

$$= -x\left(x^2 + y^2 + z^2\right)^{-3/2}$$

$$\frac{\partial^2 u}{\partial x^2} = +\frac{3}{2}x\left(x^2 + y^2 + z^2\right)^{-5/2} \times (2x)$$

$$= +3x^2\left(x^2 + y^2 + z^2\right)^{-5/2}$$

Similarly $\frac{\partial^2 u}{\partial y^2} = +3y^2\left(x^2 + y^2 + z^2\right)^{-5/2}$

$$\frac{\partial^2 u}{\partial z^2} = +3z^2\left(x^2 + y^2 + z^2\right)^{-5/2}$$

$$\frac{\partial^2 u}{\partial x^2} + \frac{\partial^2 u}{\partial y^2} + \frac{\partial^2 u}{\partial z^2} = 3x^2\left(x^2 + y^2 + z^2\right)^{-5/2} + 3y^2\left(x^2 + y^2 + z^2\right)^{-5/2} + 3z^2\left(x^2 + y^2 + z^2\right)^{-5/2}$$

$$= 3\left(x^2 + y^2 + z^2\right)^{-5/2}\left(x^2 + y^2 + z^2\right)$$

$$= 3\left(x^2 + y^2 + z^2\right)^{-5/2+1}$$

$$= 3\left(x^2 + y^2 + z^2\right)^{-3/2}$$

$$= 3\left[\left(x^2 + y^2 + z^2\right)^{-1/2}\right]^3$$

$$= 3\,(u)^3 \qquad \therefore u = \left(x^2 + y^2 + z^2\right)^{-1/2}$$

$$= 3\,u^3$$

Example-6: Verify Euler's theorem for the following

$$z = \frac{x^3 + y^3}{x + y}$$

Solution: We have $z = \dfrac{x^3 + y^3}{x + y}$

Then $$z = \frac{(\lambda x)^3 + (\lambda y)^3}{\lambda x + \lambda y}$$

$$= \frac{\lambda^3 x^3 + \lambda 3 y^3}{\lambda x + \lambda y}$$

$$= \frac{\lambda^3 (x^3 + y^3)}{\lambda (x + y)}$$

$$= \lambda^2 z$$

$\therefore$ z is a homogeneous function of degree 2, so by Euler's theorem

$$x\frac{\partial z}{\partial x} + y\frac{\partial z}{\partial y} = 2z$$

Now we find out

$$\frac{\partial z}{\partial x} = \frac{\partial}{\partial x}\left(\frac{x^3 + y^3}{x + y}\right)$$

$$= \frac{(x + y)\frac{\partial}{\partial x}(x^3 + y^3) - (x^3 + y^3)\frac{\partial}{\partial x}(x + y)}{(x + y)^2}$$

$$= \frac{(x + y)(3x^2) - (x^3 + y^3)(1)}{(x + y)^2}$$

$$= \frac{3x^3 + 3x^2y - x^3 - y^3}{(x+y)^2}$$

$$= \frac{2x^3 - y^3 + 3x^2y}{(x+y)^2}$$

$$x\frac{\partial z}{\partial x} = \frac{2x^4 - xy^3 + 3x^3y}{(x+y)^2} \longrightarrow (1)$$

$$\text{Also } \frac{\partial z}{\partial y} = \frac{2y^3 - x^3 + 3y^2x}{(x+y)^2}$$

$$y\frac{\partial z}{\partial y} = \frac{2y^4 - yx^3 + 3y^3x}{(x+y)^2} \longrightarrow (2)$$

Adding (1) and (2), we get

$$x\frac{\partial z}{\partial x} + y.\frac{\partial z}{\partial y} = \frac{2x^4 - xy^3 + 3x^3y + 2y^4 - x^3y + 3y^3x}{(x+y)^2}$$

$$= \frac{2x^4 + 2y^4 + 2x^3y + 2xy^3}{(x+y)^2}$$

$$= \frac{2(x^3 + y^3)(x+y)}{(x+y)^2}$$

$$= 2\frac{x^3 + y^3}{x+y}$$

$= 2z$

Hence Euler's theorem is verified

Example-7: Compute the degree of homogeneity and verify Euler's theorem for the production function $x = f(l,k)\ (al^4 + bk^4)1/2$

Solution: The production function is given by

$$x = f(l,k)\ (al^4 + bk^4)1/2$$

$$x = \left[a(\lambda l)^4 + b(\lambda k)^4\right]^{1/2}$$

$$= \left[a\lambda^4 l^4 + b\lambda^4 k^4\right]^{1/2}$$

$$= \left(\lambda^4\right)^{1/2} \left[al^4 + bk^4\right]^{1/2}$$

$$= \lambda^2 f(l,k)$$

Therefore 'x' is a homogenous function of degree 2.

To verify Euler's theorem, we must verify that

$$l \cdot \frac{\partial x}{\partial l} + k\frac{\partial x}{\partial k} = 2x$$

$$\frac{\partial x}{\partial l} = \frac{1}{2}\left(al^4 + bk^4\right)^{\frac{-1}{2}} \times 4al^3$$

$$= \frac{2al^3}{\left(al^4 + bk^4\right)^{1/2}}$$

$$l \cdot \frac{\partial x}{\partial l} = \frac{2al^4}{\left(al^4 + bk^4\right)^{1/2}}$$

and $\dfrac{\partial x}{\partial k} = \dfrac{1}{2}\left(al^4 + bk^4\right)^{-1/2} \cdot 4bk^4$

$$= \frac{2bk^4}{\left(al^4 + bk^4\right)^{1/2}}$$

$$l.\frac{\partial x}{\partial l}+k.\frac{\partial x}{\partial k}=\frac{2al^4}{\left(al^4+bk^4\right)^{1/2}}+\frac{2bk^4}{\left(al^4+bk^4\right)^{1/2}}$$

$$=\frac{2\left(al^4+bk^4\right)}{\left(al^4+bk^4\right)^{1/2}}$$

$$=2\left(al^4+bk^4\right)^{1/2}$$

$$=2x$$

Hence, the Euler's theorem is verified.

Exercise-3

1. If $z = AL^{\alpha} K^{1-\alpha}$ then find out the degree of homogeneity and verify Euler's theorem.

2. If $u = \log\frac{x^2+y^2}{x+y}$, prove that $x\frac{\partial u}{\partial x}+y\frac{\partial u}{\partial y}=1$

3. If $u=\frac{xy}{x+y}$, verify that $x\frac{\partial u}{\partial x}+y\frac{\partial u}{\partial y}=4$

4. If $u=\frac{xy}{x+y}$, verify that $x^2\frac{\partial^2 u}{\partial x^2}+2xy\frac{\partial^2 u}{\partial x\partial y}+y^2\frac{\partial^2 u}{\partial y^2}=0$

Total differentials

The derivative $\frac{dy}{dx}$ as a single symbol denoting the limit of $\frac{\Delta y}{\Delta x}$ as Δx approaches zero. The derivative $\frac{dy}{dx}$ may also be treated as a ratio of differentials in which dy is the differential of y and dx the differential of x. Given a function of single independent variable $y=f(x)$, the differential of y, dy, measures the change in y resulting from a small change in x, written dx.

If z = f(x, y) be a function of two variables *x* and *y*, then the expression

$$dz = fx\ dx + fy\ dy$$

Where and $fx = \frac{\partial z}{\partial x}$ and $fy = \frac{\partial z}{\partial y}$

is called the total differential of the function Z and it is also called first order total differentials.

The second order total differential of z, denoted by, is given by

$$d^2z = fxx(dx)^2 + 2fxy\ dx\ dy + fyy(dy)^2$$

Where $fxx = \frac{\partial^2 z}{\partial x^2}$, $fyy = \frac{\partial^2 z}{\partial y^2}$

$$fxy = \frac{\partial^2 z}{\partial x \partial y}$$

Example-1: Find the first and second order total differentials of the following

a) $Z = x^4 + 8xy + 3y^3$

b) $Z = 3x^2 + xy - 2y^2$

Solution: a) given $z = x^4 + 8xy + 3y^3$

$$\frac{\partial z}{\partial x} = 4x^3 + 8y$$

$$\frac{\partial z}{\partial y} = 8x + 9y^2$$

$$dz = fx\ dx + fy\ dy$$

$$dz = (4x^3 + 8y)dx + (8x + 9y^2)dy$$

Then the second order total differentials

$$\frac{\partial^2 z}{\partial x^2} = \frac{\partial}{\partial x}\left(4x^3 + 8y\right) = 12x^2$$

$$\frac{\partial^2 z}{\partial y^2} = \frac{\partial}{\partial y}\left(8x + 9y^2\right) = 18y$$

$$\frac{\partial^2 z}{\partial x \partial y} = \frac{\partial}{\partial x}\left(8x + 9y^2\right) = 8$$

$$\therefore\ d^2 z = fxx(dx)^2 + 2\,fxy\ dx\ dy + fyy(dy)^2$$

$$d^2 z = 12x^2(dx)^2 + 16\,dx\ dy + 18y(dy)^2$$

b) Given $z = 3x^2 + xy - 2y^2$

$$\frac{\partial z}{\partial x} = 6x + y$$

$$\frac{\partial z}{\partial y} = x - 4y$$

$$dz = fx\ dx + fy\ dy$$

$$dz = (6x + y)dx + (x - 4y)dy$$

Then the second order total differential is

$$\frac{\partial^2 z}{\partial x^2} = \frac{\partial}{\partial x}(6x + y) = 6$$

$$\frac{\partial^2 z}{\partial y^2} = \frac{\partial}{\partial y}(x - 4y) = -4$$

$$\frac{\partial^2 z}{\partial x \partial y} = \frac{\partial}{\partial x}(x-4y) = 1$$

$$d^2 z = fxx(dx)^2 + 2fxy\ dx\ dy + fyy(dy)^2$$

$$d^2 z = 6(dx)^2 + 2\ dx\ dy - 4(dy)^2$$

Differentiation of implicit function:

If we write, we say that 'y' is an explicit function of *x*; if $x = g(y)$, then x is an explicitly function of y. when relationships between two variables are written in the explicit forms, it is easy to obtain directly *dy/dx* or *dx/dy*. Sometimes a relationship between two variables may be written in the form

$$f(x,y) = 0$$

This is called an implicit function of *x* and *y*.

Let z = *f*(*x*, *y*) when z = 0 for all (*x*, *y*)

$$\text{The } dz = \frac{\partial z}{\partial x}dx + \frac{\partial z}{\partial y}dy$$

(or)

$$dz = fx\ dx + fy\ dy$$

Since z = 0; for all (*x*, *y*)

$$dz = 0$$

thus $fx\ dx + fy\ dy = 0$

$$dy = -\frac{fx}{fy}dx$$

$$\text{Or } \frac{dy}{dx} = -\frac{fx}{fy}$$

This expression $\frac{dy}{dx}$ in terms of partial derivation of f

Example-1: Find $\frac{dy}{dx}$ for the following implicit function

$$x^2 + y^2 - 2xy = 0$$

Solution: Let $f(x, y) = x^2 + y^2 - 2xy = 0$

$$fx = \frac{\partial f}{\partial x} = 2x - 2y$$

$$fy = 2y - 2x$$

$$\therefore \frac{dy}{dx} = -\frac{fx}{fy} = -\frac{2x-2y}{2y-2x}$$

Example-2: Find $\frac{dy}{dx}$ if $x^2 + 2xy - y^2 = 0$

Solution: Let $f(x, y) = x^2 + 2xy - y^2 = 0$

Then $fx = \frac{\partial f}{\partial x} = 2x + 2y$

$$fy = 2x - 2y$$

$$\therefore \frac{dy}{dx} = \frac{2x+2y}{2x-2y}$$

Example-3: Find $\frac{dy}{dx}$ if $x^3 + y^2 - xy + x^2 + 4 = 0$

Solution: Let $f(x, y) = x^3 + y^2 - xy + x^2 + 4 = 0$

Then, $fx = \frac{\partial f}{\partial x} = 3x^2 - y + 2x$

$fy = 2y - x$

$$\therefore \frac{dy}{dx} = -\frac{fx}{fy} = \frac{-3x^2 - y + 2x}{2y - x}$$

Exercise-4

1. Find $\frac{dy}{dx}$ if $x^2 + y^2 - 4x = 0$

2. Find $\frac{dy}{dx}$ if $3x^3 + 2y^2 + x^2y + 3xy^2 = 0$

3. Find $\frac{dy}{dx}$ if $\log y + \log x + 2 = 0$

4. Find $\frac{dy}{dx}$ if $e^x + e^y - 2\log y + 5 = 0$

5. Find $\frac{dy}{dx}$ if $x^3 + y^3 + x^3 = 0$

6. Find $\frac{dy}{dx}$ if $x^3 + x^2y + xy = 0$

Maxima and minima of two variables

Now we consider the problem of maximizing and minimizing function $f(x, y)$ involving two variables. In this case we follow the following criterion for maximum minimum values:

Given $z = f(x,y)$

1. Find f_x *and* f_y
2. Find the critical points by solving $f_x = 0$ *and* $f_y = 0$
3. Find f_{xx} , f_{xy} *and* f_{yy}.
4. a) if $f_{xy}\, f_{yy} - (f_{xy})^2 > 0$ *and* $f_{xx} < 0$, f has maximum.

   b) if $f_{xx}\, fyy_{yy} - (f_{xy})^2 > 0$ *and* $f_{xx,} > 0$, f has minimum.

   c) if $fxx\, fyy - (f_{xy})^2 < 0$ f has neither maximum nor minimum

   d) if $fxx\, fyy - (f_{xy})^2 = 0$ the test fails and further investigation is required.

Example-1: Find the maximum or minimum for $z = x^2 + y^2 - 4x$

Solution: we have $z = x^2 + y^2 - 4x$

$$f_x = \frac{\partial z}{\partial x} = 2x - 4$$

$$f_y = \frac{\partial z}{\partial y} = 2y$$

$2x - 4$ and $2y = 0$

$2x = 4$

$x = 2 \quad y = 0$

$\therefore (x, y) = (2, 0)$

And $f_{xx} = \dfrac{\partial^2 z}{\partial x^2} = \dfrac{\partial}{\partial x}(2x-4) = 2$

$$f_{yy} = \frac{\partial^2 z}{\partial y^2} = \frac{\partial}{\partial y}(2y) = 2$$

$$f_{xy} = \frac{\partial^2 z}{\partial x \partial y} = \frac{\partial}{\partial x}(2y) = 0$$

$$\therefore f_{xx}\, f_{yy} - (f_{xy})^2 = 4 - 0 = 4 > 0$$

And $f_{xx} = 2 > 0$

This shows that there exists a minimum at (2, 0)

At (1, 0) = 12(1) = 12 > 0

And $f_{xx} = 6x = 6(1) = 6 > 0$, therefore f has a minimum at (1,0).

And at (-1,0) = 12(-1) = -12 < 0

And f_{xx} = -6<0, therefore f has maximum nor minimum at (-1, 0)

Example-2: If $z = f(x, y) = x^2y^2 - 5x^2 - 8xy - 5y^2$ then finding the extreme values.

Solution: we have $z = f(x, y) = x^2y^2 - 5x^2 - 8xy - 5y^2$

$$f_x = \frac{\partial z}{\partial x} = 2xy^2 - 10x - 8y$$

$$f_y = \frac{\partial z}{\partial y} = 2x^2y - 8x - 10y$$

For critical points $f_x = 0$ *and* $f_y = 0$

$$2xy^2 - 10x - 8y = 0 \quad \rightarrow 1$$

$$2x^2y-8x-10y=0 \qquad \rightarrow 2$$

For equation 1 $\Rightarrow 2xy(y-x)-10(x-y)-8(y-x)=0$

For equation 2 $\Rightarrow (y-x)(2xy+10-8)=0$

$y=x$ or $2xy=-2$

$xy=-1$

Example-3: If $z = x^3 - 3x + y^2$ then find out maxima and minima values.

Solution: we have $z = x^3 - 3x + y^2$

$$f_x = \frac{\partial z}{\partial x} = 3x^2 - 3$$

$$f_y = \frac{\partial z}{\partial y} = 2y$$

Then $f_x = 0$ *and* $f_y = 0$

$3x^3 - 3 = 0 \qquad 2y = 0$

$3x^2 = 3 \qquad y = 0$

$x^2 = 1$

$x = \pm 1$

x= 1, -1 $\qquad y = 0$

$(x,y) = (1,0)$ and $(x,y) = (-10)$

$$f_{xx} = \frac{\partial^2 z}{\partial x^2} = \frac{\partial}{\partial x}\left(3x^2-3\right) = 6x$$

$$f_{yy} = \frac{\partial^2 z}{\partial y^2} = \frac{\partial}{\partial y}(2y) = 2$$

$$f_{xy} = \frac{\partial^2 z}{\partial x \partial y} = \frac{\partial}{\partial x}(2y) = 0$$

$$\therefore f_{xx} \cdot f_{yy} - (f_{xy})^2 = (6x)(2) - (0)^2 = 12x$$

Substituting x for y in the equation (1), we have

$$y = x \Rightarrow \quad 2x^3 - 10x - 8x = 0$$

$$2x(x^2 - 9) = 0$$

$$x = 0 \quad \text{or} \quad x = \pm 3$$

And also $y = -\frac{1}{x} \Rightarrow 2x\left(\frac{-1}{x}\right)^3 - 10x + \frac{8}{x} = 0$

$$\frac{10}{x} - 10x = 0$$

$$x^2 = 1$$

$$x = \pm 1$$

Thus the critical values are

(0,0) (3,3), (-3, -3), (1, -1), (-1, 1).

Then $f_{xx} = 2y^2 - 10$

$$f_{xy} = 4xy - 8$$

$$f_{yy} = 2x^2 - 10$$

a) at (0,0)

$$f_{xx} f_{yy} - (f_{xy})^2 = (-10)(-10) - (-8)^2 = 36 > 0$$

And $f_{xx} = -8 < 0$

∴ f has a maximum at (0,0)

b) A(3,3)

$$f_{xx}\, f_{yy} - (f_{xy})^2 = (8)^2 - (28)^2 < 0$$

And $f_{xx} = 8 > 0$

∴ f has a maximum nor minimum

at (3,3)

c) At (-3, -3)

$$fxx.fyy - (fxy)^2 = (8)^2 - (28)^2 < 0$$

∴ f has neither a maximum nor minimum at (-3,-3)

d) At (1, -1)

$$fxx.fyy - (fxy)^2 = (-8)(-8) - (-4-8)^2 < 0$$

∴ f has neither a maximum nor minimum at (1,-1)

e) At (-1, 1)

$$fxx.fyy - (fxy)^2 = (-8)(-8) - (-4-8)^2 < 0$$

∴ f has neither a maximum nor minimum at (-1,1)

∴ Hence f has a maximum value at (0,0)

Exercise-5

1. Find the extreme value of $z = x^2 + 2y^2 - 4y$
2. Find the extreme value of $z = x^2 + 3y^2 - 2x + 7y + 2$
3. Find the extreme value of $z = x^2 - xy + y$
4. Find the extreme value of $z = x^2 - y^2$

5. Find the extreme value of $z = x^2 - 2y^2 + xyz$

6. Find the extreme value of $z = 20 - 2x^2 + 4y - y^2$

7. Find the extreme value of $z = 3x^2 + y^2 - 3xy$

8. Find the extreme value of $z = 6xy - x^3 - y^3$

9. Find the extreme value of

$$z = 2x^2 + 2y^2 + 9 - 6x + 6y - 2xy$$

10. Find the extreme value of $z = x^3 + x^2 - xy + y^2 + 4$

Applications of Partial Differentiation

Name of the commodities

Let x_1 and x_2 he the two commodities, having demand laws $x_1 = f(P_1, P_2)$ and x_2 g (P_1, P_2) and where P_1, P_2 being the prices. Then the two commodities are complementary

$$\text{if } \frac{\partial x_1}{\partial P_2} < 0 \, and \, \frac{\partial x_2}{\partial P_1} < 0$$

and also the two commodities are competitive or substitute if

$$\frac{\partial x_1}{\partial p_2} > 0 \quad and \quad \frac{\partial x_2}{\partial p_1} > 0$$

If $\frac{\partial x_1}{\partial P_2}$ and $\frac{\partial x_2}{\partial P_1}$ have opposite signs, the two commodities are neither complementary nor competative.

Example-1: The demand functions for the two commodities x_1 and x_2 are each a function of the prices of x_1 and x_2 and are given by:

$$x_1 = P_1^{-0.5} \; e^{-0.3 P_2} \quad \text{and} \quad x_2 = P_2^{-0.4} \; e^{-0.3 P_1}$$

Where P_1 and P_2 denote the price and x_1, x_2 are the quantities of the two goods respectively. Find the four partial marginal demand function. Also discuss whether x_1 and x_2 are complementary or substitutes.

Solution: $x_1 = P_1^{-0.5} \; e^{-0.3P_2}$ and $x_2 = P_2^{-0.4} \; e^{-0.3P_1}$

$$\frac{\partial x_1}{\partial p_1} = -0.5\,p^{-1.5}\; e^{0.3p_2}$$

$$\frac{\partial x_1}{\partial p_2} = 0.3\,p_1^{-0.5}\; e^{0.3p_2}$$

$$\frac{\partial x_2}{\partial p_1} = 0.3\,p_2^{-0.4}\; e^{0.3p_1}$$

$$\frac{\partial x_2}{\partial p_2} = -0.4\,p_2^{-1.4}\; e^{0.3p_1}$$

Since $\frac{\partial x_1}{\partial p_2}$ and $\frac{\partial x_2}{\partial p_1}$ are both positive

∴ The two commodities are substitutes.

Example-2: The demand functions for two commodities are given below:

$$x_1 = \frac{-p_1}{p_2^2}, \quad x_2 = \frac{p_1^2}{p_2}$$

Where p_1, p_2 are prices and x_1, x_2 denote the quantities of the two commodities respectively. Show that the two commodities are substitutes for one another.

Solution: we have $x_1 = \frac{-p_1}{p_2^2} = -p_1 \cdot p_2^{-2}$

$$x_2 = \frac{p_1^2}{p_2} = p_1^2 . p_2^{-1}$$

$$\frac{\partial x_1}{\partial p_2} = \frac{\partial}{\partial p_2}\left(-p_1 . p_2^{-2}\right)$$

$$= -p_1.\left(-2p_2^{-3}\right)$$

$$= +2p_1 p_2^{-3}$$

$$\frac{\partial x_2}{\partial p_2} = \frac{\partial}{\partial p_2}\left(p_1^2 . p_2^{-1}\right)$$

$$= p_1^2(-1)p_2^{-2}$$

$$= -p_1^2 p_2^{-2}$$

Thus $\frac{\partial x_1}{\partial p_2}$ and $\frac{\partial x_2}{\partial p_2}$ have opposite sight. So that the two commodities are neither complementary nor competitive.

Exercise-6

1. **The demand functions for two commodities x_1 and x_2 are each a function of the prices of x_1 and x_2 and are given by**

   $x_1 = P_1^{-0.4} \quad e^{-0.2P_2}$ **and** $x_2 = P_2^{-0.6} \quad e^{-0.5P_1}$

   Where P_1 and P_2 denote the prices and x_1, x_2 are the quantities of the two goods respectively. Find the four partial marginal demand functions. Also discuss whether x_1 and x_2 are complementary or substitutes.

2. **Determine the partial elasticity's and nature of commodities for the following function**

$$x_1 = \frac{p_1}{p_2} \quad and \quad x_2 = \frac{p_1^2}{p_2}$$

3. Find out the partial elasticity's and nature of the commodities for the following demand function

$$x_1 = \frac{1}{P_1^2 \; P_2} \text{ and } x_1 = \frac{1}{P_1 \; P_2}$$

4. Determine the partial elasticity's and nature of the commodities for the following demand function

$$x_1 = P_1^{-1.5} \quad P_2^{0.4} \quad \text{and} \quad x_2 = P_2^{-0.5} \quad P_2^{-0.4}$$

5. The demand function of two commodities x_1 and x_2 are $x_1 = P_1^{-1.4} \; P_2^{0.6}$ and $x_2 = P_2^{0.5} \; .P_2^{-1.2}$ respectively, where x_1 and x_2 respectively and P_1 and P_2 are their respective prices. Find the four partial elasticity's of demand and determine whether the commodities are competitive or complementation.

6. Following are the demand function for two commodities x_1 and x_2

$$x_1 = P_1^{-1.7} \quad P_2^{-0.8} \quad \text{and} \quad x_2 = P_2^{0.5} \quad P_2^{-0.2}$$

Determine whether the commodities are complementary or competitive.

7. If the utility function involving commodities x and y is

$$x = 8x + 22y - x^2 - 2xy - y^2$$

and the budget constraint is $12 = x + 2y$ determine the values of x and y that maximum the utility.

Utility function

The level of satisfaction derived by the consumer can be written as a function of the quantities consumed x and y of two commodities x and y.

$$u = f(x,y)$$

Then we can find out the marginal utility of a commodity x

$$\text{i.e. } Mu_x = \frac{\partial u}{\partial x}$$

Similarly the marginal utility of commodity *y*

$$\text{i.e. } Muy = \frac{\partial u}{\partial y}$$

Here we have to note that utility should not be confused with usefulness. A commodity may not be useful. Yet, it may have utility for a particular individual consumer. For example, Statutory warning i.e Smoking is injurious to health, yet it satisfied the want of Smokers. Thus, utility has nothing to do with usefulness.

Budget Line

Definition: "The locus of a point representing all the possible combinations of two goods that can just be bought by a consumer given his income and the prices of the two goods is called budget line".

For example

Suppose an individual consumer has Rs.10 at his disposal to spend on apples and oranges. Let us further suppose that the price of apples in the market is Rs.2 per unit and the price of orange is Rs.1 per unit with Rs. 10.

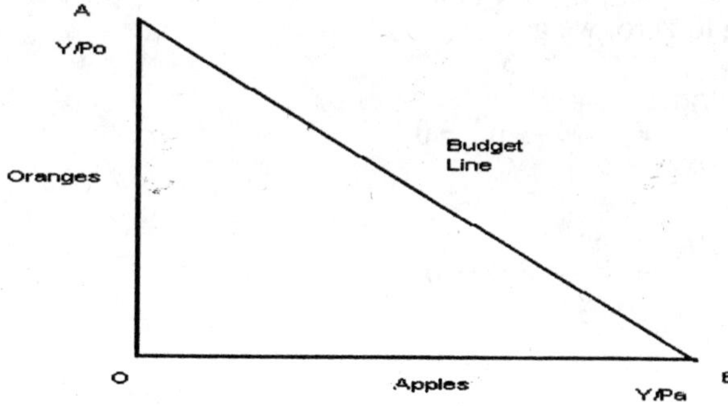

The consumer can buy 5 (=OB) apples and no oranges or 10 oranges (=OA) and no apples. By joining points A and B, we get what is called price line or price opportunity line. This line is also known as budget line or price – income line.

Consumer optimization

If a consumer has a limited purchasing power say 'y' with which he can buy a certain combination of two commodities x_1 and x_2 so as to derive the highest level of satisfaction. The prices of commodities being p_1 and p_2 respectively.

Utility Max. : $U = f(x_1, x_2)$

Subject to : $y = p_1 x_1 + p_2 x_2$

Here we apply Lagrange's Multiplier to obtain the quantities of x_1 and x_2 that yield maximum satisfaction, given the constraint. The procedure involves the following steps.

Step I: Rewrite the budget constraint in the implicit form

$$g(x, y) = y - p_1 x_1 - p_2 x_2 = 0$$

Step II: Construct a function F of three variables x_1 x_2 and λ as

$$F(x_1, x_2,) = f(x_1, x_2) + \lambda (y - p_1 x_1 - p_2 x_2)$$

Where 'λ' is Lagrangian multiplier

Step III: Now, to maximize the utility, the criterion is as follows.

Apply the *First order condition* is that

Differentiating 'F' partially with respect to x_1, x_2 and λ and equating to zero, we get

$$\frac{\partial F}{\partial x_1} = \frac{\partial f}{\partial x_1} - \lambda p_1 = 0$$

$$\frac{\partial F}{\partial x_2} = \frac{\partial f}{\partial x_2} - \lambda p_2 = 0$$

$$\frac{\partial F}{\partial \lambda} = y - p_1 x_1 - p2x_2 = 0$$

$$\frac{\partial f}{\partial x_1} = \lambda p_1 \quad and \quad \frac{\partial f}{\partial x_2} = \lambda p_2$$

$$\therefore \quad \frac{MUx_1}{MUx2} = \frac{\lambda p_1}{\lambda p_2} = \frac{p_1}{p_1}$$

i.e. the slope of indifference curve is equal to price ratio.

Now let us calculate the 'Δ' value with second order condition.

Second order condition

Find $\Delta = \begin{vmatrix} 0 & gx & gy \\ gx & fxx & fxy \\ gy & fxy & fyy \end{vmatrix}$ is called the bordered Hessian determinant. Then the function is a Maximum or Minimum depending upon whether 'Δ' is positive or negative.

Example-1 Given the utility function U = (x+2) (y+1) and the budget constraint 2x + 5y = 51, find the optimum levels of x and y purchased by the consumer.

Solution: We have to Maximize

$$U = f(x, y) = (x+2)\,(y+1)$$

Subject to the budget constraint

$$g\,(x, y) = 51 - 2x - 5y$$

The Lagrangian function is given by f(x, y,λ) = (x+2) (y+1) + λ(51-2x-5y)

Let us apply the First order condition for the given function

$$\frac{\partial F}{\partial x} = y + 1 - 2\lambda = 0 \rightarrow \text{Considered as equation-1}$$

$$\frac{\partial F}{\partial y} = x + 2 - 5\lambda = 0 \quad \rightarrow \text{Considered as equation -2}$$

$$\frac{\partial F}{\partial \lambda} = 51 - 2 - 5y = 0 \rightarrow \text{Considered as equation-3}$$

From (1) and (2), we have

$$\frac{y+1}{2} = \frac{x+2}{5} \text{ or } y = \frac{2x-1}{5}$$

Substituting the value in equation (3), we get

$2x + 2x - 1 = 51$

$4x = 52$

$x = 13$, Also $y = 5$

Thus, the optimal values of x and y are 13 and 5 respectively.

Now let us apply the second order condition. Here

$$fxx = 0, \quad fxy = \frac{\partial^2 f}{\partial x \partial y} = \frac{\partial}{\partial x}\left(\frac{\partial f}{\partial x}\right) = \frac{\partial}{\partial x}(x + 2 - 5\lambda) = 1$$

$$fyy = 0,\ gx = \frac{\partial g}{\partial x} = -2,\ gy = \frac{\partial g}{\partial y} = -5$$

$$\Delta = \begin{vmatrix} 0 & gx & gy \\ gx & fxx & fxy \\ gy & fxy & fyy \end{vmatrix}$$

$$\Delta = \begin{vmatrix} + & - & + \\ 0 & 2 & 5 \\ 2 & 0 & 1 \\ 5 & 1 & 0 \end{vmatrix}$$

$= +0\ (0-1) + 2\ (0 + 5) - 5\ (-2)$

$= + 10 + 10 = 20 > 0$

Thus, the second order condition satisfied, therefore the utility is maximum when x = 13 and y = 5

Example-2: An individual's utility function for two goods is U = (x+2) (y+1) and the budget constraint is 4x + 6y = 130. Using the Lagrangian Multiplier method, find the optimum levels of purchase of the two commodities. Is the second order condition for Maximum utility satisfied?

Solution: We have to maximize

$$U = f(x, y) = (x+2)(y+1)$$

Subject to the budget constraint

$$g(x, y) = 130 - 4x - 6y$$

The Lagrange function is given by

$$F(x, y, \lambda) = (x+2)(y+1)+\lambda(130-4x-6y)$$

First order condition is

$$\frac{\partial F}{\partial x} = y + 1 - 4\lambda = 0 \rightarrow 1$$

$$\frac{\partial F}{\partial y} = x + 2 - 6\lambda = 0 \rightarrow 2$$

$$\frac{\partial F}{\partial \lambda} = 130 - 4x - 6y = 0 \rightarrow 3$$

From (1) and (2), we have

$$\frac{y+1}{4} = \frac{x+2}{6}$$

$$6(y+1) = 4(x+2)$$

$$6y + 6 = 4x + 8$$

$$6y = 4x + 8 - 6$$

$$y = \frac{4x + 2}{6}$$

Substituting the value of 'y' in equation (3), we get

$$130 - 4x - 6y = 0$$

$$130 - 4x - 6\left(\frac{4x + 2}{6}\right) = 0$$

$$130 - 4x - 4x - 2 = 0$$

$$128 - 8x = 0$$

$$- 8x = -128$$

$$x = \frac{128}{8} = 16$$

$$130 - 4(16) - 6y = 0$$

$$130 - 64 - 6y = 0$$

$$- 6y = - 66$$

$$y = \frac{66}{6} = 11$$

Thus, the optimal values of x and y are 16 and 11 respect.

Second Order Condition is

$$fxx = \frac{\partial^2 z}{\partial x^2} = \frac{\partial}{\partial x}\left(\frac{\partial z}{\partial x}\right) = \frac{\partial}{\partial x}(y + 1 - 4\lambda) = 0$$

$$fxy = \frac{\partial^2 z}{\partial x \partial y} = \frac{\partial}{\partial x}\left(\frac{\partial z}{\partial y}\right) = \frac{\partial}{\partial x}(x + 2 - 6\lambda) = 1$$

$$fyy = 0$$

$$gx = \frac{\partial g}{\partial x} = \frac{\partial}{\partial x}(130 - 4x - 6y) = 6$$

$$gy = \frac{\partial g}{\partial y} = \frac{\partial}{\partial y}(130 - 4x - 6y) = -4$$

$$\Delta = \begin{vmatrix} + & - & + \\ 0 & -4 & -6 \\ -4 & 0 & 1 \\ -6 & 1 & 0 \end{vmatrix}$$

= +0 (0-1) +4 (-6) -6 (-4)

= - 24 + 24 = 0

Thus, the second order condition of utility maximum is also satisfied. Hence the utility maximum when x = 16 and y = 11.

Example-3: Find the marginal utilities with respect to two commodities $x_1 = 1$ and $x_2 = 2$ units of the two commodities are consumed and if the utility function of x_1 and x_2 is given by; $U = (x_1 + 3)(x_2 + 5)$

Solution: We have $U = (x_1 + 3)(x_2 + 5)$

$$\frac{\partial u}{\partial x_1} = x_2 + 5$$

and $$\frac{\partial u}{\partial x_2} = x_2 + 3$$

So at and $x_1 = 1$ and $x_2 = 2$

$$\frac{\partial u}{\partial x_1} = 7, \quad \frac{\partial u}{\partial x_2} = 4$$

Which are the required marginal utilities.

Exercise-7

1. Find the optimum commodity purchase for a consumer whose utility function and budget constrain are $U = q_1^{15} q_2$ and $3q_1 + 4q_2 = 100$ respectively.

2. Find the marginal utilites with respect to two commodities x_1 and x_2 and $x_1 = 1$ and $x_2 = 2$ units of the two commodities are consumed, if the utility function of x_1 and x_2 is given by

   $U = (x_1 + 3)(x_2 + 5)$

3. An individual's utility function for two goods is given below $U = (x + 2)(y + 1)$. It is given that $Px =$ Re. 4 $Py =$ Re. 6 and the individual's fixed income is Rs. 130. Using the Lagrange Multiplier method, find the optimum levels of purchase of the two commodities. Is the second order condition for maximum utility satisfied?

4. Find the optimum commodity purchased for a consumer whose utility function and budget constraints are $U = x^2y^3$ and $x + 4y = 10$ respectively.

5. A consumer's utility function is given as $u = \sqrt{x_1x_2}$, where x_1, x_2 denote the quantities of two production consumed by the consumer and the prices per unit of the goods are Re. 20 and Re. 10 respectively. Determine the optimum level of commodities to maximize his utility and spend his total income of Re. 640 on the two goods.

6. Use Lagrangian multiplier to find optimum commodity purchases for a consumer whose utility function is $u = x_1x_2 + 2x_1$ and prices of x_1 and x_2 are Re. 4 and Re. 2 respectively and his income is Re. 60.

7. Let the production function of firm A be

   $X = 15l + 26k + 2lk - l^2 - 2k^2$

Where l and k are respectively labour input of skills L and K. suppose the wages for L and K are respectively 3 and 2 and the firm can only expand 50 for the total labor force; find what the maximum product.

Production function

Introduction

The production function is purely technical relation which connects factor inputs and outputs. It describes the laws of proportion, i.e. the transformation of factor inputs into products (outputs) at any particular time period. The production function represents the technology of a firm of an industry or the economy as a whole.

There are widely used production functions are Cobb-Douglas production function, CES and Frontier production function. But here we are discussed the former two only.

Cobb – Douglas Production functions:

A production function of the form

$$Q = AL^{\alpha} K^{\beta}, \text{ when } 0 \le \alpha \quad \beta \le 1$$

When A is a positive constant, K and L are inputs of capital and labour respectively, is called a Cobb – Douglas production function.

If $\alpha + \beta = 1$ then it is called strict Cobb – Douglas function

$\alpha + \beta \le 1$ then it is termed as a generalized Cobb – Douglas function

Also if $\alpha + \beta = 1$, it depicts constant returns to scale

$\alpha + \beta < 1$, it depicts decreasing returns to scale

and $\alpha + \beta > 1$, it depicts increasing returns to scale

Properties

1) The marginal product of factors

a) The $MP_L = \dfrac{\partial x}{\partial L} = \dfrac{\partial}{\partial L}\left(AL^{\alpha} K^{\beta}\right)$

$= A \alpha L^{\alpha - 1} K^{\beta}$

$= \alpha \ A \ \dfrac{L^{\alpha} K^{\beta}}{L}$

$$= \alpha \cdot \frac{AL^{\alpha}K^{\beta}}{L}$$

$$= \alpha \cdot \frac{Q}{L}$$

$$= L \cdot (AP_L)$$

AP_L is the average product of labour

b) Similarly $MP_K = \beta \frac{Q}{K} = \beta \cdot (AP_K)$

2) The marginal rate of substitution

$$MRS_{L,K} = \frac{\partial Q / \partial L}{\partial Q / \partial K} = \frac{\alpha\left(\frac{Q}{L}\right)}{\beta\left(\frac{Q}{K}\right)} = \frac{\alpha}{\beta} \cdot \frac{K}{L}$$

3) The elasticity of substitution

$$\sigma = \frac{d(K/L) \Big/ \left(\frac{K}{L}\right)}{d(MRS)/(MRS)} = 1$$

$$\sigma = \frac{d(K/L) / \left(\frac{K}{L}\right)}{d\left(\frac{\alpha}{\beta} \cdot \frac{K}{L}\right) \Big/ \left(\frac{\alpha}{\beta} \cdot \frac{K}{L}\right)} = 1$$

$$= \frac{d(K/L)\left(\frac{\alpha}{\beta}\right)}{\left(\frac{\alpha}{\beta}\right) d\left(\frac{K}{L}\right)} = 1$$

Given that $\frac{\alpha}{\beta}$ is constant and does not affect the derivative.

4) Factor intensity

In the C-D function factor intensity is measured by the ratio $\frac{\alpha}{\beta}$ the higher this ratio the more labour intensive the technique. Similarly the lower the ratio $\frac{\alpha}{\beta}$ the more capital intensive the technique.

5) The efficiency of production:

The efficiency in the organization of the factors of production is measured by the coefficient 'A'. intuitively it is clear that if two forms have the same K, L, b_1 and b_2 and still produce different quantities of output, the difference can be due to the superior organization and entire premiership of the one of the firms, which results different efficiencies, it is very important to note that the more efficient firm will have a larger 'A' than the less efficient one.

5) *The returns to scale*: The main conditions are already mentioned earlier

CES Production Function:

A production function which belongs to the CES class has two major characteristics

1. It is homogeneous degree one
2. It has a constant elasticity of substitution

The above which lack one or both it is not belong to the CES class.

For example $Q = AL^{\alpha} K^{1-\alpha} + L$

$$= A(\lambda L)^{\alpha} (\lambda K)^{1-\alpha} + (\lambda L)$$

$$= AL^{\alpha} K^{1-\alpha} (\lambda) + \lambda L$$

$$= \lambda\, AL^{\alpha} K^{1-\alpha} + L$$

It is the homogenous of degree one but it does not have a constant elasticity of substitution and is not a member of the CES class.

Properties

1. By advanced methods it has been shown that the class of CES production functions may be expressed in the form

   $$Q = A\left[\alpha\, x_1^{-\rho} + (1-\alpha)x_2^{-\rho}\right]^{-1/\rho}$$

   Where the parameters $A > 0$ and $0 < \alpha < 1$. It is easily verified that the above form is homogenous degree one.

2. The marginal product of the inputs are

$$\frac{\partial q}{\partial x_2} = \frac{\alpha}{A^{\rho}}\left(\frac{q}{x_1}\right)^{\rho+1}$$

$$\frac{\partial q}{\partial x_2} = \frac{1-\alpha}{A^{\rho}}\left(\frac{q}{x_2}\right)^{\rho+1}$$

   and $x_{1,}\ x_2 > 0$

3. The rate of technical substitution is

$$\text{RTS} = \frac{\alpha}{1-\alpha}\left(\frac{x_2}{x_1}\right)^{P+1}$$

The RTS is decreasing and the iso-quants convex for $P > -1$

4. The elasticity of substitution is

$$\sigma = \frac{f_1 f_2\,(x_1 f_1 + x_2 f_2)}{f_{12}(x_1 f_1 + x_2 f_2)^2}$$

$$\sigma = \frac{f_1\, f_2}{f_{12}\, q} \quad \text{(Euler's theorem)}$$

$$f_{12} = \frac{(1+P)\alpha\,(1-\alpha)q^{1+2P}}{A^{2P}\,(x_1 x_2)^{1+P}}$$

By evaluating the above, finally we get

$$\sigma = \frac{1}{1+\rho}, \qquad \rho = \frac{1-\sigma}{\sigma}$$

Thus, the parameter 'p' is closely related to the CES.

Monopoly and joint production:

A producer produces two commodities x_1 and x_2 which are sold at price P_1 and P_2. He is a monopolist in the production of both the commodities.

In this situation, the total revenue is the combination of two commodities

i.e. $TR = P_1 x_1 + P_2 x_2$

Similarly the cost function is $TC = C_1 + C_2$

$$\therefore \pi = TR - TC$$

$$\pi = P_1 x_1 + P_2 x_2 - (C_1 + C_2)$$

The condition for profit maximum is

1. $\dfrac{\partial \pi}{\partial x_1} = \dfrac{\partial \pi}{\partial x_2} = 0$

2. $\left(\dfrac{\partial^2 \pi}{\partial x_1^2}\right)\left(\dfrac{\partial^2 \pi}{\partial x_2^2}\right) - \left(\dfrac{\partial^2 \pi}{\partial x_1 \partial x_2}\right)^2 > 0$

and $\dfrac{\partial^2 \pi}{\partial x_1^2} < 0$ and $\dfrac{\partial^2 \pi}{\partial x_2^2} < 0$

Example-1: A monopolist produces two commodities x_1 and x_2 which have the following demand functions; $P_1 = 100 - 2x$, $P_2 = 80 - x_2$, where P_1 and P_2 are their respective prices and x_1 & x_2 are their respective quantities. If TC = $20x_1 + 20x_2$ = then find out the prices and quantities that would maximum its profits.

Solution: We have $P_1 = 100 - 2x_1$

$$P_2 = 80 - x_2$$

and $TC = 20x_1 + 20x_2$

Then we find out $TR = P_1 x_1 + P_2 x_2$

$$P_1 x_1 = (100 - 2x_1) x_1 = 100x_1 - 2x_1^2$$

$$P_2 x_2 = (80 - x_2) x_2 = 80x_2 - x_2^2$$

$$TR = 100x_1 - 2x_1^2 + 80x_2 - x_2^2$$

$$TR = 100x_1 + 80x_2 - 2x_1^2 - x_2^2$$

Then $\Pi = TR - TC$

$$\Pi = 100x_1 + 80x_2 - 2x_1^2 - x_2^2 - 20x_1 - 20x_2$$

$$\Pi = 80x_1 + 60x_2 - 2x_1^2 - x_2^2$$

For maximizing profit

$$\frac{\partial \Pi}{\partial x_1} = \frac{\partial \Pi}{\partial x_2} = 0$$

$$\frac{\partial \Pi}{\partial x_1} = \frac{\partial}{\partial x1}\left(80x_1 + 60x_2 - 2x_1^2 - x_2^2\right)$$

$$= 80 - 4x_1 = 0$$

$$= -4x_1 = -80$$

$$= x_1 = \frac{80}{4}$$

$$x_1 = 20$$

$$\frac{\partial \Pi}{\partial x_2} = \frac{\partial}{\partial x_2}\left(80x_1 + 60x_2 - 2x_1^2 - x_2^2\right)$$

$= 60 - 2x_2 = 0$

$= 2x_2 = 60$

$x_2 = 30$

and the sufficient condition for maximum profit is

$$\frac{\partial^2 \Pi}{\partial x_1^2} = \frac{\partial}{\partial x_1}(80 - 4x_1) = -4 < 0$$

$$\frac{\partial^2 \Pi}{\partial x_2^2} = \frac{\partial}{\partial x_2}(60 - 2x_2) = -2 < 0$$

$$\frac{\partial^2 \Pi}{\partial x_1 \partial x_2} = \frac{\partial}{\partial x_1}\left(\frac{\partial \Pi}{\partial x_2}\right) = \frac{\partial}{\partial x_1}(60 - 2x_2) = 0$$

then $\frac{\partial^2 \Pi}{\partial x_1^2}\left(\frac{\partial^2 \Pi}{\partial x_2^2}\right) - \left(\frac{\partial^2 \Pi}{\partial x_1 \partial x_2}\right)^2$

$= (-4)(-2) - (0)^2$

$= 8 > 0$

Therefore the profits are maximized at $x_1 = 20$ and $x_2 = 30$

The prices are $P_1 = 100 - 2x_1$

$P_1 = 100 - 2(20)$

$P_1 = 100 - 40$

$P_1 = 60$

and $P_2 = 80 - x_2$

$P_2 = 80 - 30$

$P_2 = 50$

and the maximum profit is

$\Pi = 80(20) + 60(30) - 2(20)^2 - (30)^2$

$\Pi =$ Re. 1700

Example-2: Assume that a monopolist sells his product in two separate markets and the demand functions are $P_1 = 12 - x_1$, $P_2 = 20 - 3x_2$. The total cost function for his product in given by $TC = 3 + 2(x_1 + x_2)$ determine the prices that the monopolist will changes and the quantities he will sell in each of the markets to maximize his profit.

Solution: Given $P_1 = 12 - x_1$

$$P_2 = 20 - 3x_2$$

And $TC = 3 + 2x_1 + 2x_2)$

Then $TR = p_1x_1 + p_2x_2$

$$P_1x_1 = (12 - x_1)\, x_1$$

$$= 12\,x_1 - x_1^2$$

$$P_2\,x_2 = (20 - 3x_2)\, x_2$$

$$20x_2 - 3x_2^2$$

$$TR = 12x_1 - x_1^2 + 20x_2 - 3x_2^2$$

$$TR = 12x_1 - 20x_2 - x_1^2 - 3x_2^2$$

$$\Pi = 12x_1 + 20x_2 - x_1^2 - 3x_2^2 - 3 - 2x_1 - 2x_2$$

$$\Pi = 10x_1 + 18x_2 - x_1^2 - 3x_2^2 - 3$$

For maximizing profit, the necessary condition is

$$\frac{\partial \Pi}{\partial x_1} = \frac{\partial \Pi}{\partial x_2} = 0$$

$$\frac{\partial \Pi}{\partial x_1} = \frac{\partial}{\partial x_1}\left(10x_1 + 18x_2 - x_1^2 - 3x_2^2 - 3\right) = 0$$

$$10 - 2x_1 = 0$$

$$2x_1 = 10$$

$$x_1 = 5$$

$$\frac{\partial \Pi}{\partial x_2} = \frac{\partial}{\partial x_2}\left(10x_1 + 18x_2 - x_1^{\,2} - 3x_2^{\,2} - 3\right) > 0$$

$18 - 6x_2 = 0$

$6x_2 = 18$

$x_2 = 3$

and the sufficient conditions are

$$\frac{\partial^2 \Pi}{\partial x_1^2} = \frac{\partial}{\partial x_1}(10 - 2x_1) = -2 < 0$$

$$\frac{\partial^2 \Pi}{\partial x_2^2} = \frac{\partial}{\partial x_2}(18 - 6x_2) = -6 < 0$$

$$\text{and } \frac{\partial^2 \Pi}{\partial x_1 \partial x_2} = \frac{\partial}{\partial x_1}(18 - 6x_2) = 0$$

$$\left(\frac{\partial^2 \Pi}{\partial x_1^2}\right)\left(\frac{\partial^2 \Pi}{\partial x_2^2}\right) - \left(\frac{\partial^2 \Pi}{\partial x_1\,\partial x_2}\right)$$

$= (-2)\,(-6) - (0)^2 = 12 > 0$

Therefore the profit is maximum at (5, 3)

The prices are $P_1 = 12 - 5$

$P_1 = 7$

and $P_2 = 20 - 3(3)$

$= 20 - 9$

$P_2 = 11$

$\Pi = 10(5) + 18(13) - (5)^2 - 3\,(3)^2 - 3$

$= 50 + 54 - 25 - 27 - 3$

$= 104 - 55$

$\Pi = 49$

Example-3: In a monopolistic competition producers, must determine the price that will maximize their profit. Assume that a producer offers two different brands of a product, for which the demand function are product, for which the demand functions are:

$x_1 = 14 - 0.25P_1$

$x_2 = 24 - 0.5P_2$

and the joint-cost function is

$$TC = x_1^2 + 5x_1x_2 + x_2^2$$

Find the prices and profit maximizing level of output.

Solution: We have $x_1 = 14 - 0.25P_1$

i.e. $P_1 = 56 - 4x_1$

$x_2 = 24 - 0.5P_2$

i.e. $P_2 = 48 - 2x_2$

$TR = P_1x_1 + P_2x_2$

$P_1x_1 = (56 - 4x_1)\, x_1$

$P_1x_1 = 56x_1 - 4x_1^2$

$P_2x_2 = (48 - 2x_2)\, x_2$

$P_2x_2 = 48x_2 - 2x_2^2$

$TR = 56x_1 - 4x_1^2 + 48x_2 - 2x_2^2$

$TR = 56x_1 - 48x_2 + 4x_1^2 - 2x_2^2$

$\Pi = TR - TC$

$\Pi = 56x_1 - 48x_2 + 4x_1^2 - 2x_2^2 - x_1^2 - 5x_1x_2 - x_2^2$

$\Pi = 56x_1 - 48x_2 - 5x_1x_2 - 5x_1x_2 - 5x_1^2 - 3x_2^2$

For maximizing profit, the necessary condition is $\dfrac{\partial \Pi}{\partial x_1} = \dfrac{\partial \Pi}{\partial x_2} = 0$

$$\frac{\partial \Pi}{\partial x_1} = \frac{\partial}{\partial x_1}\left(56x_1 + 48x_2 - 5x_1x_2 - 5x_1^2 - 3x_2^2\right)$$

$= 56 - 5x_2 - 10x_1 = 0 \rightarrow (1)$

$$\frac{\partial \Pi}{\partial x_2} = \frac{\partial}{\partial x_2}\left(56x_1 + 48x_2 - 5x_1x_2 - 5x_1^2 - 3x_2^2\right)$$

$= 48 - 5x_1 - 6x_2 = 0 \rightarrow (2)$

By solving eq (1) & (2)

$-5 \times -10x_1 - 5x_2 = -56$

$-10 \times -5x_1 - 6x_2 = -48$

$50x_1 + 25x_2 = 280$

$50x_1 + 60x_2 = 480$

— — —

$-35x_2 = -200$

$x_2 = 6.57$

$-10x_1 - 5x_2 = -56$

$-10x_1 - 5(6.57) = -56$

$-10x_1 - 32.85 = -56$

$-10x_1 = -56 + 32.85$

$-10x_1 = -23.15$

$$x_1 = \frac{23.15}{10}$$

$x_1 = 2.32$

Then the sufficient condition is

$$\frac{\partial^2 \Pi}{\partial x_1^2} = \frac{\partial}{\partial x_1}(56 - 5x_2 - 10x_1) = -10 < 0$$

$$\frac{\partial^2 \Pi}{\partial x_2^2} = \frac{\partial}{\partial x_2}(48 - 5x_1 - 6x_2) = -6 < 0$$

$$\frac{\partial^2 \Pi}{\partial x_1 \partial x_2} = \frac{\partial}{\partial x_1}(48 - 5x_1 - 6x_2) = -5$$

$$\therefore \left(\frac{\partial^2 \Pi}{\partial x_1^2}\right)\left(\frac{\partial^2 \Pi}{\partial x_2^2}\right) - \left(\frac{\partial^2 \Pi}{\partial x_1 \partial x_2}\right)^2$$

$$(-10)(-6) - (-5)^2 = 60 - 25 = 35 > 0$$

$\therefore$ The profit is maximum at (2.31, 6.57). Thus the prices are $P_1 = 46.76$ and $P_2 = 34.86$

Exercise-8

1. The demand function for x and y facing a monopolist are $x_1 = 36 - 4P_1$, $x_2 = 24 - 2P_2$ and his joint cost function is $T.C = x_1^2 + x_2^2$ find the profit – maximizing levels of output and of price.

2. The demand curves for commodities x_1 and x_2 facing the monopolist are

   $x_1 = 5 - P_1 + 2P_2$

   $x_1 = 4 - P_1 - 3P^2$

   and the cost function is $Tc = x_1^2 + x_2^2$

   Find the approximate profit maximizing levels of output and of price.

3. A monopolist producing two commodities x and y, faces the following market demands

$x_1 = 12 - P_1, \quad x_2 = 8 - ½P_2$

If the joint cost function is $TC = 3x_1^2 + x_1x_2 + 2x_1^2$ find maximum – profit levels of output and of prices.

4. A monopolist producing two commodities x_1 and x_2 is faced with the demand function

   $P_1 = 8 - x_1 + 3x_2$

   $P_2 = 7 + x_1 + 2x_2$

   And joint cost function is $TC = x_1^2 + 2x_2^2$. Find the monopolist equilibrium levels of output and price

5. A monopolist firm produces commodities of two types x_1 and x_2 at constant average cost Re. 2.50 and Re. 3.00 per item respectively. If P_1 and P_2 are the prices charged and the market demands are $x_1 = 5P_2 - 5P_1$ and $x_2 = 32 + 5P_1 - 10P_2$, find the prices of two commodities for maximum joint monopoly profit.

6. A firm produces two items x_1 and x_2. The market prices are given by $P_1 = 100 - 2x_1$, and $P_2 = 125 - 3x_2$. The cost of production is $12x_1 + 11x_2 + 4x_2x_2$ for producing x_1 and x_2 items. Find how many items of each should be produced to have the joint profit maximum.

5

Integration

Reversing the process of differentiation and findings the original function from the derivative is called integration or anti-differentiation.

If $f(x)$ is a function of x such that $\frac{d}{dx}[F(x)] = f(x)$

$$\therefore \int f(x)\, d(x) = F(x)$$

Thus, $\frac{d}{dx}[F(x)] = f(x)$

$$\Rightarrow \int f(x)\, dx = f(x) + C$$

The left-hand side of the equation is read, "The indefinite integral of f of x with respect to x". The symbol $\int$ is an integral sign, $f(x)$ is the integrated, and 'C' is the constant of integration.

Rules of Integration

1. $\int K\, dx = Kx + C$
2. $\int 1\, dx = x + C$

3. $\int x^n \, dx = \frac{x^{n+1}}{n+1} + C$ when $n \neq -1$

4. $\int x^{-1}$ or $\int \frac{1}{x} dx = \log x + C$

5. $\int e^x \, dx = e^x + C$

6. $\int k \, f(x) dx = k \int f(x) dx$

7. $\int a^x dx = \frac{a^x}{\log a} + C$

Examples

Example-1: Evaluate $\int (x^2 + 4x - 3) dx$

Solution: Given $\int (x^2 + 4x - 3) dx$

$$= \int x^2 dx + 4 \int x dx - 3 \int 1 dx$$

$$= \frac{x^{2+1}}{2+1} + 4 \cdot \frac{x^{1+1}}{1+1} - 3 \cdot x + C$$

$$= \frac{x^3}{3} + 4 \cdot \frac{x^2}{2} - 3x + C$$

$$= \frac{x^3}{3} + 2x^2 - 3x + C$$

Example-2: Evaluate $\int \left(2x^3 + 4x^{-3} - 3x + \frac{1}{\sqrt{x}} + \frac{7}{x} \right) dx$

Solution: We have $\int \left(2x^3 + 4x^{-3} - 3x + \frac{1}{\sqrt{x}} + \frac{7}{x} \right) dx$

$$= 2\int x^3 dx + 4\int x^{-3} dx - 3\int x dx + \int x^{-1/2} dx + 7\int \frac{1}{x} dx$$

$$= 2\cdot\frac{x^4}{4} + 4\cdot\frac{x^{-2}}{-2} - 3\cdot\frac{x^2}{2} + \frac{x^{1/2}}{1/2} + 7\log x + C$$

$$= \frac{x^4}{2} - \frac{2}{x^2} - \frac{3x^2}{2} + 2\sqrt{x} + 7\log x + C$$

Example-3: Evaluate $\int (x^2 + x^3 + 2x) dx$

Solution: Given $\int (x^2 + x^3 + 2x) dx$

$$= \int x^2 dx + \int x^3 dx + 2\int x\, dx$$

$$= \frac{x^3}{3} + \frac{x^4}{4} + 2\frac{x^2}{2} + C$$

$$= \frac{x^3}{3} + \frac{x^4}{4} + x^2 + C$$

Example-4: Evaluate $\int \frac{x^2 + x + 1}{x} dx$

Solution: We have $\int \frac{x^2 + x + 1}{x} dx$

$$= \int \frac{x^2}{x} dx + \int \frac{x}{x} dx + \int \frac{1}{x} dx$$

$$= \int x\, dx + \int 1\, dx + \int \frac{1}{x} dx$$

$$= \frac{x^2}{2} + x + \log x + C$$

Example-5: Evaluate $\int\left(x-2x^2-\frac{7}{x}\right)dx$

Solution: Given $\int\left(x-2x^2-\frac{7}{x}\right)dx$

$$=\int x\,dx-2\int x^2dx-7\int\frac{1}{x}dx$$

$$=\frac{x^2}{2}-2\cdot\frac{x^3}{3}-7\log x+C$$

$$=\frac{x^2}{2}-\frac{2x^3}{3}-7\log x+C$$

Example-6: Evaluate $\int\frac{x-1}{\sqrt{x}}\,dx$

Solution: Given $\int\frac{x-1}{\sqrt{x}}\,dx$

The given function can be written as $\int\frac{x-1}{x^{1/2}}\,dx$

$$=\int x^{\frac{1}{2}}\,dx-\int x^{-\frac{1}{2}}\,dx$$

$$=\frac{x^{3/2}}{3/2}-\frac{x^{1/2}}{1/2}+C$$

$$=\frac{2}{3}x^{3/2}-2x^{1/2}+C$$

Example-7: Evaluate $\int \left(x^2 + \frac{1}{x^2} \right)^3 dx$

Solution: Given $\int \left(x^2 + \frac{1}{x^2} \right)^3 dx$

$$= \int \left(x^6 + \frac{1}{x^6} + 3x^2 + \frac{3}{x^2} \right) dx$$

$$= \int x^6 dx + \int x^{-6} dx + 3\int x^2 dx + 3\int x^{-2} dx$$

$$= \frac{x^7}{7} + \frac{x^{-5}}{-5} + \frac{3x^3}{3} + \frac{3x^{-1}}{-1} + C$$

$$= \frac{x^7}{7} - \frac{1}{5x^5} + x^3 - \frac{3}{x} + C$$

Example-8: Evaluate $\int \left(e^{a \log x} + e^{x \log a} \right) dx$

Solution: $\int \left(e^{a \log x} + e^{x \log a} \right) dx = \int (x^a + a^x) dx$

$$= \int x^a dx + \int a^x dx$$

$$= \frac{x^{a+1}}{a+1} + \frac{a^x}{\log a} + C$$

Exercise – 1

1. Evaluate $\int \left(\frac{5x^4 + 12x^3 + 7x^2}{x^x + x} \right) dx$

2. Evaluate $\int \frac{x^3}{(2x+1)} dx$

3. Evaluate $\int \left(2x^3 + 4x^{-3} - 3x + \frac{1}{\sqrt{x}} + \frac{7}{x}\right) dx$

4. Evaluate $\int \left(\frac{4}{x^3} + \frac{2}{x^4} + x^2 + e^x\right) dx$

5. Evaluate $\int \frac{e^{5\log x} - e^{3\log x}}{e^{4\log x} - e^{2\log x}} dx$

6. Evaluate $\int \left(\sqrt{x} + \frac{1}{\sqrt{x}}\right)^3 dx$

7. Evaluate $\int \left(x^a + a^x + \frac{x}{a} + \frac{a}{x} + ax\right) dx$

8. Evaluate $\int \left(e^{3a\log x} + e^{3x\log a}\right) dx$

9. Evaluate $\int \left(\frac{2x^2 + x}{x - 1}\right) dx$

10. Evaluate $\int \frac{x}{a + bx} dx$

Integration by substitution:

Suppose we want to evaluate $\int f(x)\, dx$. Then making substitution $x = h(y)$, thus it is sometimes easier to evaluate the given integral.

Example-1: Evaluate $\int \frac{2x+4}{x^2+4x-9}$

Solution: Here $\frac{d}{dx}\left(x^2+4x-9\right)=2x+4$

$\therefore$ we put $x^2+4x-9=t$

This gives $(2x+4)dx = dt$

$$\int \frac{2x+4}{x^2+4x-9}\ dx = \int \frac{1}{t}\,dt = \log t + C$$

$= \log (x^2+4x-9) + C$

Example – 2: $\int \frac{2x+3}{x^2+3x+7}\,dx$

Solution: Here $\frac{d}{dx}\left(x^2+3x+7\right)=2x+3$

Therefore, we put $x^2 + 3x + 7 = t$

$(2x + 3)\ dx = dt$

$$\int \frac{2x+3}{x^2+3x+7}\,dx = \int \frac{1}{t}\,dt$$

$= \log t + c$

$= \log (x^3 + 3x + 7) + C$

Example-3: Evaluate $\int \frac{1}{x(1+\log x)}\,dx$

Solution: Given $\int \frac{1}{x(1+\log x)}\,dx$

Put 1+logx = t

$$\frac{1}{x}dx = dt$$

$$\int \frac{1}{x(1+\log x)}dx = \int \frac{1}{t}dt = \log t + c$$

= log (1+logx) +C

Integration by parts

If we want to integrate a product of two functions. The following rule known as integration by parts.

If u and v are two function of x, then

$$\int (uv)dx = u.\int vdx - \int \left[\frac{d}{dx}(u)\int vdx\right]dx$$

In words, integral of the product of two functions = first function X integral of the second - integral of (differential first X integral of the second function)

Example-1: Evaluate $\int xe^x dx$

Solution: we have $\int xe^x dx$

$$\int uvdx = \text{u.} \int vdx - \int (u^1 \int vdx)dx$$

Let u = x

v = e^x

Then $\int xe^x dx = \text{x} \int e^x dx - \int \left(\frac{d}{dx}(x)\int e^x dx\right)dx$

$$= xe^x - \int e^x dx$$

$$= xe^x - e^x + C$$

$$= e^x(x-1) + C$$

Example-2: Evaluate $\int \left(x^n \log x\right) dx$

Solution: let $u = \log x$

$v = x^n$

$$\int uv\,dx = u \cdot \int v\,dx - \int \left[\frac{d}{dx}(v) . \int v\,dx\right] dx$$

$$\int (\log x)\, x^n = \log x \int x^n\,dx - \int \left[\frac{1}{x} \cdot \int x^n\,dx\right] dx$$

$$= \log x \cdot \frac{x^{n+1}}{n+1} - \int \frac{1}{x} \cdot \frac{x^{n+1}}{n+1}\,dx$$

$$= \log x \cdot \frac{x^{n+1}}{n+1} - \frac{1}{n+1} \int \left(x^{-1} \cdot x^{n+1}\right) dx$$

$$= \log x \cdot \frac{x^{n+1}}{n+1} - \frac{1}{n+1} \cdot \int x^n\,dx$$

$$= \log x \cdot \frac{x^{n+1}}{n+1} - \frac{1}{n+1} \cdot \frac{x^{n+1}}{n+1} + C$$

$$= \frac{x^{n+1}}{n+1}\left[\log x - \frac{1}{n+1}\right]$$

Example-3: $\int x^2 e^{3x}\,dx$

Solution: we know $\int uv\,dx = u \cdot \int v\,dx - \int \left[\frac{d}{dx}(v) \cdot \int v\,dx\right] dx$

Let $u = x^2 \quad v = e^{3x}$

$$\int x^2 e^{3x} = x^2 \int e^{3x}\,dx - \int\left[\frac{d}{dx}(x^2)\cdot \int e^{3x}\,dx\right]dx$$

$$= x^2 \cdot \frac{e^{3x}}{3} - \int 2x \cdot \frac{e^{3x}}{3}\,dx$$

$$= x^2 \cdot \frac{e^{3x}}{3} - \frac{2}{3}\int x e^{3x}\,dx$$

$$= x^2\,\frac{e^{3x}}{3} - \frac{2}{3}\left[x\frac{e^{3x}}{3} - \int 1 \cdot \frac{e^{3x}}{3}\,dx\right]$$

$$= x^2\,\frac{e^{3x}}{3} - \frac{2}{3}\left[x\frac{e^{3x}}{3} - \frac{e^{3x}}{9}\right]$$

$$= \frac{x^2}{3}e^{3x} - \frac{2}{9}xe^{3x} + \frac{2}{27}e^{3x} + C$$

Exercise-2

1. Evaluate $\int 2x^3\, e^{x^2}\, dx$
2. Evaluate $\int \log x\, dx$
3. Evaluate $\int \log\left[x + \sqrt{1+x^2}\right]dx$
4. Evaluate $\int e^x\left[\frac{1}{x} - \frac{1}{x^2}\right]dx$
5. Evaluate $\int x\, e^{2x}\, dx$

6. Evaluate $\int x e^{-x} \, dx$

7. Evaluate $\int \frac{\log x}{\sqrt{x}} \, dx$

8. Evaluate $\int x^3 \, e^x \, dx$

9. Evaluate $\int \frac{4x+1}{\sqrt{2x^2+x-3}} \, dx$

10. Evaluate $\int \frac{2x+5}{\sqrt{x^2+2x+5}} \, dx$

Definite integrals

Suppose $f(x)$ and $g(x)$ be two functions of x such that $\int f(x) \, dx = g(x)$.

Then, the definite integral of over the interval [a, b], denoted by

$$\int_a^b f(x) \, dx \text{ is defined as } \int_a^b f(x) \, dx = [gx]_a^b = g(b) - g(a)$$

When a and b are the lower and upper limits of real numbers.

Example-1: Evaluate $\int_2^4 \frac{1}{x} \, dx$

Solution: $\int_a^b f(x) \, dx = [g(x)]_a^b$

$$= [\log x]_2^4$$
$$= \log 4 - \log 2$$
$$= \log 2^2 - \log 2$$

$= 2\log 2 - \log 2$

$= \log 2$

Example-2: Evaluate $\int_0^2 (4 - x^2)\,dx$

Solution: we have $\int_a^b f(x)dx = [g(x)]_a^b$

$$\int_0^2 (4 - x^2)dx = \int_0^2 4\,dx - \int_0^2 x^2\,dx$$

$$= [4x]_0^2 - \left[\frac{x^3}{3}\right]_0^2$$

$$= [8] - \left[\frac{8}{3} - 0\right]$$

$$= 8 - \frac{8}{3}$$

$$= \frac{24-8}{3} = \frac{16}{3}$$

Exercise-3

1. Evaluate $\int_0^3 3x^2\,dx$

2. Evaluate $\int_1^2 (x^2 + 4x + 2)dx$

3. Evaluate $\int_0^1 (1-t)^{1/2}\, dt$

4. Evaluate $\int_{10}^{100} \frac{2}{x}\, dx$

5. Evaluate $\int_0^1 e^{-2y}\, dy$

Applications to Economics

We know that if the Total cost function 'TC' is given, then we find out the Marginal cost function i.e. MC $= \frac{d}{dx}(TC)$

If we find out the total cost function, as given Marginal cost then we are using Integration.

i.e. TC $= \int Mc\, dx + k$

Where 'k' is the constant of integration.

Example-1: The Marginal cost function of manufacturing 'x' shoes is $6+10x-6x^2$ The total cost producing a pair of shoes is Re.12 Find the total and Average cost function.

Solution: we know that MC $= \frac{d}{dx}(TC)$

Thus TC $= \int Mc\, dx + k$

$= \int (6 + 10x - 6x^2)\, dx + k$

$= 6x + 10\frac{x^2}{2} - 6\frac{x^3}{3} + k$

$= 6x + 5x^2 - 2x^3 + k$

at x = 2, TC = 12

$\therefore 12 = 6\ 2 + 10\ \times\frac{4}{2} - 6\times\frac{8}{3} + k$

k = -4

Hence the total cost function is $TC = 6x + 5x^2 - 2x^3 - 4$

$$TC = 6x + 10\ \frac{x^2}{2} - 6\frac{x^3}{3} - 4$$

$$AC = TC/x = 6 + 5x - 2x^2 - \frac{4}{x}$$

Example-2: A Manufacture's Marginal cost function is: $MC = 0.003x^2 - 0.6x + 40$, where x is the number of units of a product. If x increases from 100 to 200 units, find the total increase in cost.

Solution: Given $Mc = 0.003x^2 - 0.6x + 40$

The total increase in cost when x increases from 100 to 200 units is

$$TC = \int_{100}^{200} Mc\, dx$$

$$= \int_{100}^{200} (0.003x^2 - 0.6x + 40)\, dx$$

$$= \left[0.003\frac{x^3}{3} - 0.6\frac{x^2}{2} + 40x\right]_{100}^{200}$$

$= (8000 - 12000 + 8000) - (1000 - 3000 + 4000)$

TC = 2000

Example-3: If the Marginal revenue function is MR = $5 + 102x - 9x^2$

Then find out TR given that total revenue is 230 when x = 2

Solution: We have MR = $5 + 102x - 9x^2$

$$TR = \int MR\, dx + k$$

$$= \int (5 + 102x - 9x^2)\, dx + k$$

$$= 5x + 102\frac{x^2}{2} - 9\frac{x^3}{3} + k$$

$$TR = 5x + 51x^2 - 3x^3 + k$$

When x = 2

$$TR = 5(2) + 51(2)^2 - 3(2)^3 + K$$

$$230 = 10 + 204 - 24 + K$$

$$230 = 190 + K$$

$$K = 230 - 190$$

$$K = 40$$

Example-4: Suppose the marginal cost of a product is given by $25 + 30x - 9x^2$ and fixed cost is known to be 55. Find the total cost and average cost functions.

Solution: We have, MC = $25 + 30x - 9x^2$

$$\text{Then TC} = \int MC\ dx + k$$

$$= \int (25 + 30x - 9x^2)\, dx + k$$

$$= 25x + 30\frac{x^2}{2} - 9\frac{x^3}{3} + k$$

$$= 25x + 15x^2 - 3x^3 + k$$

It is given that TC = 55, when $x = 0$

$\therefore$ k = 55

Hence TC $= 25x + 15x^2 - 3x^3 + 55$

$$\text{AC} = \frac{TC}{x} = 25 + 15x - 3x^2 + \frac{55}{x}$$

Example-5: If the marginal revenue function for a commodity is MR = 9 – 4x² find the demand function

Solution: We have MR = 9 – 4x²

$$\text{TR} = \int MR\ dx + k$$

$$= \int (9 - 4x^2) dx + k$$

$$= 9x - \frac{4x^3}{3} + k$$

Since TR = 0, When x = 0

$\therefore$ k = 0

$$\text{TR} = 9x - \frac{4x^3}{3}$$

If 'p' is the Price TR = p. x and so the demand function is

$$\therefore \text{P} = \frac{TR}{x} = 9 - \frac{4x^2}{3}$$

Exercise-4

1. The Marginal cost function of a firm is given by MC = 3000 $e^{0.3x} + 50$, where x is the quantity produced. If the fixed cost is Re. 80,000, find the total cost of the firm.

2. The Marginal cost of production is found to be MC = 2000 – 40x + 3x² where 'x' is the number of units produced. The fixed cost of production is Re. 18,000. Find the total cost function and the average cost function.

3. If the marginal cost of firm be 100–10x - 0.1x² where x is the output obtain the total cost function of the firm under the assumption that its fixed cost is Re. 500.

4. If the marginal cost function is MC = 4+3eˣ and the fixed cost is Re. 50, find the total and average cost functions.

5. The marginal cost of production (in Re.) is $3+\frac{x}{3000}+e^{-0.03x}$, where x denotes the number of units. Find the cost of producing 100 units (∴ $e^{-3} = 0.05$)

6. A firm has a marginal revenue function is given by MR = 275 – x – 0.3x². Find the increase in the firm's total revenue if production is increased from 10 to 20 units.

Consumer's surplus

In what has become a classical discussion of the relationship between value and utility, Alfred Marshall advanced the concept of consumer's surplus. The central idea is that a person always has in his mind a price that he would be willing to pay rather than go without a certain commodity, and that the degree of satisfaction as measured by the price, the consumer is willing to pay is greater than the price he actually pays in the market. The difference between the price he would be willing to pay rather than go without the commodity and the actual price he pays is the "economic measure" of his surplus satisfaction such as excess of satisfaction over market price is called consumer's surplus.

Therefore, the difference between what consumers' are willing to pay and what they would actually pay in the absence of price discussed is called consumers' surplus.

$$\text{C.S.} = \int_0^{x_e} f(x)dx - p_e.x_e$$

Where f(x) is demand function

p_e – is the market price

x_e – quantity of commodity

Producer's surplus

Similarly, the difference of the total revenue actually achieved and the revenue that would have been generated by the willingness of some producers to changeless is producer surplus.

$$P.S = p_e x_e - \int_0^{x_e} g(x)\, dx$$

Where g(x) – supply function

p_e – the market price

x_e – is the quantity of a commodity

Example –1: If the market demand curve is P = 20 – 2x, Where P and x are respectively the price and the amount of commodity x, find the consumers' surplus when P = 4 and P = 8

Solution: Given the demand function: P = 20 – 2x

$$C.S = \int_0^{xe} f(x)dx - p_e . x_e$$

When P = 4 ⇒ P = 20 – 2x

4 = 20 – 2x

2x = 24

x = 12

x_e = 12

∴ The value of x_e = 12 substituting in demand function, we get P_e value

P = 20 – 2x

= 20 – 12

P_e = 8

$$C.S. = \int_0^{12} (20 - 2x)\, dx - (8 \times 12)$$

$$= \left[20x - x^2\right]_0^{12} - 96$$

$$= [240 - 144] - 96$$

$$C.S = 106 - 96 = 10$$

When P = 8 $\quad P = 20 - 2x$

$$8 = 20 - 2x$$

$$2x = 28$$

$$x = 14$$

$$x_e = 14$$

Then the value of $x_e = 14$ subsisting in the demand function, we get P_e value

$$P = 20 - 2x$$

$$= 20 - 14$$

$$P_e = 6$$

$$C.S. = \int_0^{x_e} f(x)\, dx - (P_e \times x_e)$$

$$= \int_0^{14} (20 - 2x)\, dx - (14 \times 6)$$

$$= \left[20x - x^2\right]_0^{14} - 84$$

$$= [280 - 196] - 84$$

$$= 84 - 84$$

$$C.S \quad = 0$$

When P = 4, the consumer surplus is 10,

Whereas P = 8, the consumer surplus is '0'

Example-2: Given the demand and supply functions $P_d = 4-x^2$ and $P_s = x + 2$. Find Consumer's surplus and Producer's surplus.

Solution: For market equilibrium: $P_d = P_s$

$$x + 2 = 4 - x^2$$

$$x^2 + x - 2 = 0$$

$$x^2 + 2x - x - 2 = 0$$

$$x(x + 2) - 1(x + 2) = 0$$

$$(x + 2)(x-1) = 0$$

$$x = -2 \text{ and } 1$$

Since negative value of x is not possible, we have $x = 1$.

At $x = 1$ $\quad P = 4 - x^2$

$$= 4 - 1$$

$$= 3$$

Therefore we have $x_e = 1$ and $P_e = 3$

Hence, C.S. = $\int_0^{x_e} f(x)\, dx - (P_e \times x_e)$

$$= \int_0^1 (4 - x^2)dx - (3 \times 1)$$

$$= \left[4 - \frac{x^3}{3}\right]_0^1 - [3]$$

$$= \left[4 - \frac{1}{3}\right] - 3$$

$$= \frac{11}{3} - 3 = \frac{2}{3}$$

$$\text{and P.S.} = (P_e \times x_e) - \int_0^{x_e} g(x)\,dx$$

$$= (3\times 1) - \int_0^1 (x+2)\,dx$$

$$= 3 - \left[\frac{x^2}{2} + 2x\right]_0^1$$

$$= 3 - \left[\frac{1}{2} + 2\right]$$

$$= 3 - \frac{5}{2}$$

$$\text{P.S.} = \frac{1}{2}$$

Example-3: For a free article $P_e = 0$, find the consumers surplus for this article if its demand function is given by $P = 64 - x^3$

Solution: Given $P = 64 - x^3$

When $P_e = 0$, we have $64 - x^3 = 0$

$\Rightarrow x = 4$

$$\text{Consumers surplus} = \int_0^4 (64 - x^3)\,dx - 0 X 4$$

$$= \left[64x - \frac{x^4}{4}\right]_0^4$$

$$= 64 \text{ x } 4 - \frac{(4)^4}{4}$$

$= 256 - 64$

C.S = 192.

Example-4: **The demand and supply function under perfect competition are Pd = 16 – x^2 and Ps = $2x^2$ + 4 respectively. Find the market price, consumer surplus and producer's surplus.**

Solution: For a market equilibrium

$$P_d = P_s$$
$$16 - x^2 = 2x^2 + 4$$
$$16 - x^2 - 2x^2 - 4 = 0$$
$$12 - 3x^2 = 0$$
$$3x^2 = 12$$
$$x^2 = 4$$
$$x = \pm 2$$
$$x = 2 \text{ and } -2$$

Thus the negative value in not possible so we take $x = 2$, i.e. $x_e = 2$

$$\text{at} \quad x_e = 4 \Rightarrow P_d = 16 - x^2$$
$$P_d = 16 - 2^2$$
$$= 16\text{-}4\text{=}12$$

$$\text{C.S} = \int_0^{x_e} f(x)\,dx - \left(P_e\ X\ x_e\right)$$

$$= \int_0^2 (16 - x^2)\,dx - (12\ X\ 2)$$

$$= \left[16x - \frac{x^3}{3}\right]_0^2 - 24$$

$$= 32 - \frac{8}{3} - 24 = \frac{96 - 8 - 72}{3} = 16$$

Exercise-5

1. Given the demand function, $P_d = 25 - x^2$ and the supply function $Ps = 2x + 1$, assuming pure competition, find the consumers surplus.
2. Determine consumer's surplus and producers' surplus under pure competition for the demand function $P_d = 36 - x^2$ and the supply function $P_s = 6 + \frac{x^2}{4}$
3. The demand and supply laws for a commodity are $P_d = 18 - 2x - x^2$ and $Ps = 2x - 3$. Find the consumers' surplus and producers' surplus at equilibrium price.
4. The demand and supply laws for a commodity are given as $P_d = \frac{8}{x+1} - 2$ and $P_s = \frac{1}{2}(x+3)$. Determine the consumers' surplus and production surplus.
5. Given the demand function; $P_d = 45 - \frac{x}{2}$, find the consumers surplus when $P_e = 32.5$ and $x_e = 25$.

6

Input – Output Analysis

Input – output analysis is a particular planning and forecasting technique with a wide variety of applications. W.W. Leontief has propounded the concept of Input-Output technique. It is the study of mutual interdependence of various sectors of the economy. The interdependence between individual sectors of a given system is distributed with the help of linear equations.

According to J.R Hicks, "An input is something which is bought for enterprise while an output is something which is sold by it".

This technique also deals with the industrial inter-relationships. The inputs of one industry serve as outputs of the other and vice-versa. The mutual relationships lead to achieve equilibrium between demand and supply in the economy. The supply side consists of large inter industry flows of intermediate products and the demand side of the final goods.

Basic features of the Input-Output models:

a. Input-Output analysis is concerned with production only. It determines the amounts of different inputs to be used in the production process to get a certain output. Demand theory has no role that is why Baumol calls it as a hard core of input-output analysis. It deals with only technological problems.

b. It is purely an empirical investigation and quite different from theoretical analysis of general equilibrium and as a result, it is both simplified and narrow than the usual general equilibrium theory.

c. It lays more emphasis on equilibrium phenomenon. It investigates how the various sectors, sub sectors or industries constituting an economy are inter-related. As rightly pointed out by Hirschman terminology, generally industries have both backward and forward linkages and, thus, are inter-dependent and with this interdependence of production activities seek to take account of the fact that each industry uses output of other industries as raw materials.

Uses of input–output model:

1) Input-output analysis may be used for production and forecasting purposes.

2) Input-output analysis can be used to examine the stimulation process.

3) To show the strength of linkages between activities in an economy.

4) The knowledge of input-output relationships has been found useful in growth and planning exercises of only those countries where manufacturing sector is considerably developed.

5) To portray the technology of our economy.

Since the input-output model normally encompasses a large number of industries, its framework is of necessity rather involved. To simplify the problem, the following assumptions are as rule adopted.

1. Each industry produces only one homogenous commodity.
2. Each industry uses a fixed input ratio for the production of its output.
3. Production is every industry is subject to constant returns to scale, so that a k-fold change in every input will result in an exactly k-fold change in the output.

Based on the above assumptions, in order to produce each unit of the jth commodity, the input need for the ith commodity must be a fixed amount, which is denoted by a_{ij}. More specifically, the production of each unit of the jth commodity will require a_{1j} (amount) of the first commodity, a_{2j} of the second commodity ...., and a_{nj} of the nth commodity. The a_{ij} symbol indicates an input coefficient.

For an n-industry economy, the input coefficients can be arranged into a Matrix $A = [a_{ij}]$, as in the below table, in which each column specifies the input requirements for the production of one unit of the output of a particular industry.

Input	*Out put*				
	I	*II*	*III*	....	*N*
I	a_{11}	a_{12}	a_{13}	....	a_{1n}
II	a_{21}	a_{22}	a_{23}	....	a_{2n}
III	a_{31}	a_{32}	a_{33}	....	a_{3n}
•	⋮	⋮	⋮	⋮	⋮
•					
N	a_{n1}	a_{n2}	a_{n3}	....	a_{nn}

The second column, for example, states that to produce a unit of commodity II, the inputs needed are a_{12} units of commodity I, a_{22} units of commodity II, etc. If no industry uses its own product as an input, then the elements in the principal diagonal of Matrix 'A' will be zero.

The Transaction Matrix

The starting point for an input-output analysis is the construction of a table containing entries which show, either quantitatively or in value terms, how the total output of one industry is distributed to all other industries as intermediate output (i.e. raw materials) and to the final non-producing users. Roughly, the whole economy is divided into the industry sector and the consuming sector; the industry sector, in turn, is divided into a large number of industries where each industry is assumed to be producing a homogeneous product. The following table constructed for the United States, there are about 450 industries. For a simple illustration, we shall consider a consolidated transitions matrix for U.S discussed by Chernery and Clark.

Table: 1947 Consolidated Transaction Matrix for the United States

Production sector	*Purchasing sector*			*Final use*	*Total use*
	Agriculture	*Industry*	*Service*		
Agriculture	11	19	1	10	41
Industry	5	89	10	106	240
Service	5	37	37	106	185
Primary inputs	20	95	107	21	243
Total output	41	240	185	243	659

The above table is the entries indicting the distribution of each sector's output as intermediate output to the various sectors in the economy.

For example, the agricultural sector produced the total of 41 billion dollars worth of goods in 1947. Of this total, 11 billion dollars was used as raw materials for agricultural production within its own sector, 19 billon went into industry sector as raw material; 1 billion was used up by the services sector; and 10 billion dollars worth of agricultural production was consumed by the consumers. Going vertically up and down on a column, we find the distribution of purchases of a sector from all sectors of the economy. For instance, if we take the industry sector, it purchased 19 billion dollars worth of raw materials from the agricultural sector, used up 89 billion dollars worth of its own output for production, and bought 37 billion worth of services. Furthermore, the primary input, the value-added part of the sectors output, of 95 billion dollars went into the sectors productive activities, resulting in the sector's total output of 240 billion dollars. Thus at the end of each column the sum of the column's entries gives the total output of the sector in the column; and at the end of each row is found the sum of the row entries representing uses to which a sector's output are put. The final use sector is also called the autonomous sector, meaning that the demands for outputs of various sectors constitute only the consumption of the outputs and do not contribute to production in any other sector of the economy.

Technology Matrix

The Transactions Matrix refers to rise to the production of any industry given one year period of time. At the same time the matrix also provides the information on how the output of a given industry is distributed among the industries and sectors in the rest of the economy.

For example,

$$\begin{array}{cc} & \begin{array}{ccc} A & I & S \end{array} \\ \begin{array}{c} A \\ I \\ \\ S \end{array} & \begin{bmatrix} 0.268 & 0.079 & 0.006 \\ 0.122 & 0.371 & 0.216 \\ 0.122 & 0.154 & 0.200 \\ 0.488 & 0.396 & 0.578 \end{bmatrix} \end{array}$$

Primary input 1.000 1.000 1.000

From the above example, we consider the ratio $a_{il} = X_{i1} / X_1$ for i = 1, 2 ... m. Each of these ratios are called marginal input coefficient. The table constituting of these input coefficients called a technology matrix. Referring Table – 1, we construct Table – 2 containing input coefficients.

The Table – 2 says is that, if we take Column A, for example, the technology condition in the agricultural sector is such that for it is produce 1 dollar worth of output, about 27 cents worth of raw material is needed from the agricultural sector, about 12 cents of input from each of the industry and the services sectors, and about 50 cents worth of labour input. Thus the input coefficients are "standardized" indicators of the amounts of raw materials needed from all industries of the economy for producing a certain amount of output by any industry.

There are mainly two types of input-output models:

1. The open input-output model
2. The closed input-output model

The open input-output model:

If, besides the 'n' industries, the model also contains an 'open' sector which exogenously determines a final demand for the product of each industry and which supplies a primary input not produced by the 'n' industries themselves, the model is an open model. In view of the presence of the open sector, the sum of the elements in each column of the input-coefficient matrix A (or input matrix 'A') must be less than 1.

Symbolically, this fact may be stated thus:

$$\sum_{i=1}^{n} aij < 1 \qquad (j=1,2,.........n)$$

Thus the value of the primary input needed in producing a unit of the jth commodity should be $1-\sum_{i=1}^{n} aij$

If industry I is to produce an output just sufficient to meet the input requirements of the 'n' industries as well as the final demand of the open sector, its output level x_1 must satisfy the following equation.

$$x_1 = a_{11}x_1 + a_{12}x_2 + ... + a_{1n}x_n + d_1$$

Or

$$(1-a_{11})x_1 - a_{12}x_2 - .... - a_{1n}x_n = d_1$$

Similarly the other equations are;

$$-a_{21}x_1 + (1-a_{22}x_2) - \cdots\cdots - a_{2n}x_n = d_2$$

$$\vdots \qquad\qquad \vdots \qquad \vdots$$

$$-a_{n1}x_1 - a_{n2}x_2 \qquad - \cdots\cdots + (1-a_{nn})x_n = d_n$$

In matrix notation, this may be written as

$$\begin{bmatrix} (1-a_{11}) & -a_{12} & \cdots\cdots\cdots & -a_{1n} \\ -a_{21} & (1-a_{22}) & \cdots\cdots\cdots & -a_{2n} \\ \vdots & \vdots & & \vdots \\ -a_{n1} & -a_{n2} & \cdots\cdots\cdots & (1-a_{nn}) \end{bmatrix} \begin{bmatrix} x_1 \\ x_2 \\ \vdots \\ x_n \end{bmatrix} = \begin{bmatrix} d_1 \\ d_2 \\ \vdots \\ d_n \end{bmatrix}$$

$$\text{Let } A = \begin{bmatrix} 1-a_{11} & -a_{12} & \cdots & -a_{1n} \\ -a_{21} & 1-a_{22} & \cdots & -a_{2n} \\ -a_{n1} & -a_{n2} & \cdots & 1-a_{nn} \end{bmatrix}$$

Where A is called coefficient Matrix or technology matrix

$$X = \begin{bmatrix} x_1 \\ x_2 \\ \vdots \\ x_n \end{bmatrix} \text{ is called the gross output vector}$$

$$D = \begin{bmatrix} d_1 \\ d_2 \\ \vdots \\ d_n \end{bmatrix} \text{ is called the final demand vector}$$

If $(I-A)^{-1}$ exists, then the output 'X' is given by $X = (I-A)^{-1}.D$

The closed input – output model:

If the exogenous sector of the open input-output model is absorbed into the system as just another industry, the model will became a closed model. In such a model, final demand and primary input do not appear; in their place will be the input requirements and the output of the newly conceived industry. All goods will now be intermediate in nature, because everything that is produced only for the sake of satisfying the input requirements of the n + 1 industries in the model.

In this model, whatever is produced is supposed to be consumed by the producers themselves. No one except those who participate in the production is benefited.

Example

1. Given the following transaction Matrix, find the gross output to meet the final demand of 200 units of Agriculture and 800 units of industry.

Producing sector	*Purchasing agriculture*	*Sector industry*	*Final demand*
Agriculture	300	600	100
Industry	400	1200	400

Solution

Total output for agriculture = 300 + 600 + 100 = 1000

Total output for industry = 400 + 1200 + 400 = 2000

$$\text{The technology Matrix is } A = \begin{bmatrix} \frac{300}{1000} & \frac{600}{2000} \\ \frac{400}{1000} & \frac{1200}{2000} \end{bmatrix}$$

$$= \begin{bmatrix} \frac{3}{10} & \frac{3}{10} \\ \frac{2}{5} & \frac{3}{5} \end{bmatrix}$$

Let x_1 and x_2 be the gross output of Agriculture and Industry respectively. The balance matrix equation for the two sectors is

$$\begin{bmatrix} \frac{3}{10} & \frac{3}{10} \\ \frac{2}{5} & \frac{3}{5} \end{bmatrix} \begin{bmatrix} x_1 \\ x_2 \end{bmatrix} + \begin{bmatrix} 200 \\ 800 \end{bmatrix} = \begin{bmatrix} x_1 \\ x_2 \end{bmatrix}$$

$$\frac{3}{10}x_1 + \frac{3}{10}x_2 + 200 = x_1 \rightarrow \quad (1)$$

$$\frac{2}{5}x_1 + \frac{3}{5}x_2 + 800 = x_2 \rightarrow \quad (2)$$

$$\frac{3}{10}x_1 + \frac{3}{10}x_2 + 200 - x_1 = 0$$

$$\frac{3}{10}x_1 - x_1 + \frac{3}{10}x_2 + 200 = 0$$

$$\frac{-7}{10}x_1 + \frac{3}{10}x_2 = -200$$

$$\frac{7}{10}x_1 - \frac{3}{10}x_2 = 200$$

Similarly for equation (2) is $\frac{2}{5}x_1 - \frac{2}{5}x_2 = 800$

Solving the above equations by Cramer's rule, we get

$$x_1 = \frac{D_1}{D} = \frac{-6000}{3} = -2000$$

$$x_2 = \frac{D_{21}}{D} = \frac{-8000}{3} = 2665$$

Hawkins – Simon Conditions:

The input – output solution can also give a negative answers implying that more than 1 unit of the product is being used as an input in producing 1 unit of that particular product. To avoid such situations, the following Hawkins - Simon conditions are imposed.

1. The determinant $|I-A|$ of the Leontief Matrix must be positive.
2. The diagonal elements: $1-a_{11}$, $1-a_{22}$ ..... $1-a_{nn}$, of the Leontief Matrix (I – A) should all be positive.

Example-1: Find the demand vector, which is consistent with the input-output matrix

$$A = \begin{bmatrix} 0.2 & 0.3 & 0.2 \\ 0.4 & 0.1 & 0.2 \\ 0.1 & 0.3 & 0.2 \end{bmatrix} \text{ and the output vector } X = \begin{bmatrix} 25 \\ 21 \\ 18 \end{bmatrix} \text{ also}$$

test Hawkins – Simon Conditions for the viability of the system.

Solution: We have X = AX + D

$$\therefore D = (I - A).\ X$$

$$\text{Now}\quad I - A = \begin{bmatrix} 1 & 0 & 0 \\ 0 & 1 & 0 \\ 0 & 0 & 1 \end{bmatrix} - \begin{bmatrix} 0.2 & 0.3 & 0.2 \\ 0.4 & 0.1 & 0.2 \\ 0.1 & 0.3 & 0.2 \end{bmatrix}$$

$$= \begin{bmatrix} 0.8 & -0.3 & -0.2 \\ -0.4 & 0.9 & -0.2 \\ -0.1 & -0.3 & 0.8 \end{bmatrix}$$

$$\therefore D = (I - A)\, X = \begin{bmatrix} 0.8 & -0.3 & -0.2 \\ -0.4 & 0.9 & -0.2 \\ -0.1 & -0.3 & 0.8 \end{bmatrix} \begin{bmatrix} 25 \\ 21 \\ 18 \end{bmatrix}$$

$$= \begin{bmatrix} 10.1 \\ 5.3 \\ 5.6 \end{bmatrix}$$

$$|I - A| = \begin{vmatrix} + & - & + \\ 0.8 & -0.3 & -0.2 \\ -0.4 & 0.9 & -0.2 \\ -0.1 & -0.3 & 0.8 \end{vmatrix}$$

$$= +0.8 \begin{vmatrix} 0.9 & -0.2 \\ -0.3 & 0.8 \end{vmatrix} + 0.3 \begin{vmatrix} -0.4 & -0.2 \\ -0.1 & 0.8 \end{vmatrix} - 0.2 \begin{vmatrix} -0.4 & 0.9 \\ -0.1 & -0.3 \end{vmatrix}$$

$= 0.8\ (0.72 - 0.6) + 0.3\ (-0.32 - 0.02) - 0.2\ (0.12 + 0.09)$

$= 0.096 + 0.102 + 0.042$

$= 0.24$

Since $(I - A) = 0.24 > 0$ and elements of the Principal diagonal of $|I - A|$ are positive, the Simon – Hawkins conditions are satisfied. Hence the system is viable.

Example-3: A three sector economy has the following input-output coefficient Matrix

$$A = \begin{bmatrix} 0 & 0.5 & 0 \\ 0.2 & 0 & 0.5 \\ 0.4 & 0 & 0 \end{bmatrix}$$

The labour days required per unit of output of the three sectors are 0.4, 0.7 and 1.2 respectively and their consumer output targets are 1000, 5000 and 4000 units respectively. Find the gross output of each sector and how many total labour days required.

Solution: The technology matrix is

$$A = \begin{bmatrix} 0 & 0.5 & 0 \\ 0.2 & 0 & 0.5 \\ 0.4 & 0 & 0 \end{bmatrix}$$

and the final demand Matrix is

$$D = \begin{bmatrix} 1000 \\ 5000 \\ 4000 \end{bmatrix}$$

Let the gross output of the three sectors be and respectively.

The balance Matrix equation for the three sectors is

$$\begin{bmatrix} 0 & 0.5 & 0 \\ 0.2 & 0 & 0.5 \\ 0.4 & 0 & 0 \end{bmatrix} \begin{bmatrix} x_1 \\ x_2 \\ x_3 \end{bmatrix} + \begin{bmatrix} 1000 \\ 5000 \\ 4000 \end{bmatrix} = \begin{bmatrix} x_1 \\ x_2 \\ x_3 \end{bmatrix}$$

We know $AX + D = X$

$(I - A)X = D$

$\therefore X = (I - A)^{-1} \cdot D$

$$\text{Here } I - A = \begin{bmatrix} 1 & 0 & 1 \\ 0 & 1 & 0 \\ 0 & 0 & 1 \end{bmatrix} - \begin{bmatrix} 0 & 0.5 & 0 \\ 0.2 & 0 & 0.5 \\ 0.4 & 0 & 0 \end{bmatrix}$$

$$= \begin{bmatrix} 1 & -0.5 & 0 \\ -0.2 & 1 & -0.5 \\ -0.4 & 0 & 1 \end{bmatrix}$$

$$\therefore |I-A| = \begin{vmatrix} 1 & -0.5 & 0 \\ -0.2 & 1 & -0.5 \\ -0.4 & 0 & 1 \end{vmatrix}$$

$$= +1(1+0) + 0.5(-0.2-0.2) + 0$$

$$= 1 - 0.20 + 0 = 0.8$$

Since $|I-A| = 10$ $(I-A)^{-1}$ exists

Thus X = $(I - A)^{-1}$. D

$$= \frac{1}{0.8}\begin{bmatrix} 1 & 0.5 & 0.25 \\ 0.4 & 1 & 0.5 \\ 0.4 & 0.2 & 0.9 \end{bmatrix} \begin{bmatrix} 1000 \\ 5000 \\ 4000 \end{bmatrix}$$

$$= \frac{10}{8}\begin{bmatrix} 1000 & + & 2500 & + & 1000 \\ 400 & + & 5000 & + & 2000 \\ 400 & + & 1000 & + & 3600 \end{bmatrix}$$

$$= \frac{10}{8}\begin{bmatrix} 4500 \\ 7400 \\ 5000 \end{bmatrix}$$

$$= \begin{bmatrix} 5625 \\ 9250 \\ 6250 \end{bmatrix}$$

$\therefore x_1 = 5625$ units $\quad x_2 = 9250$ units

$\therefore$ The total labour days required

$$= \begin{bmatrix} 5625 \\ 9250 \\ 0250 \end{bmatrix} \begin{bmatrix} 00.4 & 0.7 & 1.2 \end{bmatrix}$$

$$= \begin{bmatrix} 2250 + 6475 + 7500 \end{bmatrix}$$

$$= 16225$$

Example-4: A three sector economy has the following input-output coefficient Matrix A and demand D

$$A = \begin{bmatrix} 0.3 & 0.2 & 0.2 \\ 0.2 & 0.1 & 0.5 \\ 0.2 & 0.4 & 0.2 \end{bmatrix} \quad D = \begin{bmatrix} 80 \\ 30 \\ 50 \end{bmatrix}$$

Find the gross output of each sector to meet the final demand.

Solution

Let x_1, x_2 and x_3 be the gross output of the three sectors to meet the final demand.

We have $AX + D = X$

i.e. $(I - A)X = D$

$X = (I - A)^{-1} \cdot D$

$$\text{Here } I - A = \begin{bmatrix} 1 & 0 & 1 \\ 0 & 1 & 0 \\ 0 & 0 & 1 \end{bmatrix} - \begin{bmatrix} 0.3 & 0.2 & 0.2 \\ 0.2 & 0.1 & 0.5 \\ 0.2 & 0.4 & 0.2 \end{bmatrix}$$

$$= \begin{bmatrix} 0.7 & -0.2 & -0.2 \\ -0.2 & 0.9 & -0.5 \\ -0.2 & -0.4 & 0.8 \end{bmatrix}$$

$$|I-A| = \begin{vmatrix} 0.7 & -0.2 & -0.2 \\ -0.2 & 0.9 & -0.5 \\ -0.2 & -0.4 & 0.8 \end{vmatrix}$$

$= 0.26$

Thus $X = (I - A)^{-1} . D$

$$= \frac{1}{0.26}\begin{bmatrix} 0.52 & 0.24 & 0.28 \\ 0.26 & 0.52 & 0.39 \\ 0.26 & 0.32 & 0.59 \end{bmatrix}\begin{bmatrix} 80 \\ 30 \\ 50 \end{bmatrix}$$

$$= \frac{1}{0.26}\begin{bmatrix} 62.8 \\ 55.9 \\ 59.9 \end{bmatrix}$$

$$= \frac{1}{0.26}\begin{bmatrix} 241.54 \\ 215 \\ 230.38 \end{bmatrix}$$

Hence $x_1 = 241.54$ units, $x_2 = 215$ units and $x_3 = 230.38$ units.

Exercise – 1

1. Given the input Matrix and final demand vector:

$$A = \begin{bmatrix} 0.05 & 0.25 & 0.34 \\ 0.33 & 0.10 & 0.72 \\ 0.19 & 0.38 & 0.00 \end{bmatrix} \qquad D = \begin{bmatrix} 1800 \\ 200 \\ 900 \end{bmatrix}$$

i. Explain the economic meaning of the element 0.33, 0.00 and 200

ii. Explain the economic meaning of the third column sum.

iii. Explain the economic meaning of the third row sum

2. You are given the following technology Matrix for a two industry economy.

	Steel	*Coal*
Steel	0.2	0.2
Coal	0.4	0.1

Write down the input-output table for the economy, when the final demand targets are Re.100 crore in steel and Re. 20 crore in coal.

3. Explain the difference between the open and close input-output models developed by Leontief.

4. Given the following technology Matrix

$$A = \begin{bmatrix} 0.5 & 0.1 & 0.1 \\ 0.2 & 0.6 & 0.2 \\ 0.1 & 0.2 & 0.6 \end{bmatrix}$$

i. Test Simon – Hawkins conditions for the viability of the system

ii. Define the gross output vector X, given the demand vector

$$D = \begin{bmatrix} 2100 \\ 4200 \\ 6300 \end{bmatrix}$$

5. If the final consumer requirements are RS. 80 million of railway transports determine the final output goal of each industry.

	Steel	*Coal*	*Railway transport*
Steel	0.2	0.2	0.2
Coal	0.4	0.1	0.3
Rail transport	0.1	0.3	0.1
Labour	0.3	0.4	0.3

Also estimate the labour requirements for final output of the three industries.

6. From the following transaction Matrix, determine the input–output Matrix

	Users		
Producers	*A*	*B*	*Projected Demand*
A	200	400	100
B	300	800	300

7. Assume that an economy consist of only two industries, A and B and has the following transactions matrix for the year 200 B.C (figures are in '000s of dollars)

	A	*B*	*Final Demand*	*Total Output*
A	20	15	45	80
B	15	15	10	40
Primary input	35	10	5	40

Find the technology matrix of this economy.

8. What are the basic features of input-output analysis?

9. Discuss the uses of input-output analysis?

10. Briefly explain the following with a suitable examples:

    i. Transactions Matrix

    ii. Technology Matrix

11. Given the technology matrix of a Leontief input-output Matrix as

$$A = \begin{bmatrix} 0.4 & 0.1 & 0.2 \\ 0.1 & 0.3 & 0.3 \\ 0.2 & 0.1 & 0.2 \end{bmatrix}$$

and the domestic consumption vector $D = \begin{bmatrix} 10 \\ 20 \\ 10 \end{bmatrix}$

To

i. Test Simon – Hawkins conditions for the viability of the system.

ii. Write the balancing equation

iii. Obtain the gross output

12. The input-output technology matrix for three industries is

$$\begin{bmatrix} 0.2 & 0.3 & 0.1 \\ 0 & 0.5 & 0.2 \\ 0 & 0 & 0.5 \end{bmatrix}$$

and the final demand is $\begin{bmatrix} 100 \\ 200 \\ 300 \end{bmatrix}$

Find the gross output.

7

Linear Programming and Game Theory

Linear programming is a technique for determining an optimum schedule of interdependent activities in view of the available resources. Programming is just another word for 'planning' and refers to the process of determining a particular plan of action from amongst several alternatives. The word linear stands for indicating that all relationships involved in a particular problem are linear.

In this chapter, we shall study how a linear programming problem is formulated as a mathematical model and ways to solve such a problem.

General Formulation of Linear Programming Problems

The mathematical structure of the general liner-programming problem is as follows:

Maximize $Z = c_1 x_1 + c_2 x_2 + \ldots\ldots + c_n x_n$

Subject to

$$a_{11} x_1 + a_{12} x_2 + \ldots\ldots + a_{1n} x_n \leq r_1$$

$$a_{21} x_1 + a_{22} x_2 + \ldots\ldots + a_{2n} x_n \leq r_2$$

$$\ldots\ldots \quad \ldots\ldots \quad \ldots\ldots$$

$$\ldots\ldots \quad \ldots\ldots \quad \ldots\ldots$$

$$a_{m1} x_1 + a_{m2} x_2 + \ldots\ldots + a_{mn} x_n \leq r_m$$

and $x_j \geq 0$ $(j = 1, 2 \ldots n)$

Where

a. The variable $x_1, x_2 \dots x_n$ whose values are to be determined are called the decision variables.

b. The linear function Z is given by which is minimized or maximized is called the objective function of the LPP

c. The conditions given by equation (2) are termed as the constraints of the LPP.

d. The set of inequalities equation (3) is known as the set of non-negative restrictions of the LPP.

e. The constraints c_1, c_2, ...c_n are the parameters of the problem.

f. The expression ($\leq$, = $\geq$) indicates that any one of the three signs would hold for a particular constraint.

Formulation

The following basic steps involves for formulating LPP ;

1. Identify the decision variables whose values we wish to determine and assign symbols x_1, x_2 ...... to them.
2. Express the objective quantitatively as a linear function of the decision variables.
3. Identify the set of constraints or restrictions, stated interms of the decision variables in the form of liner relationships.
4. Write down the non-negative restrictions for the decision variables.

Examples on

Formulation of the Linear Programming Problems:

Example-1: A resourceful home decorator manufactures two types of lamps say A and B. Both lamps go through two technicians, first a cutter, second a cutter, second a finisher. Lamp A requires 2 hours of the cutter's time and 1 hour of finisher's time. Lamp B requires 1 hour of cutter's time and 2 hours of finisher's time. The cutter has 104 hours and the finisher 76 hours of time available each month.

Profit on one lamp A is Re. 6.0 and one lamp B is Re. 11.0. Assuming that he can sell that he produces, formulate the problem as a linear programming model to obtain the best return.

Solution: Let x_1 = is the number of lamps of type A to be produced.

x_2 = the number of lamps of type B to be produced.

The total profit is $z = 6x_1 + 11x_2$

The total time of the cutter used in preparing x_1 lamps of type A and x_2 lamps of type B is $2x_1 + x_2$

Since the cutter has 104 hours only for each month

$\therefore\ 2x_1 + x_2 \le 104$

The total time of the finisher used in preparing x_1 lamps of type A and x_2 lamps of type B is

$x_1 + 2x_2 \le 76$

and $x_1 \ge 0,\ x_2 \ge 0$

Hence Max $z = 6x_1 + 11x_2$

Subject to constraints: $2x_1 + x_2 \le 104$

$x_1 + 2x_2 \le 76$

and $x_1\ x_2 \ge 0$

Example-2: Food X contains 6 units of vitamin A and 7 units of vitamin B per gram and costs 12 p/gm. Food y contains 8 units and 12 units of A and B per grams respectively and costs 20 p/gm. The daily requirements of vitamin A and B are at least 100 unit and 120 units respectively. Formulate the above as an LPP to minimize the cost.

Solution: Let x_1= the number of units contained in vitamin A

x_2 = the number of units contained in vitamin B

Total cost is $z = 12x_1 + 20x_2$

Total daily requirements of vitamin A and

Food x and y is $6x_1 + 8x_2$

Since the vitamin A is atleast 100 units

$\therefore\ 6x_1 + 8x_2 \geq 100$

Similarly vitamin B is

$7x_1 + 12x_2 \geq 20$

Also $x_1 \geq 0, x_2 \geq 0$

Hence, the given problem has reformulated as

Min $z = 12x_1 + 20x_2$

Subject to

$6x_1 + 8x_2 \geq 100$

$7x_1 + 12x_2 \geq 120$

And $x_1, x_2 \geq 0$

Example-3: The manager of an oil refinery must decide the optimal mix of the possible blending process of which the input and output per production run are as under:

Process	*Input (Units)*		*Output (Units)*	
	Crude A	*Crude B*	*Gasoline X*	*Gasoline Y*
12	54	35	54	84

The maximum quantities available of crude A and B are 200 units and 150 units respectively. Market requirements show that at least 100 units of Gasoline X and 80 units of Gasoline Y must be produced. The profits per production run for process 1 and process 2 are Re. 300 and Re. 400 respectively. Formulate the problem as LPP model to maximize profit.

Solution: Let x_1 and x_2 be the amount of produced in the two processes.

Profit is $z = 300x_1 = + 400x_2$

Amount of crude A used is $5x_1 + 4x_2$ units, which should naturally be less than or equal to the amount available. Hence, $5x_1 + 4x_2 \leq 200$

similarly for crude B is $3x_1 + 5x_2 \leq 150$ Gasoline X produced in two process in $5x + 4y$ units. Because of market requirements $5x_1 + 4x_2 \geq 100$, considering the amount gasoline y produced in the two processes, we get

$$8x_1 + 4x_2 \geq 80$$

or

$$2x_1 + x_2 \geq 20$$

and $x_1, x_2 \geq 0$

Thus the Mathematical formulation of the given LPP is

Maximize $z = 300x_1 + 400x_2$

Subject to

$$5x_1 + 4x_2 \leq 200$$
$$3x_1 + 5x_2 \leq 150$$
$$5x_1 + 4x_2 \geq 100$$
$$2x_1 + x_2 \geq 20$$

and $x_1 \; x_2 \geq 0$

Exercise – 1

1. A diet to contain atleast 400 units of carbohydrate, 500 units of fat and 300 units of protein. Two foods are available F_1, which costs Res. 2 per unit and F_2, which costs Re. 4 per unit. A unit of F-$_1$ contains 10 units of carbohydrate, 20 units of fat and 15 units of proteins; a unit of food F_2 contains 25 units of carbohydrate, 10 units of fat and 20 units of protein. Find the minimum cost for a diet that consists of a mixture of these two foods and also meet the minimum nutrition requirements. Formulate the problem as a linear programming problem.

2. A person requires 10, 12 and 12 units of chemicals A, B and C respectively for his garden. A liquid product contains 5, 2 and 1 units of A, B and C respectively per Jar. A dry product contains

1, 2 and 4 units of A, B and C per carton. If the liquid product sells for Re. 3 per Jar and the dry product sells for Re. 2 per carton, formulate an LPP, showing how may of each should be purchased with the object of minimizing the cost and meeting the requirements.

3. An agriculturalist has a farm with 125 acres. He produces Radish, Mutter and Potato. Whatever he raises is fully sold in the market. He gets Re.5 for Radish per kg., Re. 4 for mutter per kg. and Re.5 for potato per kg. the average yield 1,500 kg. of Radish per acre, 1,800 kg. of mutter per acre and 1,200 kg of Potato per acre. To produce each 100kg. of Radish and mutter and to produce each 80kg. of Potato, a sum of Re,12.50 has to be used for manure. Labour required for each acre to raise the crop is 6 man days for radish and potato each and 5 man days for mutter. A total of 500 man days of labour at a rate of Re.40 per man day are available. Formulate this as a linear programming model to maximize the Agriculturalist's total profit?

4. A company is making two products A and B. the cost of producing one unit of product A and B is Re. 60 and Re.8 respectively. As per the agreement, the company has to supply at least 200units of product B to its regular customers. One unit of product A requires one machine hours whereas product B has machine hours available abundantly within the company total machine hours available for product A are 400 hours. One unit of each product A and B requires one labour hour each and total of 500 labour hours are available. The company wants to minimize the cost of production by satisfying the given requirements. Formulate the problem as a linear programming problem.

5. Anita Electric Company produces two products P_1 and P_2 that are produced and sold on a weekly basis. The weekly production cannot exceed 25 for product P_1 and 35 for product P_2 because of limited available facilities. The company employs a total of 60 workers, product P_1 requires 2 man – weeks of labour where as P_2 requires only one. Profit margin on P_1 is

Re. 60 and P_2 is Re. 40. Formulate it as LPP and solve for maximum profit.

6. A company has two factories, one each at Mumbai and Kolkata and two warehouses, one each at Delhi and Chennai. Units produced at the factories are transported to Delhi and Chennai. If the factory at Mumbai produces 300 units and that at Kolkata 200 units, and if the warehouse at Delhi can store 280 units and that at Chennai 220 units, determine the units to be transported from the factories to the warehouses when it is known that the cost of transportation of 1 unit from Mumbai to Chennai Re. 7, from Kolkata to Delhi Re 8 and from Kolkata to Chennai is Re.12.

LPP by Graphical approach

Example-1: Solve the Linear Programming Problem by Graphical method

$$\text{Maximize } Z = 6x_1 + 11x_2$$

$$\text{Subject to } 2x_1 + x_2 \leq 104$$

$$x_1 + 2x_2 \leq 76$$

$$\text{and } x_1, x_2 \geq 0$$

Solution: The given inequal constraints are converting into equalities

$$2x_1 + x_2 = 104 \rightarrow (1)$$

$$x_1 + 2x_2 = 76 \rightarrow (2)$$

Take the fist equation

$$2x_1 + x_2 = 104$$

$$\text{Put } x_1 = 0 \Rightarrow 2(0) + x_2 = 104$$

$$x_2 = 104$$

$$\text{Put } x_2 = 0 \Rightarrow 2x_1 + 0 = 104$$

$$2x_1 = 104$$

$$x_1 = \frac{104}{2} = 52$$

$x_1 = 52$

$\therefore (x_{1.}, x_2) = (52, 104)$

Take the second equation

$x_1 + 2x_2 = 76$

Put $x_1 = 0 \Rightarrow 0 + 2x_2 = 76$

$2x_2 = 76$

$x_2 = \frac{76}{2}$

$x_2 = 38$

Put $x_2 = 0 \Rightarrow x_1 + 2(0) = 76$

$x_1 = 76$

$\therefore (x_{1,} x_2) = (76, 38)$

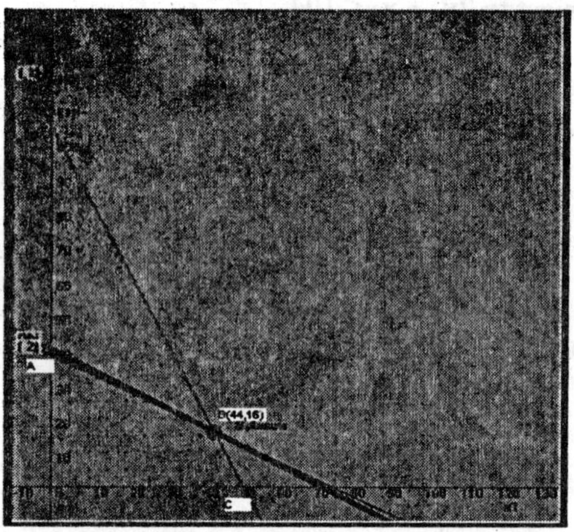

For point B, we can solve the (1) & (2) equations

$$1 \times 2x_1 + x_2 = 104$$
$$2 \times x_1 + 2x_2 = 76$$

$$2x_1 + x_2 = 104$$
$$2x_1 + 4x_2 = 152$$

$$-3x_2 = -48$$

$$x_2 = \frac{48}{3} = 16$$

Then the value of 'x_2' substituting in any above equation, we get x_1 value

$$x_1 + 2x_2 = 76$$
$$x_1 + 2(16) = 76$$
$$x_1 = 76 - 32$$
$$x_2 = 44$$
$$\therefore (x_1\ x_2) = (44, 16)$$

Therefore OABC is the feasible region, the corner point of the feasible region are 0 (0,0), A(52,0), B (44,16), C(0,38)

The values of the objective function at these corner points are

$Z = 6x_1 + 11x_2$

At 0 (0, 0) $\Rightarrow$ z = 6(0) + 11(0) = 0

A (52, 0) $\Rightarrow$ z = 6(52) + 11(0) = 312

B (44, 16) $\Rightarrow$ z = 6(44) + 11(16) = 440

C (0, 38) $\Rightarrow$ z = 6(0) + 11(38) = 418

The Maximum value of z is 440 at the point B(44, 16) i.e. $x_1 = 44$ and $x_2 = 16$

Example-2: Solve the Linear Programming Problem by Graphical method

$$\text{Maximize } z = 40x_1 + 35x_2$$

$$\text{Subject to } 2x_1 + 3x_2 \leq 60$$

$$4x_1 + 3x_2 \leq 96$$

$$\text{and } x_1, x_2 \geq 0$$

Solution: Given Maximize $Z = 40x_1 + 35x_2$

$$\text{Subject to } 2x_1 + 3x_2 \leq 60$$

$$4x_1 + 3x_2 \leq 96$$

$$\text{and } x_1, x_2 \geq 0$$

The above mentioned inequal constraints are converted into equalities.

$$2x_1 + 3x_2 = 60 \rightarrow \quad (1)$$

$$4x_1 + 3x_2 = 96 \rightarrow \quad (2)$$

Now we take the first equation,

$$2x_1 + 3x_2 = 60$$

Put $x_1 = 0$

$$2(0) + 3x_2 = 60$$

$$3x_2 = 60$$

$$x_2 = \frac{60}{3} = 20$$

Put $x_2 = 0$

$$2x_1 + 3(0) = 60$$

$$2x_1 = 60$$

$$x_1 = \frac{60}{2} = 30$$

$$\therefore (x_1, x_2) = (30, 20)$$

Take the second equation

$$4x_1 + 3x_2 = 96$$

Put $x_1 = 0$

$$4(0) + 3x_2 = 96$$

$$3x-_2 = 96$$

$$x_2 = \frac{96}{3} = 32$$

Put $x_2 = 0$

$$4x_1 + 3(0) = 96$$

$$4x_1 = 96$$

$$x_1 = \frac{96}{4} = 24$$

$$\therefore (x_{1,}\ x_2) = (24, 32)$$

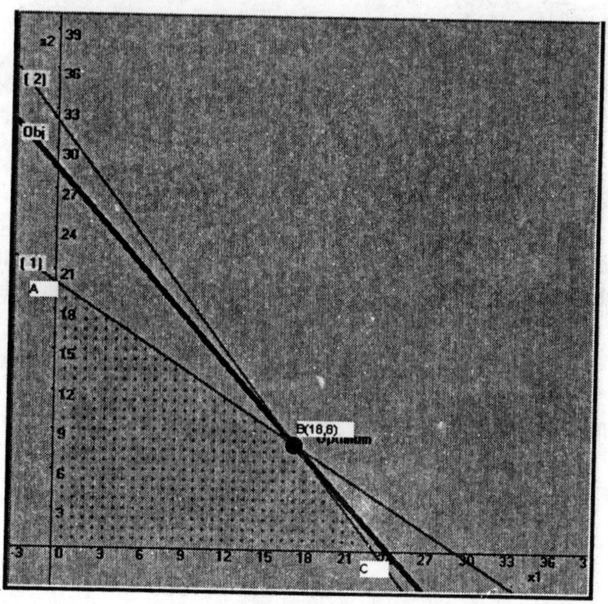

For point B, we can solve the (1) & (2) equations

$$4\times\ 2x_1 + 3x_2 = 60$$
$$2\times\ 4x_1 + 3x_2 = 96$$

$$8x_1 + 12x_2 = 240$$
$$8x_1 + 6x_2 = 192$$

$$6x_2 = 48$$

$$x_2 = \frac{48}{6} = 18$$

Then the value of 'x_2' substituting in any above equation, we get, x_1 value

$$2x_1 + 3x_2 = 60$$
$$2x_1 + 3(8) = 60$$
$$2x_1 + 24 = 60$$
$$2x1 = 36$$
$$x_1 = \frac{36}{2} = 18$$

$$\therefore\ (x_1\ x_2) = (18,\ 8)$$

Therefore OABC is the feasible region, the corner point of the feasible region are 0 (0, 0), A (0, 20), B (18, 8), C (24, 0). The values of the objective function at these corner points are

$$Z = 40x_1 + 35x_2$$

at O (0, 0) $\Rightarrow$ $z = 40(0) + 35(0) = 0$

A (0, 20) $\Rightarrow$ $z = 40(0) + 35(20)$

$= 0 + 700 = 700$

B (18, 8) $\Rightarrow$ $z = 40(18) + 35(8)$

$= 720 + 280 = 1000$

$$C(24, 0) \Rightarrow \quad z = 40(24) + 35(0)$$
$$= 960$$

The Maximum value of z is 1000 at the point C (18, 8) i.e.

$$x_1 = 18 \text{ and } x_2 = 8$$

Example – 3: Solve the Linear Programming Problem by Graphical method Minimize $z = 5x_1 + 6x_2$

Subject to $2x_1 + 3x_2 \geq 24$

$$3x_1 + x_2 \geq 12$$

$$2x_1 + 2x_2 \geq 16$$

And $x_1, x_2 \geq 0$

Solution: Given Minimize $z = 5x_1 + 6x_2$

Subject to $2x_1 + 3x_2 \geq 24$

$$3x_1 + x_2 \geq 12$$

$$2x_1 + 2x_2 \geq 16$$

And $x_1, x_2 \geq 0$

The above mentioned inequal constraints are converted into equalities

$$2x_1 + 3x_2 \geq 24 \rightarrow 1$$

$$3x_1 + x_2 \geq 12 \rightarrow 2$$

$$2x_1 + 2x_2 \geq 16 \rightarrow 3$$

Now we take the first equation

$$2x_1 + 3x_2 \geq 24$$

Put $x_1 = 0 \Rightarrow 2(0) + 3x_2 = 24$

$$3x_2 = 24$$

$$x_2 = \frac{24}{3} = 8$$

Put $x_2 = 0 \Rightarrow 2x_1 + 3(0) = 24$

$$2x_1 = 24$$

$$x_1 = \frac{24}{2} = 12$$

$$\therefore (x_1, x_2) = (12, 8)$$

Take the second equation

$$3x_1 + x_2 = 12$$

Put $x_1 = 0 \Rightarrow 3(0) + x_2 = 12$

$$x_2 = 12$$

Put $x_2 = 0 \Rightarrow 3x_1 + 0 = 12$

$$3x_1 = 12$$

$$x_1 = \frac{12}{3} = 4$$

$$\therefore (x_1, x_2) = (4, 12)$$

The third equation is $2x_1 + 2x_2 = 16$

Put $x_1 = 0 \Rightarrow 2(0) + 2x_2 = 16$

$$2x_2 = 16$$

$$x_2 = \frac{16}{2} = 8$$

Put $x_2 = 0 \Rightarrow 2x_1 + 2(0) = 16$

$$2x_1 = 16$$

$$x_1 = 8$$

$$\therefore (x_1, x_2) = (8, 8)$$

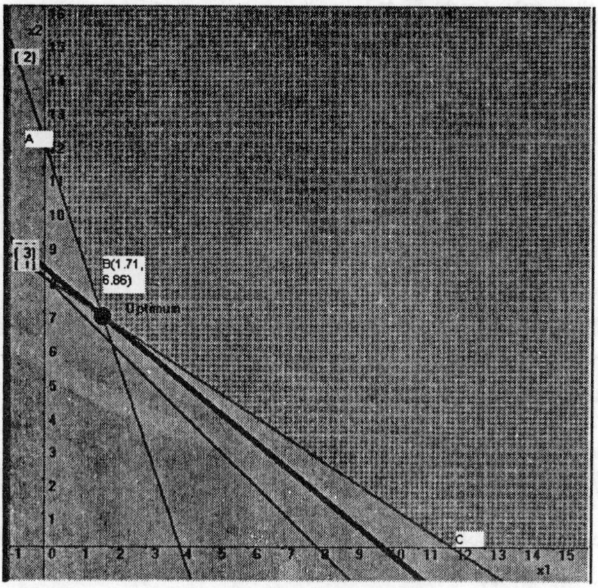

For point B, we can solve the (1) & (2) equations

$$3 \times 2x_1 + 3x_2 = 24$$
$$2 \times 3x_1 + x_2 = 12$$

$$6x_1 + 9x_2 = 72$$
$$6x_1 + 2x_2 = 24$$

$$7x_2 = 48$$
$$x_2 = \frac{48}{7} = 6.86$$

Then the value of 'x_2' substituting in any above equation, we get x_1 value

$$2x_1 + 3x_2 = 24$$

$$2x_1 + 3(6.86) = 24$$

$$2x_1 = 20.58 = 24$$

$$2x_1 = 3.42$$

$$x_1 = \frac{3.42}{2} = 1.71$$

$\therefore (x_1\ x_2) = (1.71, 6.86)$

Therefore ABC is the feasible region, the corner point of the feasible region are A (0, 8), B (1.71, 6.86), C (4, 0). The values of the objective function at these corner points are

$Z = 5x_1 + 6x_2$

A (0, 12) $\Rightarrow$ z = 5(0) + 6(12) = 0 + 72 = 72

B (1.76, 6.86) $\Rightarrow$ z = 5(1.71) + 6(6.86) = 8.55 + 41.16

= 49.71

C (12, 0) $\Rightarrow$ z = 5(12) + 6(0) = 60 + 0 = 60

The Maximum value of z is 49.71 at the point B (1.71, 6.86) i.e. $x_1 = 1.71$ and $x_2 = 6.86$

Example – 4: Solve the Linear Programming Problem by Graphical method Minimize $z = 40x_1 + 24x_2$

Subject to $20x_1 + 50x_2 \geq 4{,}800$

$80x_1 + 50x_2 \geq 7{,}200$

And $x_1, x_2 \geq 0$

Solution: the given inequal constraints are converted into equalities.

$20\,x_1 + 50x_2 = 4,800 \rightarrow 1$

$80\,x_1 + 50x_2 = 7,200 \rightarrow 2$

Now we take the first equation

$$20\,x_1 + 50x_2 = 4,800$$

Put $x_1 = 0 \Rightarrow 20(0)+50\,x_2 = 4{,}800$

$$50x_2 = 4{,}800$$

$$x_2 = \frac{4{,}800}{50}$$

$$x_2 = 96$$

Put $x_2 = 0 \Rightarrow 20x_1+50(0) = 4{,}800$

$$20x_1 = 4{,}800$$

$$x_1 = \frac{4800}{20} = 240$$

$$\therefore (x_1, x_2) = (240, 96)$$

Take the second equation $80x_1 + 50x_2 = 7{,}200$

Put $x_1 = 0 \Rightarrow 80(0)+50\,x_2 = 7{,}200$

$$50x_2 = 7{,}200$$

$$x_2 = \frac{7200}{50} = 144$$

Put $x_2 = 0 \Rightarrow 80x_1+50(0) = 7{,}200$

$$80x_1 = 7{,}200$$

$$x_1 = \frac{7200}{80} = 90$$

$$\therefore (x_1, x_2) = (90, 144)$$

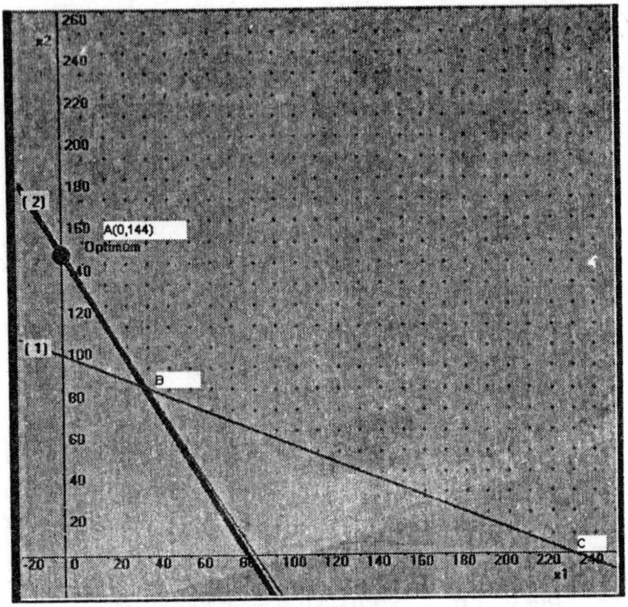

For point B, we can solve the (1) & (2) equations

$$20x_1 + 50x_2 = 4800$$

$$80x_1 + 50x_2 = 7200$$

$$-60x_1 = -2400$$

$$-60x_1 = 2400$$

$$x1 = 40$$

The value of 'x_1' substituting in any of the above equations

$$20x_1 + 50x_2 = 4800$$

$$20(40) + 50x_2 = 4800$$

$$800 + 50x_2 = 4800$$

$50x_2 = 4800$

$x_2 = 80$

$\therefore (x_1\ x_2) = (40, 80)$

Therefore ABC is the feasible region, the corner point of the feasible region are A (0, 144), b (40,80), C (240,0). The values of the objective function are

$$Z = 40x_1 + 24x_2$$

A (0, 144) $\Rightarrow$ $z = 40(0) + 24(144) = 0 + 3456 = 3456$

B (40, 6.86) $\Rightarrow$ $z = 40(40) + 24(80) = 1600 + 1920$
$= 3520$

C (240, 0) $\Rightarrow$ $z = 40(240) + 24(0) = 9600 + 0 = 9600$

The minimum value of 'z' is 3456 at point A (40, 80) i.e $x_1 = 40$ and $x_2 = 80$.

Example – 5: Solve the Linear Programming Problem by Graphical method Maximize $z = 2x_1 + 5x_2$

Subject to $x_1 \leq 4$

$x_2 \leq 3$

$x_1 + 2x_2 \leq 8$

and $x_1, x_2 \geq 0$

Solution: The given inequal constraints are converted into equalities

$x_1 = 4 \quad \rightarrow (1)$

$x_2 = 3 \quad \rightarrow (2)$

$x_1 + 2x_2 = 8 \quad \rightarrow (3)$

For the equation (1) $(x_1, x_2) = (4, 0)$

Similarly equation (2) is $(x_1, x_2) = (0, 3)$

For equation (3)

$x_1 + 2x_2 = 8$

Put $x_1 = 0 \Rightarrow 2(0) + x_2 = 8$

$x_2 = 4$

Put $x_2 = 0 \Rightarrow x_1 + 2(0) = 8$

$x_1 = 8$

$\therefore (x_1, x_2) = (8, 4)$

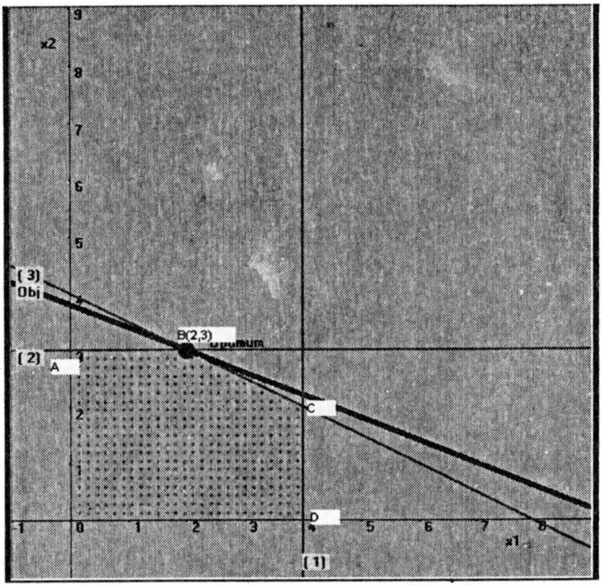

For point B, we can solve the (2) & (3) equations

$x_2 = 3$

$x_1 + 2x_2 = 8$

$x_1 + 2(3) = 8$

$x_1 + 6 = 8$

$x_1 = 2$

$(x_1, x_2) = (2, 3)$

For point C we can solve (1) & (3) equations

$$x_1 = 4$$
$$x_1 + 2x_2 = 8$$
$$4 + 2x_2 = 8$$
$$2x_2 = 4$$
$$x_2 = 2$$
$$(x_1, x_2) = (4, 2)$$

Therefore OABCD is the feasible region. The corner points of the feasible region are 0 (0, 0), A (0, 3), B (2, 3) C (4, 2) D (4, 0). The values of the objective function at these corner point is

$Z = 2x_1 + 5x_2$

0 (0, 0) $\Rightarrow$ $z = 2(0) + 5(0)$

$= 0 + 0 = 0$

A (0, 3) $\Rightarrow$ $z = 2(0) + 5(3)$

$= 0 + 15 = 15$

B (2, 3) $\Rightarrow$ $z = 2(2) + 5(3)$

$= 4 + 15 = 19$

C (4, 2) $\Rightarrow$ $z = 2(4) + 5(2)$

$= 8 + 10 = 18$

D (4, 0) $\Rightarrow$ $z = 2(4) + 5(0)$

$= 8 + 0 = 8$

Therefore the maximum value of z is 19 at point B (2, 3) i.e. $x_1 =$ and $x_2 = 3$

Problem – 6: Solve the Linear Programming Problem by Graphical method Maximize $z = 40x_1 + 60x_2$

Subject to $2x_1 + x_2 \geq 70$

$x_1 + x_2 \leq 40$

$$x_1 + 3x_2 \geq 90$$

$$\text{and } x_1, x_2 \geq 0$$

Solution: The given inequal constraints are converted into equalities.

$$2x_1 + x_2 = 70 \quad \rightarrow (1)$$

$$x_1 + x_2 = 40 \quad \rightarrow (2)$$

$$x_1 + 3x_2 = 90 \quad \rightarrow (3)$$

For the first equation

$2x_1 + x_2 = 70$

Put $x_1 = 0 \Rightarrow x_2 = 70$

Put $x_2 = 0 \Rightarrow x_1 = 35$

$\therefore (x_1, x_2) = (35, 70)$

Second equation is $x_1 + x_2 = 40$

Put $x_1 = 0 \Rightarrow x_2 = 40$

Put $x_2 = 0 \Rightarrow x_1 = 40$

$\therefore (x_1, x_2) = (40, 40)$

The Third equation is

$x_1 + 3x_2 = 90$

Put $x_1 = 0 \Rightarrow 3x_2 = 90$

$x_2 = 30$

$x_2 = 0 \Rightarrow x_1 = 00$

$\therefore (x_1, x_2) = (90, 30)$

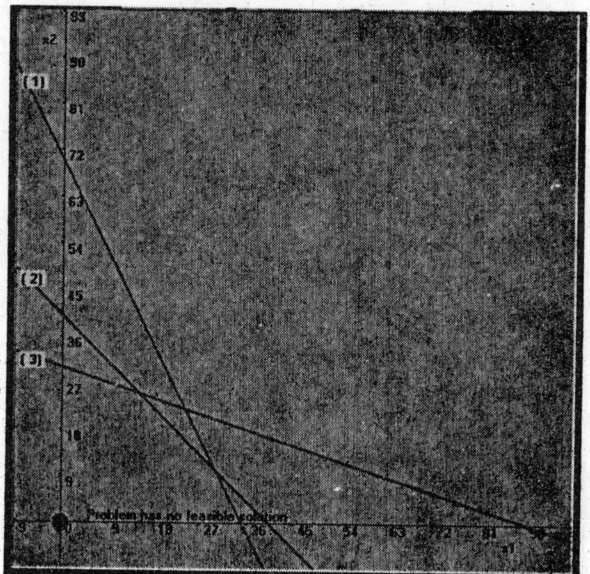

Therefore the feasible region cannot be obtained as all the constraints are not satisfied simultaneously. Hence, the solution is infeasible.

Example – 6: Solve the Linear Programming Problem by Graphical method Minimize $z = 20x_1 + 10x_2$

$$\text{Subject to } x_1 + 2x_2 \leq 40$$

$$3x_1 + x_2 \geq 30$$

$$4x_1 + 3x_2 \geq 60$$

$$\text{and } x_1, x_2 \geq 0$$

Solution: The Given inequal constraints are converted into equalities.

$$x_1 + 2x_2 = 40 \quad \rightarrow (1)$$

$$3x_1 + x_2 = 30 \quad \rightarrow (2)$$

$$4x_1 + 3x_2 = 60 \quad \rightarrow (3)$$

Take the first equation

$x_1 + 2x_2 = 40$

Put $x_1 = 0 \Rightarrow 2x_2 = 40$

$x_2 = \frac{40}{2} = 20$

Put $x_2 = 0 \Rightarrow x_1 = 40$

$\therefore (x_1, x_2) = (40, 20)$

The second equation is

$3x_1 + x_2 = 30$

Put $x_1 = 0 \Rightarrow x_2 = 30$

Put $x_2 = 0 \Rightarrow 3x_1 = 30$

$x_1 = 10$

$\therefore (x_1, x_2) = (10, 30)$

The Third equation is

$4x_1 + 3x_2 = 60$

Put $x_1 = 0 \Rightarrow 3x_2 = 60$

$x_2 = 20$

Put $x_2 = 0 \Rightarrow 4x_1 = 60$

$x_2 = 15$

$\therefore (x_1, x_2) = (15, 20)$

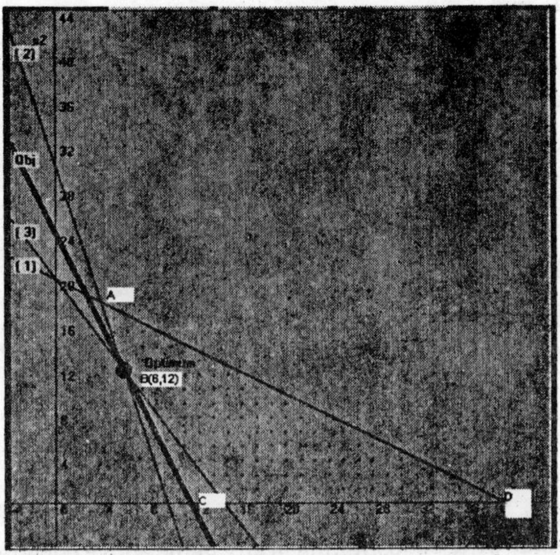

For point A, we can solve the (2) & (1) equations

$$3 \times x_1 + 2x_2 = 40$$

$$1 \times 3x_1 + x_2 = 30$$

$$3x_1 + 6x_2 = 120$$

$$3x_1 + x_2 = 30$$

$$5x_2 = 90$$

$$x_2 = \frac{90}{5}$$

$$x_2 = 18$$

The value of 'x_2' substituting in any of the above equations

$$x_1 + 2x_2 = 40$$

$$x_1 + 2(18) = 40$$

$x_1 = 40-36$

$x_1 = .4$

$\therefore (x_1\ x_2) = (4, 18)$

For point B, we can solve the (2) & (3) equations

$4 \times 3x_1 + 2x_2 = 30$

$3 \times 4x_1 + 3x_2 = 60$

$12x_1 + 4x_2 = 120$

$12x_1 + 9x_2 = 180$

$-5x_2 = -60$

$$x_2 = \frac{60}{5} = 12$$

The value of 'x_2' substituting in any of the above equation, we get x_1 value

$3x_1 + x_2 = 30$

$3x_1 + 12 = 30$

$3x_1 = 18$

$$x_1 = \frac{18}{3} = 6$$

$\therefore (x_1\ x_2) = (6, 12)$

Therefore ABCD is the feasible region. The corner points of the feasible region are A (4, 18), B (6, 12), C (15, 20) D (40, 0). The values of the objective function of these values are:

$Z = 20x_1 + 10x_2$

A (4, 18) $\Rightarrow$ $z = 20\ (4) + 10\ (18)$

$= 80 + 180$

$= 260$

B (6, 12) $\Rightarrow$ z = 20 (6) + 10(12)

= 120 + 120

= 240

C (15, 20) $\Rightarrow$ z = 20 (15) + 10(20)

= 300 + 200

= 500

D (40, 0) $\Rightarrow$ z = 20 (40) + 10(0)

= 800 + 0

= 800

The maximum value of 'z' is 240 at point B (6, 12) i.e. x_1 =6 and x_2 = 12

Example –8: Solve the Linear Programming Problem by Graphical method Maximize $z = 3x_1 + 2x_2$

Subject to $x_1 + x_2 \leq 3$

$x_1 - x_2 \geq 2$

$x_1 \leq 1$

and $x_1, x_2 \geq 0$

Solution: The Given inequal constraints are converted into equalities.

$x_1 + x_2 = 3$ $\rightarrow$ (1)

$x_1 + x_2 = 2$ $\rightarrow$ (2)

$x_1 = 1$ $\rightarrow$ (3)

Take the first equation

$x_1 + x_2 = 3$

Put $x_1 = 0 \Rightarrow x_2 = 3$

$x_2 = 0 \Rightarrow x_1 = 3$

$\therefore x_1, x_2 = (3, 3)$

The second equation is

$$x_1 + x_2 = 2$$

Put $x_1 = 0 \Rightarrow x_2 = -2$

$x_2 = 0 \Rightarrow x_1 = 2$

The Third equation is

$$x_1 = 1$$

$$\therefore (x_1, x_2) = (1, 0)$$

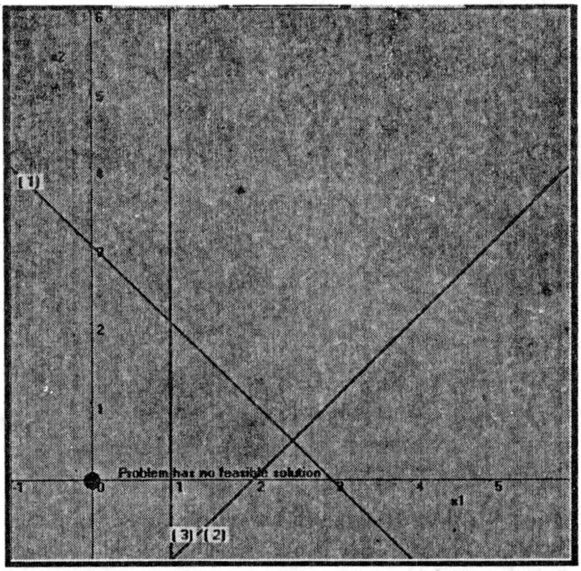

The above graph indicates that the feasible region to be the unbounded and the problem has an unbounded solution.

Exercise-2

Solve the following LPP by graphical method

1. Maximize $Z = 3x_1 + 2x_2$

   Subject to $x_1 - x_2 \geq 12$

   $x_1 + x_2 \leq 5$

   $2x_1 + 3x_2 \leq 12$

   and $x_1, x_2 \geq 0$

2. Maximize $Z = 2x_1 + 5x_2$

   Subject to $x_1 + 4x_2 \leq 24$

   $3x_1 + x_2 \leq 21$

   $x_1 + x_2 \leq 9$

   and $x_1, x_2 \geq 0$

3. Minimize Maximize $Z = 5x_1 + 4x_2$

   Subject to $4x_1 - x_2 \geq 4$

   $2x_1 + 3x_2 \geq 90$

   and $x_1, x_2 \geq 0$

4 Minimize Maximize $Z = -x_1 + 2x_2$

   Subject to $-x_1 - 3x_2 \leq 10$

   $x_1 + x_2 \leq 6$

   $x_1 - x_2 \leq 2$

   and $x_1, x_2 \geq 0$

Game Theory

Many practical problems require decision-making in a competitive – situation where there are two or more opposing parties with conflicting interest and where the action of one depends upon the one taken by opponent.

In a competitive situation the courses of action for each competitor may be either finite or infinite. A competitive situation is called a game.

Properties of the Games:

The game has the following properties

1. There are finite number of competitors are called players
2. Each player in game has a finite number of strategies available to him.
3. A play of the game takes place when each player employs his strategy.
4. The pay-off is fixed and known in advance.

Types of Games

Game theory can be classified in the following games

a. Two person – zero sum game

Where the gain of the winning player exactly corresponds to loss of the other.

b. Two person - non zero sum game

If the sum of gains or losses is not equal to zero, then the game is of non-zero sum character.

c. N – person Games

Where there are large number of competitors all trying for the best trade off.

Terminology used in Game theory:

Player: The competitors in the game are known as players. A player may be individual or group of individuals.

Thus the pay-off matrix of a rectangular game given by

Player B

$$\text{Player A}\ \begin{matrix} \\ A_1 \\ A_2 \\ A_3 \\ \vdots \\ A_m \end{matrix} \begin{matrix} B_1 & B_2 & B_3 & \cdots & B_n \\ \left[\begin{matrix} a_{11} \\ a_{21} \\ a_{31} \\ \vdots \\ a_{m1} \end{matrix}\right. & \begin{matrix} a_{12} \\ a_{22} \\ a_{32} \\ \\ a_{m2} \end{matrix} & \begin{matrix} a_{13} \\ a_{23} \\ a_{33} \\ \\ a_{m3} \end{matrix} & \begin{matrix} \cdots \\ \cdots \\ \cdots \\ \\ \cdots \end{matrix} & \left.\begin{matrix} a_{1n} \\ a_{2n} \\ a_{3n} \\ \\ a_{mn} \end{matrix}\right] \end{matrix}$$

The above the table may be interpreted as;

1. Player A has m strategies, namely A_1, A_2 .... A_m and the player B has n strategies.
2. The pay-off a_{ij} is the gain of A if he adopts the ith strategy and when B adopts the jth strategy.
3. The pay-off a_{ij} in the loss of B if he adopts the jth strategy when A adopts the ith strategy.

Dominance property

Sometimes, it is observed that one of the pure strategies of either player is always interior to at least one of the remaining ones. The superior strategies are said to dominate the inferior ones. Clearly, a player would have no incentive to use inferior strategies which are dominated by the superior ones. In such cases the dominance property used.

The Rules of Dominance Property

1. If all the elements of a row, say kth, and less than or equal to the corresponding elements of any other row, say rth, then kth row is dominated by the rth row.
2. If all the elements of a column, say kth are greater than or equal to the corresponding elements of any other column, say rth, then kth column is dominated by the rth column.

3. Dominated rows or columns may be deleted to reduce the size of pay of matrix, as the optimal strategies will remain unaffected.

Modified Dominance Property

The dominance property is not always based on the superiority of pure strategies only. A given strategy can also be said to be dominated if it is inferior said to an average of two or more other pure strategies. More generally, if some convex linear combination of some rows dominates the ith row, then i^{th} row will be deleted similar arguments follow for columns.

The Maxmin – Minmax principle

For player A, minimum value in each row represents the least gain (pay off) to him if he chooses his particular strategy. These are written in the matrix by row minima. He will then select the strategy that maximizes his minimum gains. This choice of player A is called maxmin principle, and the corresponding gain is called the maxmin value of the game.

For player B, on the other hand, likes to minimize his losses. The maximum value in each column represents the maximum loss to him if he chooses his particular strategy. These are written in the matrix by column maxima. He will then select the strategy that minimizes his maximum losses. The choice of player B is called the minimax principle and the corresponding loss is the minimax value of the game.

If the maximin value equals the minimum value, then the game is said to have a saddle point and the corresponding strategies are called optimum strategies.

Example –1 : Solve the game whose pay off matrix is as follows

		Player B	
		B_1	B_2
	A_1	9	2
Player A	A_2	8	6
	A_3	6	4

Solution:	9	2	2	Min (Max)
	8	6	6	6
	6	4	4	
Max (Min)	9	6	6	

6

$$\begin{bmatrix} 9 & 2 \\ 8 & 6 \\ 6 & 4 \end{bmatrix}$$

Column Max (min) = { 9 6 } = { 6 }

Row Min (Max) = {2, 6, 4} = { 6 }

∴ Max (min) = Min (min)

Saddle point = 6

Strategy: It is an alternative course of action available to a player in advance by which he selects the course of action to be adopted. Strategy may be classified into two types:

a) Pure strategy

If the player selects the same strategy each time, it is referred as a pure strategy. In this case each player knows what the other player is going to do against his selected strategy.

b) Mixed strategy

When the player use a combination of strategies and each player always kept guessing as to which course of action is to be selected by the other player at a particular occasion then this is known as a mixed strategy.

3. Optimum strategy

A course of action or play which puts the player in the most preferred position, irrespective of the strategy of his competitor is called the optimum strategy.

4. Pay off matrix

When the player select their particular strategies, the payoff's can be represented in the form of a matrix is called the payoff matrix.

5. Value of the game

The expected payoff of play when all the players of the game follow their optimum strategies. If the value of the game is zero it is called the game is fair, and it is non – zero refers to unfair.

Examples

Example-1: Solve the game whose payoff matrix is a follows.

Solution: Player B

$$\text{Player A}\quad \begin{array}{c} \\ A_1 \\ A_2 \\ A_3 \end{array} \begin{array}{c} B_1 \quad\quad B_2 \\ \begin{bmatrix} 8 & 2 \\ 9 & 6 \\ 6 & 4 \end{bmatrix} \end{array} \begin{array}{c} \text{Row Min} \\ 2 \\ 6 \\ 4 \end{array}$$

$$\text{Column max} \quad 9 \quad 6$$

$$\text{Row max (min)} = \{ 2, 6, 4\} = \{ 6 \}$$

$$\text{Column max(min)} = \{ 9, 6 \} = \{ 6 \}$$

$$\therefore \text{Max (Min)} = \text{Min (Max)}$$

$$\therefore \text{Saddle point} = 6$$

The game strictly determinate and fair

From the point of view of A, the best strategy should be A_2 which gives his maximum gains, where from the B's point of view, strategy B_2 makes him the minimum loser. Hence, A_2 B_2. combination is called the optimum solution of the game.

Example-2: Solve the following game

$$\text{Player A} \begin{matrix} A_1 \\ A_2 \\ A_3 \end{matrix} \overset{\text{Player B}}{\overset{\begin{matrix} B_1 & B_2 & B_3 \end{matrix}}{\begin{bmatrix} 12 & -8 & -2 \\ 6 & 7 & 3 \\ -10 & -6 & 2 \end{bmatrix}}}$$

Solution:

		B_1	B_2	B_3	*Row Min*
Player A	A_1	12	−8	−2	−8
	A_2	6	7	3	3
	A_3	−10	−6	2	−10
Column max		12	7	3	

Then

Column → max (min) = {12, 7, 3} = {3 }
Row → max (min) = {-8, 3,-10} = {3 }

∴ Max (Min) = Min (Max)

The value of the game is strictly determinable and fair

From the point of view of A, the best strategy should be A_2 which gives him maximum gains, where as from the B's point of view, strategy B_3 makes him the minimum loser. Hence, A_2 B_3- combination is called the optimal solution of the game. Since it is point of equilibrium for both the player i.e. optimum gain of A is the optimum loss of B, it is called saddle point.

Therefore the value of the game is 3

Example-3: Solve the following game

$$\text{Player A} \begin{matrix} A_1 \\ A_2 \\ A_3 \end{matrix} \overset{\text{Player B}}{\overset{\begin{matrix} B_1 & B_2 & B_3 & B_4 \end{matrix}}{\begin{bmatrix} 1 & 7 & 3 & 4 \\ 5 & 6 & 4 & 5 \\ 7 & 2 & 0 & 3 \end{bmatrix}}}$$

Solution

$$\text{Player A}\;\begin{matrix} \\ A_1 \\ A_2 \\ A_3 \end{matrix}\begin{matrix} B_1 & B_2 & B_3 & B_4 \\ \end{matrix}\left[\begin{matrix} 1 & 7 & 3 & 4 \\ 5 & 6 & 4 & 5 \\ 7 & 2 & 0 & 3 \end{matrix}\right]\begin{matrix} \textit{Row Min} \\ 1 \\ 4 \\ 0 \end{matrix}$$

Column max 7 7 7 5

Row min (max) = {1, 4, 0} = {4 }

Column max (min) = {7, 7, 4, 5} = {4 }

∴ Max (Min) = Min (Max)

Saddle point = 4

The game is strictly determinable and fair

From the point of view of A, the best strategy should be A_2 which gives him maximum gains, where from the B's point of view; strategy B_3 makes him the minimum loser. Hence, A_2 B_3 combination is called the optimum solution of the game. Since it is point of equilibrium for both the player i.e. optimum gain of A is the optimum loss of B, it is called saddle point.

∴ Value of the game = 4

Example-4: Solve the following game

Player B

$$\text{Player A}\;\begin{matrix} \\ A_1 \\ A_2 \\ A_3 \end{matrix}\begin{matrix} B_1 & B_2 & B_3 \end{matrix}\left[\begin{matrix} 9 & 8 & -7 \\ 3 & -6 & 4 \\ 6 & 7 & 7 \end{matrix}\right]$$

Solution:

Player B

		B_1	B_2	B_3	*Row Min*
Player A	A_1	9	8	−7	−7
	A_2	3	−6	4	−6
	A_3	6	7	7	6
Column max		9	8	7	

Row min (max) = { -7, -6, 6} = { 6 }

Column max (min) = { 9, 8, 7, 5} = { 7 }

$\therefore$ Max (Min) $\neq$ Min (Max)

The game is not strictly determinable and not fair and then we are using dominance property for reducing the matrix into 2 x 2.

First we can seen the row's side, that payoff relating to A_2 are less or equal to those of A_3. Hence, row A_2 are less or equal to those of A_3. Hence row A_2 is dominated by A_3 and can be deleted.

$$\begin{array}{c} \\ A_1 \\ A_3 \end{array}\begin{array}{c} \begin{array}{ccc} B_1 & B_2 & B_3 \end{array} \\ \begin{bmatrix} 9 & 8 & -7 \\ 6 & 7 & 7 \end{bmatrix} \end{array}$$

From the column side B_2 is dominated by B_3 and hence B_2 can be deleted.

$$\begin{array}{c} \\ A_1 \\ A_3 \end{array}\begin{array}{c} \begin{array}{cc} B_1 & B_3 \end{array} \\ \begin{bmatrix} 9 & -7 \\ 6 & 7 \end{bmatrix} \end{array}$$

Here also there is no saddle point and then different methods have to be adopted.

Method –I: Algebraic method.

$$p_1 = \frac{a_{22} - a_{21}}{a_{11} + a_{22} - a_{12} - a_{21}}$$

$$p_2 = \frac{a_{11} - a_{12}}{a_{11} + a_{22} - a_{12} - a_{21}}$$

$$q_1 = \frac{a_{22} - a_{12}}{a_{11} + a_{22} - a_{12} - a_{21}}$$

$$q_2 = \frac{a_{11} - a_{21}}{a_{11} + a_{22} - a_{12} - a_{21}}$$

$$V = \frac{a_{11}a_{22} - a_{12}a_{21}}{a_{11} + a_{22} - (a_{12} + a_{21})}$$

Here $a_{11} = 9$, $a_{12} = -7$, $a_{21} = 6$, $a_{22} = 7$

$$p = \frac{7-6}{(9+7)-(-7+6)} = \frac{1}{17}$$

$$q = \frac{7-(-7)}{(9+7)-(-7+6)} = \frac{14}{17}$$

$$V = \frac{(9X7)-(-7X\,6)}{(9+7)-(-7+6)} = \frac{63+42}{17} = \frac{105}{7}$$

Method-II

Let player A be playing strategy A_1, with the probability p and A_2 with (1-p)

∴ Expected pay –off for A (B using B_1 strategy)

$= 9p + 6(1-p) = 3p + 6$

Similarly Expected pay-off for A (B using B_3 strategy)

$= 7p + 7(1-p) = 3 - 14p$

By optimum strategy, the payoff of A should be the same. Hence, equating these two pay – off is

$$3p + 6 = 3 - 14p$$

$$17p = 1 \quad or \quad p = \frac{1}{17}$$

A similar analysis can be done for B expected payoff for B_1(A using A_1)

$$= 9p - 7(1-p) = 9p - 7 + 7q$$
$$= 16q - 7$$

Similarly B_3 is $= 6q + 7(1-p)$

$$= 6q + 7 - 7q = 7 - q$$

By optimal strategy, the payoff B should be the same. Hence, equating these two-payoff

$$16q - 7 = 7 - q$$
$$17q - 14 = 0$$
$$17q = 14$$
$$q = \frac{14}{17}$$

Hence player A will select strategy A_1 with probability 1/17 and strategy A_3 with probability 16/17. Similarly player B selects strategy B_1 with probability 14/17 and B_3 with probability 3/17.

The value of the game can be calculated by putting the values of p or q in any one of the above relationships.

$$V = 3p + 6 = 3 \times \frac{1}{17} + 6 = 105/17$$

or

$$V = 7 - q = 7 - \frac{14}{17} = \frac{119-19}{17} = 105/17$$

This is expected optimal gain of 'A' and expected optimal loss of 'B'

Example-5: For the game with following payoff matrix, determine the optimum strategies and the value of the game.

Player B

$$\text{Play A} \begin{matrix} A_1 \\ A_2 \end{matrix} \begin{bmatrix} 5 & 1 \\ 3 & 4 \end{bmatrix}$$

Solution: Let player A be playing A_1 with the probability of p and A_2 with (1 - p)

$\therefore$ Expected pay-off for A (B using B_1 strategy)

$= 5p + 3(1 - p)$

$= 5p + 3 - 3p = 2p + 3$

Similarly expected pay-off for A (B using B_2 strategy)

$p + 4(1 - p)$

$= p + 4 - 4p$

$= -3p + 4$

By optimum strategy, the payoff for A (A using B_2 strategy) should be the same. Hence, equating these two pay offs

$2p + 3 = -3p + 4$

$2p + 3p + 3 - 4 = 0$

$5p - 1 = 0$

$5p = 1$

$p = \frac{1}{5}$

A similar analysis can be done for B. The expected pay off for B_1. (A using A_1)

$5q + 1(1 - q)$

$= 5q + 1 - q$

$= 4q + 1$

Expected pay off for B_2 is $3q + 4(1 - q)$

$3q + 4 - 4q$

$= -q + 4$

By optimal strategy, the pay off of B should be the same, then equating these two pay-offs

$4q + 1 = -q + 4$

$4q + 1 + q - 4 = 0$

$5q - 3 = 0$

$q = 3/5$

Hence player A will select strategy A_1 with probability $\frac{1}{5}$ and strategy A_2 with 4/5. Similarly player B selects strategy B_1 with 3/5 and B_2 with 2/5.

Value of the game can be calculated by putting the values of p or q in any one of the above relationship.

$$V = 2p + 3 = 2\left(\frac{1}{5}\right) + 3$$

$$= \frac{2}{5} + \frac{3}{1} = \frac{2 + 15}{5} = 17/5$$

Or

$$V = 4q + 1 = 4\left(\frac{3}{5}\right) + 1$$

$$= \frac{12}{5} + \frac{1}{1} = \frac{17}{5}$$

This is the optimal gain of A and expected optimal lose of B.

Exercise-1

1. Find the value of the game for the following;

$$A\overset{B}{\begin{bmatrix} 0 & 2 \\ -1 & 4 \end{bmatrix}}$$

2. Determine which of the following two-persons zero-sum games are strictly determinable and fair

a) Player B

$$\text{Player A} \quad \begin{array}{c} \\ A_1 \\ A_2 \end{array} \begin{array}{c} \begin{array}{cc} B_1 & B_2 \end{array} \\ \begin{bmatrix} -5 & 2 \\ -7 & -4 \end{bmatrix} \end{array}$$

b) Player B

$$\text{Player A} \quad \begin{array}{c} \\ A_1 \\ A_2 \end{array} \begin{array}{c} \begin{array}{cc} B_1 & B_2 \end{array} \\ \begin{bmatrix} 10 & 6 \\ 8 & 2 \end{bmatrix} \end{array}$$

3. Solve the game whose pay-off matrix is given by

$$\begin{array}{c} \\ A_1 \\ A_2 \\ A_3 \end{array} \begin{array}{c} \begin{array}{ccc} B_1 & B_2 & B_3 \end{array} \\ \begin{bmatrix} -3 & -2 & 6 \\ 2 & 0 & 2 \\ 5 & -2 & -4 \end{bmatrix} \end{array}$$

4. Solve the game whose pay-off matrix is given by

$$\begin{array}{c} \\ A_1 \\ A_2 \\ A_3 \end{array} \begin{array}{c} \begin{array}{ccc} B_1 & B_2 & B_3 \end{array} \\ \begin{bmatrix} -2 & 15 & -2 \\ -5 & -6 & -4 \\ -5 & 20 & -8 \end{bmatrix} \end{array}$$

5. Solve the game for the following

$$\text{Player A}\begin{array}{c}\text{Player B}\\ \begin{bmatrix} 10 & 5 & -2 \\ 6 & 7 & 3 \\ 4 & 8 & 4 \end{bmatrix}\end{array}$$

6. Solve the game for the following

$$\begin{bmatrix} 9 & 3 & 1 & 8 & 0 \\ 6 & 5 & 4 & 6 & 7 \\ 2 & 4 & 3 & 3 & 8 \\ 5 & 6 & 2 & 2 & 1 \end{bmatrix}$$

7. Solve the game whose pay off matrix is given below

$$\begin{bmatrix} -2 & 0 & 0 & 5 & 3 \\ 3 & 2 & 1 & 2 & 2 \\ -4 & -3 & 0 & -2 & 6 \\ 5 & 3 & -4 & 2 & -6 \end{bmatrix}$$

Exercise - 2

1. For the game with the following pay off matrix, determine the optimum strategies and the value of the game.

$$A\begin{array}{c}B\\ \begin{bmatrix} 6 & -3 \\ -3 & 0 \end{bmatrix}\end{array}$$

2. Solve the game and determine the value of game

$$A\begin{array}{c}B\\ \begin{bmatrix} 6 & -3 \\ -3 & 0 \end{bmatrix}\end{array}$$

3. Solve the following game and determine the value of the game

$$\text{Player A}\quad \begin{array}{c} \\ A_1 \\ A_2 \end{array}\overset{\text{Player B}}{\begin{array}{ccc} B_1 & B_2 & B_3 \\ \end{array}}\begin{bmatrix} 2 & 5 & 6 \\ 7 & 3 & 4 \end{bmatrix}$$

4. Solve the following two person zero sum game

$$\text{Player A}\ \overset{\text{Player B}}{\begin{bmatrix} 8 & -3 & 7 \\ 6 & -4 & 5 \\ -2 & 2 & -3 \end{bmatrix}}$$

Find the optimum strategies for each of the player

5. Solve the game by using dominance property

$$\text{Player A}\ \overset{\text{Player B}}{\begin{bmatrix} 2 & -2 & 4 & 1 \\ 6 & 1 & 12 & 3 \\ -3 & 2 & 0 & 6 \\ 2 & -3 & 7 & 1 \end{bmatrix}}$$

6. Solve the game by using the concept of dominance

$$\text{Player A}\quad \begin{array}{c} A_1 \\ A_2 \\ A_3 \end{array}\overset{\text{Player B}}{\overset{\begin{array}{cccc} B_1 & B_2 & B_3 & B_4 \end{array}}{\begin{bmatrix} 8 & 10 & 9 & 14 \\ 10 & 11 & 8 & 12 \\ 13 & 12 & 14 & 13 \end{bmatrix}}}$$

7. Solve the following game

$$\text{Player A}\begin{bmatrix} 1 & -3 & 2 \\ -4 & 4 & -2 \end{bmatrix}$$

8. Solve the following game

Player B

$$\text{Player A}\begin{bmatrix} 9 & 8 & -7 \\ 3 & -6 & 4 \\ 6 & 7 & 7 \end{bmatrix}$$

Graphical approach (2 x n case)

Example-1: Solve the following game graphically and find the value of the game.

Player B

$$\text{Player A} \begin{matrix} A_1 \\ A_2 \end{matrix} \overset{\begin{matrix} B_1 & B_2 & B_3 & B_4 \end{matrix}}{\begin{bmatrix} 8 & 5 & -7 & 9 \\ -6 & 6 & 4 & -2 \end{bmatrix}}$$

Solution: Let us first find, if there exists a saddle point

Player B

		B_1	B_2	B_3	B_4	*Row* min
Player A	A_1	8	5	−7	9	−7
	A_2	−6	6	4	−2	−6
Column max		8	6	4	9	

Row min (max) = { -7 , -6} = {-6}

Column max (min) = {8, 6, 4, 9} = (4}

$\therefore$ Max (min) $\neq$ Min (max)

Hence there is no saddle point and therefore no pure strategy.

Next, we workout the expected payoff of player A corresponding to B's strategy.

B's Strategy	A's expected payoff ($\because P_2 = 1 - P_1$)
B_1	$8P_1 - 6P_2 = 14P_1 - 6$
B_2	$5P_1 + 6P_2 = 6 - P_1$
B_3	$-7P_1 + 4P_2 = 4 - 11P_1$
B_4	$9P_1 - 2P_2 = 11P_1 - P_2$

Plotting these strategies on the graph, we get the following figure

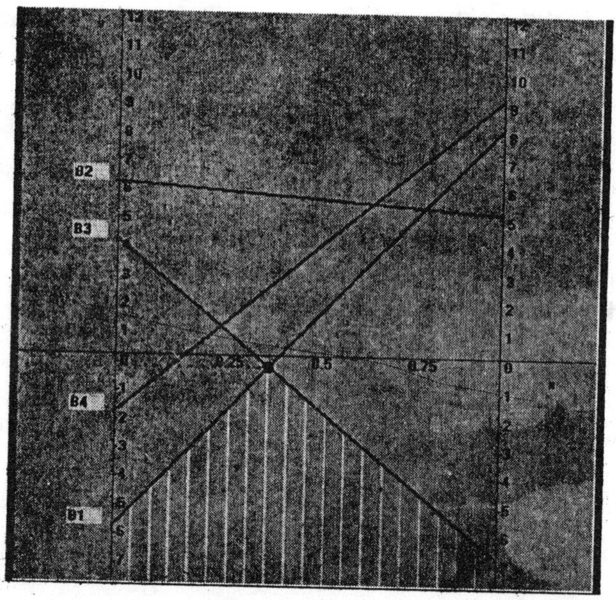

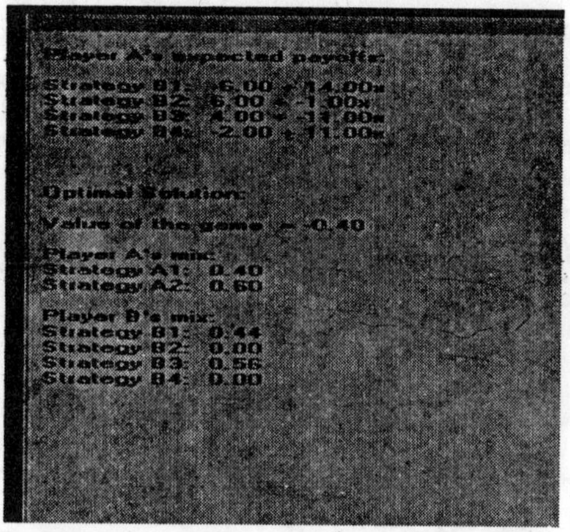

Here A's strategy are $A_1 = 0.40$ and $A_2 = 0.60$

and the value of the game is -0.4

The same solution can be obtained by solving the equations algebraically. The point of intersection for optimal strategy lies on the strategies B_1 and B_3.

Example-2: Solve the following 2 x 2 game graphically

$$\text{Player A} \begin{array}{c} \\ A_1 \\ A_2 \end{array} \overset{\text{Player B}}{\begin{array}{cccc} B_1 & B_2 & B_3 & B_4 \\ \left[\begin{array}{c} 2 \\ 1 \end{array}\right. & \begin{array}{c} 1 \\ 0 \end{array} & \begin{array}{c} 0 \\ 3 \end{array} & \left.\begin{array}{c} -2 \\ 2 \end{array}\right] \end{array}}$$

Solution: let us first find, if there exists a saddle point

$$\begin{array}{rccccc} & & & \text{Player B} & & \\ & B_1 & B_2 & B_3 & B_4 & \text{Row min} \\ \text{Player A} \quad A_1 & 2 & 1 & 0 & -2 & -2 \\ A_2 & 1 & 0 & 3 & 2 & 0 \\ \text{Column max} & 2 & 1 & 3 & 2 & \end{array}$$

Row min (max) = { -2 , 0} = {0}

Column max (min) = { 2, 1, 3, 2} = (1}

Therefore there is no saddle point and therefore no pure strategy.

Now, the expected payoff of player A corresponding to B's strategy.

B's Strategy	A's expected payoff ($\therefore P_2 = 1 - P_1$)
B_1	$2P_1 - 6P_2$
B_2	P_1
B_3	$3P_2$
B_4	$-2P_1 + 2P_2$

For $B_1 \Rightarrow 8P_1 - 6P_2$

$8P_1 - 6(1 - P_1)$

$14P_1 - 6$

$B_3 \Rightarrow -7P_1 + 4P_2$

$-7P_1 + 4(1 - P_2)$

$-11P_1 + 4$

Then equating the corresponding payoff's

$14P_1 - 6 = -11P_1 + 4$

$25P_1 = 10$

$$P_1 = \frac{10}{25} = 0.4$$

$\therefore P_2 = 1 - P_1 = 1 - 0.4 = 0.6$

$V = 14P_1 - 6 = 14(0.4) - 6 = -0.4$

Plotting these strategies on the graph, we get the following figure

Hence, $A_1 = 0.40$

$A_2 = 0.60$

and the value of the game is 0.40

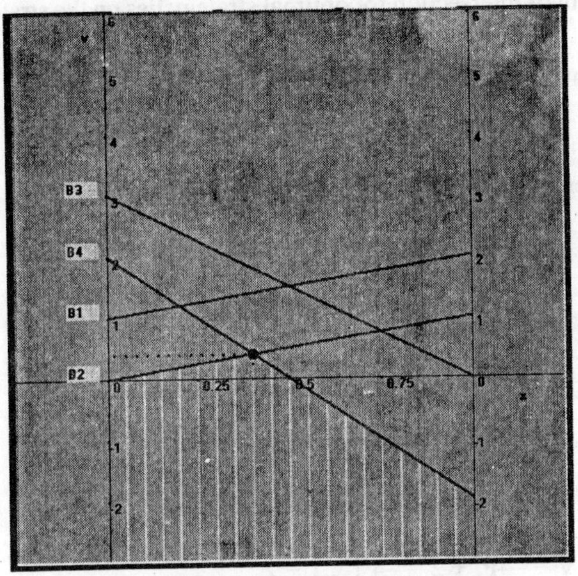

Player A's expected payoffs:

Strategy B1: 1.00 + 1.00x
Strategy B2: 0.00 + 1.00x
Strategy B3: 3.00 + -3.00x
Strategy B4: 2.00 + -4.00x

Optimal Solution:

Value of the game = 0.40

Player A's mix:
Strategy A1: 0.40
Strategy A2: 0.60

Player B's mix:
Strategy B1: 0.00
Strategy B2: 0.80
Strategy B3: 0.00
Strategy B4: 0.20

The same solution can be obtained by the equations algebraically. The point of intersection for optimal strategy lies on the strategies B_2 & B_4

$$\text{For } B_2 \Rightarrow P_1$$

$$B_4 \Rightarrow -4P_1 + 2$$

Then equating the corresponding pay offs

$$P_1 = -4P_1 + 2$$

$$5P_1 - 2 = 0$$

$$5P_1 = 2$$

$$P_1 = \frac{2}{5}$$

$$\therefore P_2 = 1 - P_1 = 1 - \frac{2}{5} = \frac{3}{5}$$

$$V = -4P_1 + 2 = -4\left(\frac{2}{5}\right) + 2$$

$$= -\frac{8}{5} + 2$$

$$= \frac{2}{5}$$

m x 2 Case

Example-1: Solve the game for the following data:

Player B

$$\text{Player A} \quad \begin{array}{c} \\ A_1 \\ A_2 \\ A_3 \\ A_4 \\ A_5 \end{array} \begin{array}{c} B_1 \quad B_2 \\ \begin{bmatrix} -6 & 7 \\ 4 & -5 \\ -1 & -2 \\ -2 & 5 \\ 7 & -6 \end{bmatrix} \end{array}$$

Solution

$$\begin{array}{cc|cc|c} & & \multicolumn{2}{c}{\text{Player B}} & \\ & & B_1 & B_2 & \text{Row Min} \\ & A_1 & -6 & 7 & -6 \\ & A_2 & 4 & -5 & -5 \\ \text{Player A} & A_3 & -1 & -2 & -2 \\ & A_4 & -2 & 5 & -2 \\ & A_5 & 7 & -6 & -6 \end{array}$$

Column Max 4 7

Row min (max) = {–6, –5, –2, –2, –6} = {–2}

Column max (min) = { 4, 7} = { 4 }

There is no saddle point and no pure strategy

Let the strategy B_1 of B be used with the probability q, the strategy B_2 used with probability (1-q). Then the expected payoff corresponding to A's strategy can be written as;

A's strategy	*expected pay-off of B's strategy*
A_1	$-6q_1 + 7q_2$
A_2	$4q_1 - 5q_2$
A_3	$-q_1 - 2q_2$
A_4	$-2q_1 + 5q_2$
A_5	$7q_1 - 6q_2$

Plotting these strategies on the graph, we get the following figure

Hence, B's strategies are

$B_1 = 11/20$

$B_2 = 9/20$

And the value of the game is $\frac{23}{20}$

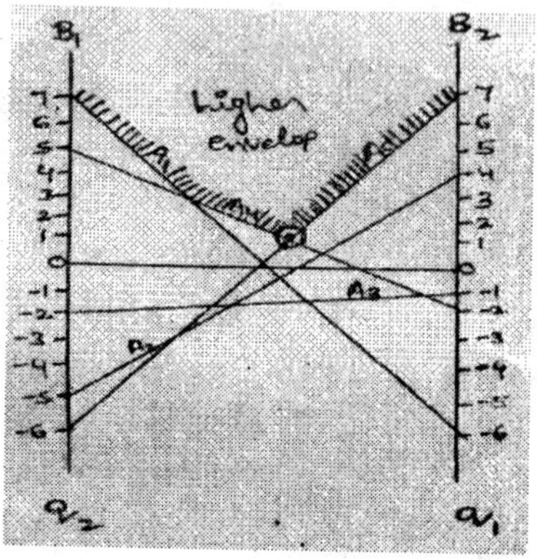

The same solution can be obtained by solving the equations algebraically. The point of intersection for optimal strategy lies on the strategies A_4 & A_5

For $A_4 \Rightarrow -2q_1 + 5q_2$

$= -2q_1 + 5(1 - q_1)$

$= -2q_1 + 5 = 5(1 - q_1)$

$= -2q_1 + 5 - 5q_1$

$= -7q_1 + 5$

$A_5 \quad 7q_1 - 6q_2$

$= 7q\text{-}_1 - 6(1 - q_2)$

$= 7q_1 - 6 + 6q_1$

$= 13q_1 - 6$

Then equating the corresponding pay offs

$-7q_1 + 5 = 13q_1 - 6$

$20q_1 - 11 = 0$

$20q_1 = 11$

$q_1 = 11/20$

$$q_2 = 1 - \frac{11}{20} = 9/20$$

$$V = -7q_1 + 5$$

$$= -7\left(\frac{11}{20}\right) + 5$$

$$= \frac{-77}{20} + 5$$

$$= \frac{-77 + 100}{20}$$

$$= \frac{23}{20}$$

Exercise-3

1. Solve the following problem graphically

Player B

$$\text{Player A} \begin{bmatrix} -3 & -3 & 4 \\ -1 & 1 & -3 \end{bmatrix}$$

2. Solve the following game by graphically

Player B

$$\text{Player A} \begin{bmatrix} 2 & 2 & 3 & -2 \\ 4 & 3 & 2 & 6 \end{bmatrix}$$

3. Solve the following game by graphically

Player B

$$\text{Player A} \begin{bmatrix} 6 & -3 & 7 \\ -3 & 0 & -6 \end{bmatrix}$$

4. Solve the following game by graphically

Player B

$$\text{Player A}\quad \begin{array}{c} \\ A_1 \\ A_2 \\ A_3 \end{array}\begin{array}{c} \begin{array}{cc} B_1 & B_2 \end{array} \\ \begin{bmatrix} 3 & -4 \\ 2 & 5 \\ -2 & 8 \end{bmatrix} \end{array}$$

5. Solve the following game by graphically

Player B

$$\text{Player A}\begin{bmatrix} 1 & 2 \\ 5 & 4 \\ -7 & 9 \\ -4 & -3 \\ 2 & 1 \end{bmatrix}$$

6. Solve the following game by graphically

Player B

$$\text{Player A}\begin{bmatrix} -2 & 0 \\ 3 & -1 \\ -3 & 2 \\ 5 & -4 \end{bmatrix}$$

7. Solve the following game by graphically

Player B

$$\text{Player A}\begin{bmatrix} -2 & 0 \\ 3 & -1 \\ -3 & 2 \\ 5 & -4 \end{bmatrix}$$

8. Solve the following game by graphically

Player B

$$\text{Player A}\begin{bmatrix} 1 & -3 \\ 3 & 5 \\ -1 & 6 \\ 4 & 1 \\ -5 & 0 \end{bmatrix}$$

9. Solve the following game by graphically

Player B

$$\text{Player A}\begin{bmatrix} -6 & 7 \\ 4 & -5 \\ -1 & -2 \\ -2 & 5 \\ 7 & 0 \end{bmatrix}$$

10. Solve the following game by graphically

Player B

$$\text{Player A}\begin{bmatrix} 2 & 2 & 3 & -2 \\ 4 & 3 & 2 & 6 \end{bmatrix}$$